VIOLENCE
IN THE SKIES

A HISTORY OF AIRCRAFT
HIJACKING AND BOMBING

PHILIP BAUM

summersdale

VIOLENCE IN THE SKIES

Summersdale Publishers Ltd
46 West Street
Chichester
West Sussex
PO19 1RP
UK

www.summersdale.com

Printed and bound by CPI Group (UK) Ltd, Croydon, CR0 4YY

ISBN: 978-1-84953-838-1

Substantial discounts on bulk quantities of Summersdale books are available to corporations, professional associations and other organisations. For details contact Nicky Douglas by telephone: +44 (0) 1243 756902, fax: +44 (0) 1243 786300 or email: nicky@summersdale.com.

Dedicated to the innocent victims of flights, who have embarked upon journeys to see the beauty our planet has to offer, but who have had their lives tragically cut short by acts of barbarism perpetrated by individuals with warped ideologies. To the heroic crew members, brave passengers and anonymous members of the security forces who have brought hijacks to safe conclusions with zero or minimal loss of life. To the men and women who, day in and day out, perform their duties professionally, often with little thanks, in an attempt to safeguard not only the flights we board but the societal values we strive to uphold. And, last but by no means least, to those I love and cherish who have enabled me to make this flight through life safely and securely.

CONTENTS

PREFACE

People often ask me how I became involved in aviation security. Perhaps it was growing up in East Sheen, on the flight path to London Heathrow. I recall gazing out of my bedroom window for hours on end at the aircraft making their final approach, and I became quite the expert at recognising airline insignia. Geography was my favourite subject at school and, while many kids of a similar age were proud to display their knowledge of cars, football players and the kings and queens of England, I wanted to be tested on my knowledge of every capital city, national flag and airline carrier.

Then again, perhaps it was because I was fortunate enough to travel frequently as a child and was always excited by the airport experience. It wasn't the aircraft themselves which appealed to me, rather the behaviour of the passengers, and those who met them or bade them farewell. The expressions of love, sadness, joy, excitement, boredom, frustration. The communication between loved ones and business colleagues, flight attendants and pilots, airport staff and the travelling public. It was fun guessing where people were travelling to – who was the tourist and who was on business, who was happy to be leaving on an adventure and who was distraught about imminent separation from a loved one they might never see again. It's a game I've converted into a profession!

However, it is more likely that I was influenced by world events. After dinner, my family always watched the BBC's

Nine O'clock News and, when I was child, aircraft hijackings took place with alarming regularity. With no sibling until I was almost 12, I had to take part in grown-up discussions about both the ills and the wonders of the world. The actions of the Palestinian terrorist groups intrigued me more than those perpetrated by, say, the Irish Republican Army, because aviation was the target. But, while I never set out to become an aviation security professional – and could never have foreseen myself sitting down for coffee with Leila Khaled in Amman on the thirtieth anniversary of the events of 6 September 1970 – somehow I knew that aviation would be part of my life.

Over the years I have followed many of the stories, generally focusing on them from a human perspective. I am fascinated by the paths taken by the perpetrators of violent acts, what led them to points of such desperation, be it hijacking, bombing or even simple unruly passenger behaviour. The stories of passengers and crew, how they responded, coped with captivity, summoned the will to survive or resigned themselves to their fate. I have brought together many of the stories that have shaped the aviation industry, together with some which have had a major impact on the world as we know it. This is by no means an exhaustive account of aviation hijackings and bombings – and some readers may feel that their favourite case study has been left out – but the ones selected are those where there is a tale to be told, a lesson to be learned or a hero to remember.

Many books have been written about individual incidents, but this history is different. The focus is less on the weapons or explosives used, the aircraft type, the tactics employed by special forces or the background political manoeuvrings, and more on the impact of the attacks on those whose lives became forever associated with violence in the skies.

PREFACE

This book would never have come about were it not for the support and encouragement of colleagues, friends and family. I am indebted to those who helped me get the ball rolling – notably Alexandra James and Louise Cooke; to those family members who helped proof – my sister, Devorah, and father-in-law, Tony – and my professional proofreader Emma Grundy-Haigh; to industry colleagues, Norman Shanks, Tony Blackiston and Amir Neeman, whose constructive criticism and feedback was invaluable; and those who commissioned it in the first place – my agent, Adrian Sington, from Kruger Cowne, and Claire Plimmer and Chris Turton at Summersdale Publishers. The publishers of *Aviation Security International* have been ever supportive of my efforts to highlight the key issues impacting upon aviation security worldwide and I am grateful for their continued faith in retaining me as the editor of the industry's mouthpiece. I express my gratitude to the staff and consultants of Green Light Ltd., who may have felt that I have been somewhat distracted from my regular duties while putting pen to paper. Glenda and Harold provided me with the hideaway and headspace to write by granting me the use of their caravan in Selsey. This book probably would never have been started were it not for the encouragement I was given by friends – in particular, Carol Bronze, who always told me that I had a book in me! My parents' faith in me has had immeasurable impact – the frequency of being told to adopt the 'I can and I will' attitude as a child; the inspiration they provide by the never-ceasing zest they continue to show for life; the unquestioning love they display for all those dear to them, values based on charity and good deeds they espouse; one can only aspire to emulate them. And last, but by no means least, my wife and daughters whose love, support and loyalty has known no bounds. They have allowed me to embark on this literary journey, while also having to cope with an often absentee spouse and father as I have travelled the globe. Kate epitomises professionalism and her desire to enable people to achieve their maximum potential is a quality that I hope I have absorbed and portray to those I encounter within the industry. While this book is dedicated to those whose lives have been shaped by hatred, it is inspired by those who love.

CHAPTER I
1911–1945

THIEVING TYPES

The aviation industry was still only in its first decade when it had to start to consider ways of ensuring the not only *safe* but *secure* transportation of passengers at high altitude above the earth, let alone the protection of its assets on the ground. Following the Wright Brothers achieving 'flight' in 1903, and the subsequent commencement of aircraft manufacturing in the early years of the last century, there have been those who have seen it as a concept that could be exploited for nefarious purposes. As a result, the industry has had to respond to the challenges posed by terrorists, criminals, psychologically disturbed individuals and asylum seekers who have sought to use aircraft as a means to prove a political point, secure the release of imprisoned colleagues, extract financial gain, reach pastures deemed greener, or even as a means to commit suicide.

However, the first criminals to target aviation did so from the safety of solid ground. According to the *Oregon News* of 9 August 1911, an aeroplane had been reported as stolen:

❝ St. Louis Police today are searching for an entirely new brand of criminal in the man or men who stole a monoplane from E. E. Lessard, a local amateur aviator. So far as known the theft is the first of its kind. ❞

It certainly wasn't the last.

The aircraft thieves of the early twentieth century were likely to be flying enthusiasts rather than hardened criminals. In 1917, the *New York Times* reported:

> NOVICE AIRMEN DIE IN 1,500-FOOT PLUNGE: Two army pupils take plane at Mineola without authority and attempt flight. They soon lose control. Crowd sees runaway biplane zigzag dizzily in the sky, then drop to earth.

And so it was that Ransom H. Merritt and Anthony D. Spileno met their premature end.

A decade later, the United Press reported that, on 26 August, Donald Charles had stolen an aircraft because he was late for a party! Charles had been a pilot in World War One, yet he had seemingly forgotten how to fly. No sooner had he taken off than he crashed the aircraft, writing it off, although walking away from the accident himself.

A year later, two German youths stole an aircraft in Winnipeg, Canada. Around the world, aircraft thefts began being reported with alarming regularity.

In Australia, on 23 September 1930, the *Sydney Morning Herald* reported that two men had been charged with the theft of an aircraft. 'Walter William Crothers, 21, a fitter, was charged at the Parramatta Court yesterday with having stolen a Moth aeroplane, valued at £850, the property of the Aero Club of New South Wales.' It was alleged that Crothers had obtained the plane from the caretaker of the Hargrave Park Aerodrome, and had intended flying it to Katoomba to perform a flying show. Jack Hart, a 21-year-old motor mechanic, was also arrested and charged in relation to the offence.

However, all of these crimes had been opportunistic in nature. Nobody was seizing aircraft in-flight and pilots were not being forced to fly against their will.

MEMORY RECALL

Unofficially – inasmuch as no report of the incident was filed by the captain at the time – the first airborne aeroplane hijacking took place in Mexico in December 1929. It was not until 1970 that pilot J. Howard 'Doc' DeCelles claimed that, back in 1929, he had been flying a postal route for the Mexican company Transportes Aeras Transcontinentales, ferrying mail from San Luis Potosi to Torreon and then on to Guadalajara, when a lieutenant under the command of Mexican revolutionary Pancho Villa ordered him to divert. DeCelles was allegedly held captive for several hours under armed guard. This was, however, not a passenger aircraft.

THE WOULD-BE ALBANIAN KING

The first 'real' hijacking to have taken place (in flight, rather than prior to take off) of a passenger-carrying aircraft may have been as early as 1919 and perpetrated by a particularly colourful character by the name of Baron Franz von Nopcsa Felső-Szilvás.

Nopsca was a Hungarian aristocrat, who became a world-renowned palaeontologist, today credited for having initiated research into the Transylvanian dinosaur following his sister's discovery of some petrified bones on the family estate in Szacsal in 1895. His research also delved into the origin of birds and the evolutionary process that has enabled them to fly; he is now regarded as one of the first scientists to have established an evolutionary link between birds and bipedal dinosaurs. Nopsca was an early proponent of the theory of 'island dwarfism', whereby animals that evolve on islands grow to a smaller size due to the limited resources available; his theory, once mocked by many, is nowadays accepted by the global scientific community.

But Nopsca was a multifaceted individual – an adventurer who developed a love of Albania, and who saw himself as the saviour of this exotic region in the Balkans. His first trip there in search of fossils came about following the commencement of a relationship with his secretary, a younger Albanian man named Bajazid Elmaz Doda. Such was his passion for the region, despite being a palaeontologist first and foremost, Nopsca is also accredited as having written 50 scientific papers on the language, history, ethnology, traditional music and laws of Albania. Committed to the country, he wished to free it from Ottoman rule and used his considerable wealth to purchase weapons to wage the first Balkan war.

Albania became independent in 1913 under the Treaty of London, and determined that it would be a monarchy. With no natural successor to the throne, the new state tried to identify suitable candidates to be king... and Nopsca thought he would be just the man for the job. However, his unabashedly camp lifestyle did not play well in early-twentieth-century Albania and he quickly found himself out of favour. So he returned to Transylvania, which was still under Hungarian rule. While continuing his research as a palaeontologist, Nopsca also spent the latter part of World War One operating as a spy for Romania... not that it was going to do him any good.

The end of World War One saw Transylvania become part of Romania, and Nopsca lost his family estate there, and the associated wealth that went with it. His fall from grace resulted in his seeking a new life in Vienna and so it was that a wealthy homosexual Hungarian palaeontologist who wanted to be King of Albania arrived, gun in hand, at Budapest Airport with false documents and ordered the pilot to fly him and Doda to Vienna. In addition to establishing the evolutionary process that enabled birds to fly, he may have inadvertently been the first of a new kind of creature of the skies – the hijacker.

Nopsca and Doda were to end their days in Vienna in 1933 when Nopsca, poor and sick, shot his lover in his sleep before turning the gun on himself.

MILITANT MAURITANIAN MOORS

The first airline to find itself the target of criminal activity was Lignes Aeriennes Latécoère (later to become Aéropostale). Between 1923 and 1926, the carrier operated mail routes across the Spanish Sahara and, on the ground below, nomadic Moors took advantage of the frequency with which these early flights were forced to land due to engine trouble or sandstorms. Pilots were frequently kidnapped and ransoms were demanded for their release. Realising that this was a profitable business, the Moors then started shooting at aircraft in flight in order to force them to land. In at least five instances, the pilots were actually killed by their captors.

LATIN AMERICAN GUERRILLAS, MONGOLIAN TRIBESMEN AND DASTARDLY DENTISTS

Given the absence of verifiable data regarding Baron Nopsca's hijacking in 1919, and the failure of 'Doc' DeCelles to report the attack on his aircraft in 1929, the aviation industry tends to treat the events of the 21 February 1931 as being the first hijacking for which detailed reports exist. In fact, it was more of a commandeering than a hijacking as all the action took place on the ground in Arequipa, Peru.

Around six months beforehand, Lt. Col. Sanchez Cerro flew to Lima from his home in Arequipa in an aircraft piloted by an American businessman by the name of Elmer Faucett (who was, subsequently, to become the founder of Peru's first airline), and seized power. By February 1931, Cerro's Arequipa-based compatriots had become disillusioned with his failure to effect the reforms he had promised, and so it was that some of them decided to take up arms and seek his removal. But Arequipa was some way from Lima and, just as Cerro himself had arrived in Lima by air, an aircraft was needed.

Captain Byron Dague Rickards was the unlucky pilot. He worked for Pan American Airways and flew Ford Tri-motors on mail routes around the Andes. On 21 February, he landed in Arequipa, on a landing strip with which he was very familiar. As he taxied towards the terminal, a group of Peruvian guerrillas bearing rifles surrounded the aircraft and advised Rickards that they were seizing the aircraft and would be utilising it to drop propaganda leaflets over cities in Peru.

Strangely enough, Rickards was not only the first captain to be 'hijacked'; he was also the first to be hijacked twice, when a Continental Airlines flight he was piloting on a domestic flight in the USA in 1961 (see p.44) was also seized. Rickards, however, can consider himself relatively fortunate since Captain Leul Abate of Ethiopian Airlines (see p.222) has been skyjacked on at least three different occasions!

The targeting of an aircraft operating a mail route was also not a one-off. On 2 July 1931, an aircraft belonging to the Eurasia Aviation Corporation was shot down near Manchuli, by Mongolian tribesmen armed with rifles. The Junkers aircraft was performing the inaugural trans-Siberian airmail route at the time; at the controls were two German pilots, Captain Johann Rathje and his flight engineer, Otto Koelber, both of whom were on loan to Eurasia Aviation by its parent-company, Lufthansa.

Rathje and Koelber were arrested and held in Outer Mongolia until September 1931, when the Nanking government in China is believed to have negotiated their release. Rathje was initially sentenced to five years imprisonment for espionage, whilst Koelber, who had been seriously injured in the initial attack, spent the three months in captivity in a hospital in Urga, where he also had his leg amputated.

SEAPLANE, SEE DANGER

The first real lesson on the risk to aviation as posed by criminal activity on the flight deck also occurred on the South American continent. On 25 September 1932, a Panair do Brasil Sikorsky S-38 seaplane was stolen from its hangar by three rebels who, having taken a hostage as protection, took off and then promptly crashed into São João de Meriti, a suburb of Rio de Janeiro. The three rebels and their hostage all died.

There is considerable debate as to when the first aircraft was blown up intentionally, but many believe that the Imperial Airways aircraft, which crashed near Dixmude in Belgium while en route from Brussels to London on 28 March 1933, may have been destroyed by one of the passengers on board. The aircraft seemingly targeted was an Armstrong Whitworth A. W. 154 Argosy II, called the *City of Liverpool*.

Observers on the ground saw the aircraft on fire before it crashed, killing all 15 people on board. The fire had been seen in the tail of the aircraft and, according to the Bureau of Aircraft Accidents Archives, the subsequent investigation showed that:

> No technical failure occurred on wings or engines. A quick and violent fire broke out in the cabin, maybe in a luggage [compartment] or in the toilet compartment for unknown reasons. This fire was very intensive as no one in the cabin was able to use the fire extinguisher.

One of the possible scenarios is that one Dr Albert Voss, a 69-year-old dentist, had started the fire intentionally. Voss' body was actually found some distance from the wreckage and the forensic investigation revealed that he had suffered burn marks to his hands and face. Witnesses on the ground claimed that they had seen a man jump from the aircraft just before the crash.

Voss' brother told investigators in London that the dentist had been considering suicide and that he may have been involved in drug smuggling. Due to his profession, Voss had easy access to anaesthetics, which at that time were highly flammable. Furthermore, it was later revealed that the flight was being monitored by the Metropolitan Police, who were already investigating Voss' alleged involvement in smuggling. His brother claimed that Voss felt it was only a matter of time before he was arrested, so perhaps he decided it was time to disappear.

THE LIQUID EXPLOSIVE PLOT OF 1933

While the loss of the Imperial Airways flight in 1933 is only suspected of being the result of sabotage, the first confirmed bombing of a commercial airliner took place on 10 October 1933, when a United Airlines aircraft, en route from

Cleveland to Chicago, exploded at an altitude of 1,000 ft over Chesterton, Indiana.

It was confirmed by Melvin Purvis, then head of the Chicago office of the United States Federal Bureau of Investigation, that their investigation demonstrated that the crash was the result of 'an explosion somehwere in the region of the baggage compartment of the rear of the plane'. Purvis reported that, 'Everything in the front of the compartment was blown forward and everything behind blown backward, and things in the side outward.' A simple fire in the fuel tanks was ruled out because 'the gasoline tanks, instead of being blowed [sic] out, were crushed in, showing there was no explosion in them'.

It was later determined that a nitroglycerine-based improvised explosive device (IED) had been concealed in the blanket compartment of the toilets. Despite the evidence, no cause or culprit were ever established. Suspects were aplenty, but the investigation was impeded by the fact that the wreckage was sold and removed from the crash site within 24 hours of the accident taking place. As the investigation dragged on from weeks to months, the lead investigators were given other issues to deal with. Purvis was also the lead agent tracking John Dillinger, the infamous gang leader who had embarked upon a series of bank robberies in May 1933; and Special Agent W. Carter Baum, who had been interviewing passengers' family members, was also assigned to the hunt for Dillinger.

On 22 April 1934, Baum was killed by 'Baby Face' Nelson, when acting on intelligence that Dillinger and members of his gang were hiding at Little Bohemia Lodge in Wisconsin. And on 22 July 1934, Purvis, having managed to track Dillinger down to the Biograph Theatre in Chicago, awaited his exit from a viewing of 'Manhattan Melodrama' to close in on his prey. Dillinger tried to escape but was shot dead. With Baum dead and Purvis having made a significant breakthrough against organised crime, FBI Director J. Edgar Hoover wanted 'Baby Face' Nelson and 'Pretty Boy' Floyd captured dead or alive, and Purvis had proven himself up to the task. As a result, the investigation into the air crash was suspended.

MURDER IN THE SKIES

The 1930s were to experience not only the first commandeering of an aircraft and the first bombing of an aircraft, but also the first act of murder in the skies. Fortunately, however, the incident took place on a light aircraft rather than on a passenger plane.

The perpetrator was Earnest Pletch, the victim Carl Bivens, who was Pletch's flying instructor, and the reason... well, nobody seems to know! Pletch was said to be a difficult man and was already on his third marriage when, on 28 October 1939, he had his final lesson with Bivens and, somewhere over Missouri, he took out a revolver and fired two shots into Bivens' head. Pletch had acquired sufficient flying skills to be able to land the training aircraft single-handedly.

This feat would not have been a surprise to those who knew Pletch, as he had been quick to brag to anybody that would listen that he had been teaching himself to fly, if only by reading books and observing the actions of trained pilots at air shows rather than by actually taking lessons. In June 1938, Pletch had stolen an aircraft from a Royal American Show and managed to take off and land the aircraft successfully, all before his first flying lesson.

Even after his arrest for the murder of Bivens, Pletch repeatedly changed his rationale for the killing, but he did plead guilty and was saved from the death penalty by Bivens' widow, who supported a life sentence with no parole.

Pletch died a free man in June 2001. Mike Dash, a Welsh historian, best known for books and articles dealing with dramatic yet little-known episodes in history, investigated the incident after Pletch had gained his freedom. He found that 'his life sentence had been commuted to one of 25 years on 9 January 1953, then further commuted on 1 March 1957, the day of his release'. Furthermore, Dash established that:

> A man by the name of Earnest Pletch had found employment as a pilot with a firm called Cox Aviation and married a woman named Mary Leap on the day after Christmas 1973. There must have been other wives as well; when Pletch died, he left 16 grandchildren and 22 great-grandchildren.

CHAPTER II
1946–1959

PEACE IN EUROPE, TERROR IN THE SKIES

Nobody was hijacking planes during World War Two. However, the end of the war in 1945 precipitated three events, or phenomena, which would become the primary political causes for attacks against aviation in the years to follow:

- Eastern Europe embraced Communism due to the success of the Red Army's actions during the war, while socialist ideals were widely taken up across the rest of Europe as the continent set about its recovery.

- The birth of the State of Israel out of the ashes of the Holocaust and the associated failure of both Israel's neighbours and the Palestinian leadership to accept the United Nations' Partition Plan which would have, back in 1948, seen a state of Palestine come into being.

- Twenty years later, the development of rebellious, youth-led, left-wing social activist movements piggybacking on to any cause which challenged the status quo or acted in support of those deemed oppressed.

The Berlin Wall had yet to be constructed when the first Eastern Europeans decided that communism was not a lifestyle choice they wished to pursue and that steps, or flights, had to be taken to escape to the West.

On 25 July 1947, three Romanian army officers hijacked their own Transporturile Aeriene Romano-Sovietice (TARS) flight, which was supposed to fly from Bucharest to Craiova. Ten minutes into the flight, the officers entered the cockpit and ordered Captain Vasile Ciobanu to divert to Turkey. Flight engineer Mitrofan Bescioti attempted to overpower the armed officers, but paid the price for his actions by being shot by Lieutenant Aurel Dobrea. Bescioti died from injuries. Ciobanu flew to Çanakkale, near Izmir in Turkey, where the officers were arrested on arrival and put on trial for the murder of Bescioti. Ciobanu returned to Romania, only to be sentenced to 16 years in prison as a traitor to the regime for allowing the hijack to succeed.

THE MISFORTUNE OF *MISS MACAU*

On 16 July 1948, a Macau Air Transport flight – a Catalina seaplane named *Miss Macau* – operating from Macau to Hong Kong was seized by four hijackers. It was well known at the time that Macau was a centre for gambling and casinos – they had been legalised there back in 1850 – while Hong Kong was a casino-free zone. Consequently, in an era that preceded credit cards, cheap flights and ease of air travel, there was an understandable belief that those passengers flying from Macau to Hong Kong were likely to be carrying large quantities of cash won on the gaming tables of Macau. Additionally, as Macau was the regional centre for the trade of gold, both maritime and airfreight operators were insured against acts of piracy. While passenger flights, such as *Miss Macau*, did not carry significant quantities of gold, their passengers were still well-to-do businessmen, bankers and merchants associated with the trade. All in all, flights between Macau and Hong Kong were likely to be carrying people able to pay significant ransoms for their freedom. At least, that was what a Chinese man by the name of Chio Tok believed. And Chio Tok was also a trained pilot.

With the plan to hijack the aircraft, replace the captain at the controls and then land the seaplane in the Pearl River estuary, Chio Tok first recruited two gunmen, Chio Cheong and Chio Kei Mun, and then a local villager, Wong Yu, who was familiar with the Pearl River, and was persuaded to join the group in return for a small financial bribe. Chio Tok went on a number of flights to familiarise himself with the aircraft, the company's operating procedures and to run through the plan in his mind. As the date approached, he dropped Chio Kei Mun from the plan, having found out that he was addicted to opium, and replaced him with Siu Chek-kam.

Around eight minutes after take off, the co-pilot, Ken McDuff, left his seat to retract the wing floats. The three gunmen sprang into action and attempted to seize control of the aircraft. McDuff immediately tried to overpower the men, while Captain Dale Cramer resisted and banked sharply to the left in order to return to Macau. The three hijackers opened fire, shooting Captain Cramer in the head; his body slumped forward over the controls and the aircraft crashed into the sea. There was one survivor – a survivor who could not only later tell the police what had happened on board *Miss Macau* but could also explain the reason for the hijack. He was Wong Yu.

Bizarrely, once he was rescued, Wong Yu could not be prosecuted because the hijack had taken place outside what was then Portuguese airspace and on board a British aircraft. Furthermore, even though he confessed to his involvement in the plan, there was insufficient evidence to prove his guilt. He was eventually released from prison in Macau after three years without a trial and was then deported to China, where he 'met with an accident' resulting in his death.

We will never know whether Chio Tok knew how much money was being carried on board the aircraft that day. The investigation revealed that four millionaires died in the accident, and that the wife of one of them had told the police her husband had been carrying HK$500,000 with him.

This incident, along with the TARS hijacking in Romania, and a number of others in the 1950s, resulted in the industry advising aircrew to comply with the demands of hijackers rather than risk in-flight shoot-outs or detonations. Even at the height of the Palestinian hijackings in the 1960s and 1970s, compliance was still recommended, given that groups perpetrating such attacks were more focussed on media coverage than killing passengers and crew en masse. However, industry standards have, understandably, changed significantly in the aftermath of the 9/11 hijackings in the United States in 2001.

CONTRACT MURDER

Although the move from hijacking towards sabotage only commenced in the mid-1980s, when terrorism was the cause, criminals had resorted to the destruction of commercial aircraft in-flight for financial benefit much earlier.

It was on 7 May 1949 that a Philippine Airlines flight, en route from Daet to Manila, crashed into the Sibuyan Sea, killing all 13 souls on board. The cause was an IED secreted on board by two contract killers hired to murder a man in order that his wife be free to marry somebody else. Obtusely, love, rather than hate, was a common theme for early acts of sabotage.

TIMED TO DIE FAMOUS

On 9 September 1949, Albert Guay put into effect a plan to kill his wife while she was a passenger on board a Canadian Pacific Airlines DC-3 operating from Montreal to Baie-Comeau via Quebec City, taking the lives of all 23 people on board with her. Rita Morrell, Guay's wife, boarded the flight in Quebec City with a timer-based IED infiltrated into her baggage. It is possible that, had the aircraft departed on time, it would have been flying over the St Lawrence River, which would have prevented any subsequent investigation as to the cause. It was no surprise that Guay chose to use a timing mechanism, as he was a jeweller and watchmaker.

Albert Guay and Rita Morrell's marriage was reported to be tempestuous, and both had had affairs. Guay's business was also floundering and his debts were on the increase, yet he found some solace in the arms of a 19-year-old waitress, Marie-Ange Robitaille. While she knew he was married, her parents did not; so, once Guay had proposed marriage and given her an engagement ring, he was introduced to them as Roger Angers. When Rita Morrell found out about the extent of the relationship, she confronted Marie-Ange's parents, showing them her own wedding photographs. Marie-Ange was thrown out of the family home.

Divorce was not an option in Quebec in the 1940s. With Marie-Ange threatening to leave him if he could not commit to their future together, more drastic action seemed necessary. Accordingly, Guay persuaded his wife to fly to Baie-Comeau on a business trip to collect some jewels; he purchased her ticket and took out a CAD$10,000 insurance policy on her life.

Marguerite Ruest-Pitre, later given the title 'Madame Raven' as she always wore black, had been organising the secret meetings of Guay and Marie-Ange and she started renting the girl a room once the teenager's father had thrown her out. Marguerite was indebted to Guay, as she had borrowed money from him and had repeatedly failed to make timely repayments. It was Marguerite's brother, who was employed by Guay as a repairman, to whom Guay turned for assistance in constructing the bomb.

Genereux Ruest's device comprised of a timing mechanism and ten pounds of dynamite, purchased by Marguerite. Once constructed, Marguerite took the package to the airport and had it shipped, on the same flight as Rita, as airmail.

Marguerite was the first suspect as witnesses had noticed her suspicious behaviour at the airport, but nobody knew her name. It was only once Guay was the subject of the police's investigation that they found Marguerite, and that was because Marie-Ange Robitaille, who no longer had any interest in Guay, led them to her. On the day that the police questioned Marguerite, she initially claimed that she thought she had been shipping a figurine. However, after she later took an overdose, which resulted in her hospitalisation, she confessed her involvement.

Guay was arrested after claiming on the life insurance policy taken out on his wife, and was sentenced to death. In an apparent effort to postpone his own execution, he further implicated Marguerite and Genereux, who was by then sick and confined to a wheelchair. They were both arrested and also sentenced to hang.

As Guay walked to the gallows, his final words were 'At least I die famous'. Sadly, this view is shared by many of today's terrorists. The siblings were also hanged, with Genereux having to be carried to the gallows and Marguerite having the dubious honour of being the last woman to be hanged in Canada.

THE FIRST TRIPLE HIJACK

The concept of using international flights as vehicles to escape to seemingly greener pastures has been repeated many times since the TARS hijacking in 1947 (see p.23). There are abundant examples of flights being hijacked from the former Soviet Union to the West, from China to Taiwan, from Iran to Israel, from poorer states in Africa and Asia to wealthier states in Europe, from Cuba to the United States and, of course, from the United States to Cuba. Coordinated attacks against aviation targeting multiple flights is, however, a tactic better associated with the likes of the Abu Nidal Organisation in the 1980s and, more recently, the al-Qaeda brand of terrorism. But there was one notable exception way back in 1950.

On 24 March 1950, three Czechoslovak State Airlines (CSA) Douglas DC-3 aircraft operating three different routes were hijacked simultaneously by their pilots. By the end of the day, all three aircraft were to be found on the ground at the US air force base in Erding, West Germany. The destination had been chosen as, to avoid arousing the suspicion of the passengers they were transporting, it had a similar flying time to the original destinations of the flights the airmen planned to hijack.

Pilots that flew for CSA who had flown for the Royal Air Force (RAF) during the war were restricted to domestic flights and their family members were never allowed to board flights they were piloting. The group of hijackers were forced, therefore, to concoct a complex plan to get themselves, their families and some trusted friends out of Czechoslovakia.

Firstly, they had to get themselves assigned to three flights, from three different cities – Brno, Ostrava and Bratislava – to Prague, flying on the same day. On 23 March, Vit Angetter, Ladislav Světlík and Oldřich Doležal met up at a coffee shop in

Prague's Ruzyně International Airport before operating their various flights to Brno, Ostrava and Bratislava, where they were to overnight before initiating their multi-flight skyjacking. They could only carry enough luggage for an overnight stay, but they were planning on leaving home for good.

Of the 85 people that boarded the three flights on 24 March, 26 knew that their flights would not be going to Prague as planned – a huge number of people not to arouse suspicion among the 'genuine' passengers.

With Vit Angetter on board the CSA flight departing Brno were Kamil Mráz, serving as the radio operator/navigator – who was also armed – and Lída Škorpíková, the flight attendant; they were part of the plot. Also in the know were Angetter's wife, Eva Veselá, who was travelling under her maiden name and Miroslav Hanzlíček, a CSA employee. Oblivious to the situation were Captain Josef Klesnil and Jan Tuček, the flight engineer, who found themselves bound and gagged by the time the plane landed. As it happens, Klesnil had been planning a similar escape, but with his family still at home in Czechoslovakia, he had to return.

On board the CSA flight departing Ostrava were Captain Ladislav Světlík, co-pilot Mečislav Kozák, Cestmír Brož, the radio operator/navigator and Gejza Holoda, the flight engineer, but only Světlík knew the plan. Among the 23 passengers, four were in the know; one of whom was CSA pilot Viktor Popelka, along with Popelka's wife, who was travelling under her maiden name, and the wife and son of Oldřich Doležal, the pilot of the Bratislava plane.

During the flight, Světlík had to leave the cockpit in order to facilitate Popelka's entry. The two men managed to overpower the other crew members and, as on the other aircraft, secure those crew members who were not part of the plan in the luggage area at the rear of the cockpit; the passengers remained oblivious to the situation.

On board the CSA flight departing Bratislava were Captain Oldřich Doležal, co-pilot Bořivoj Šmíd, Stansislav Šácha, the radio operator/navigator, Jan Královansky, the flight engineer and Eva Vysloužilová, the flight attendant. All the crew knew the plan, so it was deemed to be the easiest plan to pull off. However, it was also the last flight to leave, so there was the possibility that the loss of radio contact with the other aircraft could provoke a response from the authorities. The risk was exacerbated by the delayed departure of the aircraft, caused by the escaping passengers bringing excess luggage with them (despite instructions to the contrary). The captain had to request additional fuel, which raised concerns among airport security and resulted in all the passengers having to undergo additional document checks.

It was during these checks that the police identified the name 'Vrzánova' on the passenger manifest. One month earlier, the Czechoslovak world figure skating champion, Alena 'Áji' Vrzáňová, had defected in the West; her mother was one of the latest group of escapees!

Thirty minutes delayed, the aircraft was ready to depart but, at the last minute, they were instructed to return to the terminal. The radio operator pretended not to have heard and the aircraft departed.

Of the 85 people who landed in Erding, 27 claimed political asylum, and one American diplomat, serving in Prague, was immediately released. It took four days to arrange the repatriation of the other 57. On their arrival home, a press conference was held in which the group's spokesman said that they had 'rejected capitalist heaven'. Josef Klesnil, Mečislav Kozák and Gejza Holoda became the scapegoats and were all dismissed from CSA. A book entitled *Unos do Erdingu (Kidnap to Erding)* was published portraying the pilots as gangsters and the returning citizens as heroes. In 1953, the book was made into a film called *Unos*.

THE OAXACA BALLAD OF PACO AND ESPERANZA

In the 1950s, despite the now significant number of incidents already perpetrated, passengers were not being screened prior to boarding flights, nor, as in the case of Mexicana Airlines flight 575 on 24 September 1952, was the delivery of bags to the aircraft prohibited.

The DC-3 was preparing to depart Mexico City for Oaxaca's Xoxocotlan Airport when a man appeared at the door and delivered a bag to Irma Carranza, the flight attendant. He asked her to hold on to the bag, despite the fact that he was not a passenger; it was, allegedly, for another passenger who had yet to board. Nowadays, such a request would be treated with extreme suspicion around the world, and procedures would not permit the bag to fly... but this was 1952, when flying was fun and naivety levels high.

The flight's departure was delayed due to a crew change. Irma never actually flew to Oaxaca that day, but she did prepare the aircraft for departure while awaiting her colleague, Lilia Novelo Torres. In the process, Irma cleared the aft galley and moved the bag to the front baggage compartment, despite the man who had delivered the bag having instructed her to keep the bag at the rear of the aircraft.

Forty-five minutes after take off, the bomb, triggered by a timing mechanism, exploded. Two passengers suffered broken legs because the baggage compartment wall collapsed on them; three other passengers were injured by shrapnel, but the aircraft itself remained intact. The crew were able to successfully land at

Santa Lucia Air Force Base, where the aircraft was surrounded by armed soldiers suspicious of the unexpected arrival.

The investigation revealed a plan to benefit from payouts on life insurance policies, as well as human trafficking. Six of the passengers travelling on the Mexicana flight thought that they would be taking up employment at a hotel in Oaxaca – a hotel that did not exist. Two men had fabricated this early example of human trafficking by air. The conmen had taken out life insurance policies on the 'new hires' and were to be the beneficiaries should they meet an untimely end.

The aircraft survived the blast, probably because of the location of the bag within the cabin, so the police had little trouble in identifying the culprits. The eight employees were alive and able to give testimony, and Irma was available to provide an account of the delivery of the bag to the flight. When they identified the culprits, it sent shockwaves through Mexico.

Francisco Sierra was a baritone opera singer, married to the more famous and significantly older opera singer Esperanza Iris; he was better known as Paco Sierra, she as 'The Queen of the Operetta'. The couple mixed in high society and travelled the world, but Paco was a proud, yet greedy man who was far from content to be living off the success of his more famous wife. Paco was always in search of a way of making some extra money and it was this which led him to formulate a plan with his friend, the equally greedy Emilio Arellano, to make it big time.

Emilio made all the arrangements, including the insurance policies. He placed adverts in the newspapers to hire workers for the Oaxaca hotel and, once he had five willing candidates, he then recruited his uncle, Ramon Martinez Arellano, to be the transporter of the bomb.

When the plane landed in Santa Lucia, those passengers who thought they had jobs in Oaxaca opted to continue their journeys there the same day. This was an added reason for the identification of Arellano as the prime culprit; when they arrived in Oaxaca, nobody met them!

There had been one death, but not as a result of the bomb itself. Eugenio Pologvsky, a passenger on board, panicked and jumped from the aircraft to his death after the explosion, his body landing near Zozocolco.

As Arellano was the fixer, he was sentenced to 30 years in prison. Paco, having played a more passive role, and thanks to his numerous high society connections, was only sentenced to nine years. However, Paco appealed the sentence which he, and more importantly Esperanza, thought was excessive. This time luck was not on his side and the sentence was increased to 29 years.

Esperanza died in 1962 and Paco was released in 1971, only to marry and sing again!

ESCAPE TO XIAMEN

Criminal attacks against aviation were not only for financial gain, as was witnessed on 30 December 1952, when a Philippine Airlines flight operating a domestic route between Laoag and Aparri was hijacked by a Chinese man, Ang Chio-Kio, who was armed with a .45-calibre pistol.

The hijacker had killed a 16-year-old Chinese schoolgirl with whom he was infatuated, in front of her teacher and classmates in Manila, and had also shot the policeman who had attempted to arrest him; Ang Chio-Kio was now desperate to get to China. He boarded the flight using a false name – Hung Chu-Chun, shot and killed the first officer, and then ordered Captain Felix Gaston to fly to Xiamen in China.

As the aircraft was on its final approach, flying at only 50 ft above the sea, the unexpected DC-3 came under fire from the Chinese air force, forcing the captain to divert and land on the Taiwanese island of Quemoy. A flight attendant tried to enter the flight deck, but was also shot and killed by the hijacker. When the aircraft eventually landed on Quemoy, both the captain and the hijacker were placed under arrest, with the hijacker believing he was safely on Communist territory. They were both treated with equal suspicion and kept in the same farmhouse for interrogation.

Gaston was eventually allowed to return to the Philippines the next day; two days later his wife gave birth to their first child.

FRITZ ATTACK

The Philippine Airlines flight had *almost* been shot down by the Chinese. Almost became *actually* on 22 July 1954 when a Cathay Pacific Airways flight operating from Bangkok, Thailand to Hong Kong, was shot down by Chinese La-9 Fritz fighters near Hainan Island. There were 18 people on board, of whom only eight survived.

The attack came as a complete surprise to all on board as the aircraft was suddenly riddled with bullets. Captain Phil Blown was at the controls and he put the aircraft into a dive to avoid the onslaught. The aircraft eventually crashed into the sea and those passengers who had not been killed in their seats by the gunfire ripping through the fuselage managed to escape the wreckage. Once they were convinced that they were no longer under attack by the Chinese fighter aircraft, they inflated the life raft and awaited rescue.

China did eventually apologise to Cathay Pacific for their error and offered to pay compensation to the victims and their families.

TARGET: ZHOU ENLAI

Today's communication systems make it highly unlikely for an airliner to be shot down in the fashion described above, but if you were to ask many a modern-day airport security manager what keeps him or her awake at night, they will concede that it is the 'insider' threat – that posed by the trusted employee or individual with access to airside facilities or aircraft themselves. The insider threat may well be behind the most recent aviation disaster (at the time of writing), in which it is suspected that an airport-based employee in Sharm el-Sheikh may have infiltrated an explosive device onto a Metrojet flight bound for St. Petersburg on 31 October 2015 (see p.310). It would not have been the first time.

On 11 April 1955, an Air India flight operating from Hong Kong to Jakarta exploded and crashed into the sea near the Natuna Islands. The aircraft was carrying Chinese and Eastern European delegates to a conference when an IED concealed in the wheel bay of the aircraft detonated, perforating the fuel tank. The flight engineer, the navigator and first officer all escaped, but the remaining 16 passengers were killed.

It is believed that an aircraft cleaner, Chow-Tse Ming, an employee of the Hong Kong Aircraft Engineering Company, had infiltrated the device on board in an attempt to assassinate then Chinese Premier Zhou Enlai. When Chow-Tse Ming was questioned by the authorities, he made his escape by becoming a stowaway on board an aircraft to Taiwan. It is widely believed that Chow-Tse Ming was in fact an agent for the Kuomintang and that the group had recruited Ming specifically because of his job as a cleaner at the airport.

Zhou Enlai never actually boarded the flight and there is some speculation that he hadn't even travelled to Hong Kong, due to his having to undergo an emergency appendectomy.

Others, however, believe that Zhou Enlai was made aware of the plot and that the alleged appendectomy was merely a ruse to conceal the fact that he actually allowed the bombing to take place, knowing that he would be sacrificing some of the lesser members of his Chinese delegation.

INTERCEPTS AND SHOOT DOWNS

While conflict in the Middle East was not to become a causal factor for aircraft hijackings until the late 1960s, the region's skies were not always a safe place to be.

On 12 December 1954, two days after five Israeli soldiers had been captured in Syria, a Syrian DC-3 bound for Cairo strayed into Israeli airspace, was intercepted by Mustang fighter jets from the Israeli air force and forced to land at Lod Airport near Tel Aviv. In what was to all intents and purposes a war zone, any government could justify taking action against civilian airliners from enemy states entering its airspace; however, the subsequent action taken by Israel was, and continues to be, utilised as a political weapon to this day.

Once the aircraft was on the ground, all the passengers were interviewed by members of the Israeli security services. An American passenger, Ralph Krohn Hansen, was quickly released. So too was the aircraft's Greek pilot, although he decided to stay in Israel with his aircraft. The other crew members and passengers were detained for 48 hours, during which time the Israelis inadvertently introduced a tactic, which would be exploited by Palestinian terrorist groups years later – holding passengers hostage in return for the release of prisoners held in overseas prisons. The Israeli government wanted their five soldiers back and, in a diplomatic faux pas, they utilised their unexpected guests as a means to do so.

In the years since, Israel's action has been described by some as either a hijacking and/or a terrorist act by a sovereign state. Indeed, the Internet is awash with references to the incident, mostly citing philosopher and linguist Noam Chomsky's description of the event as 'the first airplane hijacking in the Middle East'. This statement is far-fetched; a naïve error of judgement it may have been, calculated terrorist attack it was not.

Regardless, according to the Institute of Palestinian Studies, within 48 hours, the Syrian government agreed to exchange the captured Israeli soldiers for the hostages. The short-term gain of the delayed release of passengers set a dangerous precedent, and one which certainly troubled Moshe Sharrett, then Foreign Minister of Israel. In his diaries, Sharratt wrote:

> It must be clear to you that we had no justification whatsoever to seize the plane, and that once forced down we should have immediately released it and not held the passengers under interrogation for 48 hours. I have no reason to doubt the truth of the factual affirmation of the US State Department that our action was without precedent in the history of international practice. What shocks and worries me is the narrow-mindedness and the short-sightedness of our military leaders. They seem to presume that the State of Israel may – or even must – behave in the realm of international relations according to the law of the jungle.

The threat of being shot down was also demonstrated on 27 July 1955 when an El Al Israel Airlines Lockheed Constellation, flying from London to Tel Aviv, via Vienna and Istanbul, was shot down by the Bulgarian air force, after the aircraft strayed into Bulgarian airspace during inclement weather, soon after its take off from Vienna for Istanbul.

The Bulgarian air force had scrambled two MiG-15 jets to intercept the intruder. Bulgaria quickly acknowledged that it had shot down the plane, and Israel did not dispute that its plane had crossed into Bulgaria without authorisation. The plane was ordered to land, but the aircraft altered course for Greece, possibly as a corrective measure.

Gen. Velitchko Georgiev, told the two MiG pilots, Boris Vasilev Petrov and Konstantin Krumov Sankiyski, 'If the plane is leaving our territory, disobeying orders, and there is no time left for more warnings, then shoot it down.'

The El Al aircraft crashed near the Strumitza River, close to the Yugolsav and Greek borders in south west Bulgaria killing all 51 passengers and seven crew members on board. Bulgaria apologised for the error the next day, but maintained its assertion that the El Al crew, piloted by Captain Stanley Hinks and First Officer Pini Ben-Porat, had not responded to their demands that the aircraft land. After extended negotiations, it was agreed in June 1963 that compensation be paid for the 22 Israelis who died in the crash; an agreement was signed by which Bulgaria would pay Israel a total of $195,000, far less than the $2,500,000 the Israelis had originally claimed. Each of the families of the victims received $8,236, in accordance with the maximum compensation payment fixed by the Warsaw Convention for damage claims of individuals against foreign governments.

KILLING MUM... THAT'S JUST THE WAY IT GOES

Albert Guay may have valued his wife at CAD$10,000 when he decided to do away with her on board the Canadian Pacific flight back in 1949 (see p.26), but John Gilbert Graham valued his mother, Daisie King, slightly higher. He took out a US$37,500 life insurance policy for her at the airport prior to her departure on a United Airlines flight on 1 November 1955. Graham may well have been inspired by Guay's actions in Canada six years earlier.

Initially, sabotage was not suspected, but the examination of the wreckage revealed deposits of sodium carbonate, nitrate and sulphur compounds, commensurate with nitroglycerine-based dynamite.

Graham became the prime suspect, thanks to the contents of his mother's carry-on baggage and the complete absence of her checked luggage. Daisie King's handbag was found to contain personal letters, newspaper clippings about her family, two keys and a receipt for her safety deposit boxes, as well as newspaper clippings related to Graham having been charged with forgery by the Denver County District Attorney and having been placed on the local 'most-wanted' list by that office in 1951. Graham's background was researched and it became apparent that he was set to inherit a considerable amount of money upon his mother's death, in addition to the insurance policy taken out before the United Airlines flight. As it happened, Daisie King didn't have the largest life insurance policy on the aircraft.

As well as discrepancies between his testimony and that of his wife, it was Daisie's policy which was to be Graham's downfall. He claimed not to have the policy paperwork despite having mailed it to himself from the airport; when his house was searched, the police found the policy secreted in a cedar chest. They also found some wire in a shirt pocket, the type associated with detonators. Graham realised that the game was up and admitted to bombing the aircraft. Graham was no stranger to insurance fraud: as well as the policy taken out on his mother, Graham admitted to causing an explosion at his mother's drive-in restaurant earlier in the year, and to intentionally leaving his Chevrolet on a train track and allowing it to be hit by an oncoming train. In both cases, he had benefited from insurance claims.

Graham told the police that he had constructed the bomb for the United Airlines flight from 25 sticks of dynamite, two electric primer caps, a timing device, and a six-volt battery. As Daisie King had packed her own baggage - she was a very independent woman who would never have allowed family members to do so for her - he had given the package to his mother disguised as a Christmas present, and told her not to open it until Christmas Day. As far as Graham's wife was aware, the gift comprised of drills, files and cutting tools used for creating art pieces out of seashells; she was unaware that the gift also included some added 'extras' before being wrapped.

On 17 November 1955, Graham was charged with murder; almost three weeks had passed since the crash. Graham pleaded insanity, but the psychiatrists thought he was mentally competent to stand trial. On 10 February, he tried to commit suicide in his cell.

Graham's trial was to commence on 16 April 1956, and on 5 May the jury found Graham guilty of murder in the first degree and recommended the death penalty. He was executed in the gas chamber on 11 January 1957.

The impact on his wife and children was unimaginable. Gloria Graham kept a vigil with friends on the night of her husband's execution and she buried his ashes the next morning before changing her surname, and that of her children, back to her maiden name – Elson. Gloria did remarry, but was later divorced. She died of natural causes in Colorado in 1992.

As for Graham, his final words were:

" As far as feeling remorse for these people, I don't. I can't help it. Everybody pays their way and takes their chances. That's just the way it goes. "

CHAPTER III
1960—1968

BACK TO THE USSR

Australia has been relatively untouched by the threat of terrorist hijacking. Today it is one of the most proactive states in the fight against violence in the skies with some of the most intensive aircrew security-awareness and response training programmes in the world. But there have been significant incidents, all of which perpetrated by individuals with mental-health issues rather than with terrorist or criminal intent.

The first involved a Trans Australia Airlines flight operating from Sydney to Brisbane on the evening of 19 July 1960. The hijacker was an unemployed 22-year-old Russian man, Alex Hilderbrandt. Shortly after take off, he pushed the call button and flight attendant Janeene Christie responded, only to have a sawn-off .22 rifle pointed at her neck; she was ordered to summon the captain.

While Christie was reporting the situation to the captain, a second flight attendant notified the flight deck that the man was carrying two sticks of dynamite with wires protruding from them. First Officer Tom R. Bennett made his way into the cabin while the cabin crew discreetly notified Captain Dennis Lawrence, who happened to be travelling as a passenger.

Hilderbrandt told Bennett that he wished to fly to Darwin or Singapore; his intent was to get back to Russia, having become disillusioned with the capitalist society his mother had brought him to. He cradled the bomb, which he had put together in the aircraft's toilets, as he spoke to the first officer. Bennett drew closer and Hilderbrandt fired a warning shot which hit the cabin ceiling. Bennett decided action was better than debate and threw a punch into Hilderbrandt's face and another to his stomach, before Lawrence, standing behind, then knocked him on the head with a crash axe. Despite carrying a viable IED, the two Australian pilots successfully subdued Hilderbrandt. Bennett was awarded the George Medal for his heroism.

TAKE ME TO HAVANA

While diplomatic ties between Cuba and the USA are now being normalised, this was certainly not the case in the 1960s. Indeed, Cuba became synonymous with hijacking. The first of the flights to be hijacked by pro-Castro revolutionaries took place on 21 October 1958 with the seizure of a Cubana flight by Raul Castro and members of Column 6. In the years that followed, there was an abundance of flights hijacked from Cuba to the USA and indeed from the USA to Cuba.

It could well be argued that Fidel Castro and his followers actually introduced the concept of aircraft hijacking for terrorist purposes and there is no doubt that the airport security checkpoints that we see around the globe today – i.e., archway metal detectors for passenger screening and transmission X-ray machines for hand-baggage inspection – were a response to the phenomenon of individuals armed with guns, knives, and grenades – all being dense metallic objects identifiable by such technologies.

The first American aircraft to be hijacked to Cuba was a National Airlines flight operating from Miami to Key West on 1 May 1961, when Antulio Ramirez Ortiz checked in under the name El Pirate Cofrisi, and used a knife and revolver to order co-pilot J. T. Richardson out of the cockpit and force Captain Francis Riley to alter his course for Cuba.

As detailed in Chapter I, the aviation industry regards the first hijacking to have taken place on 21 February 1931, when Captain Byron Rickards had his aircraft commandeered in Arequipa, Peru (see p.16). Rickards was also the first captain to be hijacked twice. Coincidentally, Rickards' name is also associated with the first aircraft hijacking in which an individual was sent to prison for hijacking an aircraft in the US; that hijacker's name was Leon Bearden.

Bearden, a convicted criminal, not only hijacked Continental Airlines flight 54 from Phoenix to El Paso on 3 August 1961, but he did so with the help of his 16-year-old son, Cody, in order to seek a new life for them in Cuba. Rickards managed to convince father and son that they had insufficient fuel to make the trip to Havana and the hijackers agreed that the aircraft land to refuel in El Paso, the original destination of the flight. The authorities in Texas stalled the departure of the aircraft and, in order to prevent its eventual departure, shot out its tyres, thereby immobilising the aircraft.

Bearden believed that the most valuable asset was the aircraft itself, which he wished to provide as a gift to the Cuban authorities in return for asylum. He had therefore released almost all of the passengers in El Paso, but had retained four of them as volunteer hostages. It was one of these volunteers, Leonard Gilman, who happened to be a former boxer, who seized the opportunity to knock out Leon Bearden with a punch that actually broke Gilman's hand. One of the FBI negotiators, who had been allowed to board the aircraft, overpowered Cody. This particular case resulted in a change in American legislation and aircraft hijacking became a capital offence. Leon Bearden was simply sent to Alcatraz.

DESPERATE DOTY

On 22 May 1962, Continental Airlines flight 11 became the first jet airliner to be destroyed by a bomb. It was carried on board the aircraft by Thomas Doty, who had taken out a life insurance policy on himself valued at $300,000. Doty, who was about to stand trial for an armed robbery and expected to be sentenced to imprisonment, took it upon himself to provide for his wife and 5-year-old daughter. He purchased six sticks of dynamite and detonated the device he had constructed in the aircraft's toilets while en route from Chicago to Kansas City. Forty-five passengers and crew were on board the aircraft, all but one of whom died as the aircraft hit the ground near Unionville, Missouri; the sole surviving passenger died later in hospital. It is likely that the passengers had some warning of their impending fate as the pilots were found to be wearing smoke masks and the captain was found to have the emergency checklist to hand.

FATSO AND CREWCUT

Flying an aircraft while being shot at and stabbed is no easy feat, landing it safely while oozing blood with two hijackers shooting and stabbing you is downright heroic. But that's just what Captain Anatoly Shevlev and his co-pilot, Vladimir Baydetsky, managed to do on 29 September 1964 when they were hijacked en route from Chadyr-Lunga to Izmail.

The hijackers, who were determined to leave the Soviet Union having escaped from prison the night before, took on legendary status in the Russian media; they were nicknamed 'Fatso' and 'Crewcut'. They burst into the flight deck and ordered the pilots to head towards the Black Sea. Initially, the crew complied, but they also managed to disengage the compass so that the hijackers lost their bearings. It was when the cockpit intruders caught sight of the city of Chisinau that they realised the pilots had duped them. In retaliation, Crewcut then stabbed the captain in the back and Fatso opened fire, hitting the pilot's hand. The desperate crew responded with aggressive manoeuvres in an attempt to throw the hijackers off balance, but to no avail. Worse, Fatso kept shooting while Crewcut continued to lash out with his knife. By the time the aircraft crash-landed into a vineyard, between them, the pilots had been shot seven times and stabbed four times.

Despite the severity of their injuries, the crew managed to escape the mangled aircraft and were later awarded the Order of the Red Banner.

The hijackers, whose real names were N. N. Gudumak and G. N. Karadzhi, were not to survive, despite also managing to escape the aircraft itself. Karadzhi made his way towards Chisinau, killing the vineyard's watchman on the way. The police tracked him down to a house in the city where a gun battle commenced; two policemen were to die before Karadzhi was also to succumb to a gunshot to the head, which, according to some accounts, was self-inflicted. Gudumak made his way to Chisinau Airport where he was eventually captured. On 12 February 1965 the Supreme Court of the Moldavian Regions sentenced him to death.

BOLIVIAN TRAGEDY

Insurance payouts continued to be the primary reason for detonating explosive devices on airlines in the 1960s. An Aerolíneas Abaroa DC-3 was operating a Bolivian domestic route between Tipuani and La Paz on 8 December 1964, when an explosion near the tail of the aircraft caused it to crash into the Andes, killing the 11 passengers and four crew members on board, including Gral. Cortez Villanueva, one of the airline's two founding members. His business partner, Walter Arze, had been killed in an accident in 1962. Following the deaths of both the airline's founders within two years of each other, the airline also saw its demise.

THE HIJACKERS WHO BECAME NATIONAL HEROES

The last year in which England won the FIFA World Cup, and the year the first and last hijacking of a commercial aircraft took place by a group of trade unionists, was 1966. On 28 September, an Aerolíneas Argentinas flight operating from Buenos Aires to Rio Gallegos was seized by a glamorous theatre director, Maria Christina Varrier, a journalist, Dado Cabo, and 18 members of the metal workers union (UOM) led by Augosto Timoteo Vandor.

The crew were forced to fly to the Falkland Islands. On arrival, they landed on the racecourse in Stanley, as there was no airstrip on the islands. The hijackers hoisted the Argentinian flag claiming sovereignty of the Falkland Islands and announced that they were renaming Port Stanley as Porto Revero. The Royal Marines surrounded the aircraft and the hijackers surrendered 36 hours later before being repatriated to Argentina to stand trial. As a result of the hijacking, the British government increased its military presence on the islands, but back in Argentina, the hijackers became heroes. Indeed, the hijacking, known nowadays as Operativo Cóndor ('Operation Condor'), is celebrated by leftist elements in Argentina to this day.

In 2011, on the forty-fifth anniversary of the incident, the South Atlantic News Agency, MercoPress, reported that Antonio Callo, the UOM chairman, spoke at a public ceremony, saying:

> Today is a historic day for UOM because we are honouring these true heroes who displayed no fear but much courage on taking an aircraft and have it flown to our Malvinas Islands.

THE CURIOUS CASE OF MOISE TSHOMBE

Moise Tshombe was a Congolese politician, who also managed to enter aviation security's hall of fame. He was co-founder, along with Godefroid Munongo, of the CONAKAT Party, which sought independence for what was then the Belgian Congo. Tshombe became president of one of the Congo's providences, Katanga, and was vocal in his demands that the province be made independent from the Congo. This resulted in a civil war between Katangan rebels and Patrice Lumumba's Central Congolese government.

Lumumba was overthrown in 1960 and, in 1961, flown to Katanga, being beaten up on board the Sabena aircraft on which he was being transported. He was later executed by firing squad, an act for which Tshombe was later held responsible. Katanga was not independent for long and, after a brief period of reacceptance by the new political elite in the Congo, Tshombe was forced into exile, settling in Spain in 1965 and, while there, was sentenced to death *in absentia*.

In an effort to get Tshombe back to Congo to meet his fate, a plot was hatched in which he was encouraged to invest in a property deal. He was told that he would be taken on a private aircraft to fly over the real estate in question. On 30 June 1967, a Hawker Siddeley air taxi was chartered to transport Tshombe from Ibiza to Palma by supposed businessman Francis Bodenan, who was in fact working for the Deuxième Bureau, the French counter-espionage service, and who was to become the aircraft's hijacker. Bodenan was armed and ordered the British pilots, while en route, to fly to Algeria, where the passengers, except Tshombe, were released.

The British pilots, Trevor Copleston and David Taylor, were detained for 12 weeks, during which they were repeatedly interrogated by the Algerian authorities. It was only thanks to the efforts of the International Air Line Pilots Association, and their threat to boycott Algerian airspace, that they were freed.

The incident plunged Algeria into the midst of an international dispute, with European nations demanding Tshombe's release and Algeria's African compatriots requesting that he be extradited to Congo. In the end, although the Democratic Republic of Congo became independent in 1968, Tshombe died in captivity in Algeria in June 1969, supposedly due to a heart attack.

GOODBYE VIETNAM

The late 1960s saw the height of the Vietnam War. With US casualty rates ever on the increase, the number of soldiers deserting became a key concern for military strategists. This was exemplified on 9 February 1968, when a US marine boarded a Pan Am flight in Da Nang, Vietnam, drew his pistol and ordered the pilot to 'take me to Hong Kong'. The aircraft had in fact been chartered to take 83 troops to Hong Kong for a period of rest and relaxation but the marine in question, Private William L. Clark, was not on the manifest.

The captain ordered the other troops to disembark and then summoned assistance, which came in the form of military police throwing tear gas into the cockpit. Some two years after Clark had been court martialled and dishonourably discharged, he was diagnosed as suffering from schizophrenia.

INTERNATIONAL FLIGHTS BECOME TERRORIST TARGETS

In the late 1960s, three political tsunamis were taking place in different regions of the world, which were to have a significant impact on the security of aviation in the subsequent decade.

In the United States, the assassination of Malcolm X in 1965 was instrumental in the establishment of the Black Panther Party in 1966. The Panthers believed that the non-violent campaign for black civil rights waged by Martin Luther King Jr was getting them nowhere, and that the only way that equality could be reached was through revolution. This resulted in a spate of hijackings, to both Cuba and Algeria, where the perpetrators either sought ransoms to finance their cause, or requested asylum. In addition to civil rights activism, reports coming back from the war in Vietnam fuelled anti-government sentiments and, ironically, the pacifist movement was used to justify criminal attacks against civil aviation.

Revolutionary organisations were springing up throughout Europe in the 1960s, where there was a sense that Western imperialism was leading the world towards a third world war. Nowhere was this more evident than in West Germany, where the Western contribution to both the Vietnam and Six-Day Wars was to fan the flames of social activism.

It was on 2 April 1968 that the Rote Armee Fraktion (RAF) carried out its first attack, albeit not against aviation; two students, Andreas Baader and Gudrun Ensslin, planted bombs in two Frankfurt department stores. They were arrested and charged, but their actions drew the support of lawyer Horst Mahler and journalist Ulrike Meinhof, both of whom ended up joining the RAF. By early 1970, Baader, Meinhof, Ensslin, Mahler and a number of other RAF members had left Germany for Lebanon and Jordan in order to train in Palestine Liberation Organisation camps. This period was instrumental in the link-up between what was to be called the Baader-Meinhof Gang and the Popular Front for the Liberation of Palestine (PFLP) and whose cooperation was set to have a significant impact on the hijackings of the 1970s.

Horst Mahler justified his group's actions by declaring that his organisation was participating 'in a war to end all war'.

And then there was the Middle East and the impact of the Six-Day War of June 1967 on Israel itself, their defeated Arab neighbours and the stateless Palestinian people.

While there had been previous hijackings with political intent, 23 July 1968 is often regarded as the day on which international terrorism started to challenge civil aviation globally. It was on that day that three members of the PFLP elected to hijack an El Al Israel Airlines flight, while en route from Rome to Tel Aviv. The timing was not a coincidence.

This was in the aftermath of the Six-Day War in which not only had the Arab nations failed to destroy Israel but many Palestinians – who had fled to refugee camps or villages in Jordan (West Bank), Egypt (Gaza Strip) and Syria (Golan Heights) post-1948 – now found themselves living in the same camps, but under Israeli control. The war had further distanced them from the opportunity of statehood and the world seemed not to care.

Dr George Habash, the leader of the PFLP, argued that the Palestinians needed to embrace non-traditional tactics if they were ever to destroy the Israeli state – the very kind that, they argued, had been used by Jewish activists in pre-1948 paramilitary groups, such as Lehi and the Irgun, to bring about statehood.

THE FIRST (AND LAST) SUCCESSFUL HIJACKING OF AN EL AL FLIGHT

El Al flight 426 was seized shortly after its departure from Rome on 23 July 1968 and ordered to fly to Algiers, where non-Israeli passengers were freed; for many, freedom would only come 39 days later. By 27 July, the ten remaining Israeli women and three children on board had been released, leaving only the Israeli men as hostages: seven crew members, two airline employees and five passengers. They were accommodated in army barracks near the airfield.

The Popular Front for the Liberation of Palestine were requesting the release of more than 1,000 political prisoners held in Israeli jails and the Algerian government was, understandably, initially sympathetic to their demands. However, as international pressure on Algeria again increased (the government had recent experience of the previously cited Tshombe affair, see p.48) and the threat of severed vital trade routes loomed (another boycott of Algerian airspace had been proposed, and agreed upon, by the International Federation of Airline Pilots Association on 13 August), a diplomatic solution was sought.

With the Palestinian case having been made, a final deal was struck, and on 1 September all the remaining Israeli hostages were released after more than six weeks in captivity. Israel, for its part, released 16 Palestinian prisoners as a 'humanitarian gesture' two days after their own nationals had returned home.

The mood within the PFLP was mixed. The Palestinian cause had become an international issue, yet they were furious that the Algerian government had released the prisoners and the El Al jet without consultation with them. Furthermore, even their own planning came under internal scrutiny as they had targeted that particular El Al flight as they had believed that

General Ariel Sharon (later prime minister) was a passenger on board; in fact, he was flying from Paris to Tel Aviv at the time the hijack took place.

The Israeli response to this incident was swift and designed to prevent such an attack ever succeeding again. Two security measures were introduced. Firstly, 'passenger profiling', whereby any individual intending to board an El Al flight was subjected to questioning and risk assessment. Secondly, recognising that even passenger profiling was not foolproof, a sky marshal programme, whereby armed guards were deployed on each and every El Al aircraft. Both tactics are still utilised and, granted the associated investment in training, very effectively so.

The airline has experienced hijack attempts since 1968, but none have been successful. Israel's aviation security system is now widely regarded as the gold standard of the industry's counterterrorist response.

CHAPTER IV
1969—1970

DR VASILIS TSIRONIS:
DOCTOR-CUM-HIJACKER-CUM-POLITICIAN

The hijacking of El Al flight 426 was the first of many attacks perpetrated by Palestinian groups and, later on, by those associated with Islamic fundamentalism; yet hijackings for other political reasons continued. This was notable on 16 August 1969 when Dr Vasilis Tsironis, accompanied by his wife and two sons, hijacked an Olympic Airways domestic flight en route from Athens to Agrinion.

Tsironis was the son of refugees from Asia Minor, who qualified in Athens as a medical doctor before allowing politics to shape his future. He was a left-wing liberal, widely regarded as the founder of the Party of Independence whose activities were curtailed by the Greek government.

After the 'Regime of the Colonels' came to power in Greece in April 1967, anti-left purges began and Tsironis was arrested. During a short period of parole, he boarded an Olympic Airways flight and, somewhere over the Bay of Corinth, he hijacked the aircraft to Vlorë, Albania, using the pistols that both he and his wife were carrying, and knives that had been secreted on their children. There were 31 passengers and crew on board the aircraft and, even though Tsironis surrendered on arrival, their return to Greece was hampered by the fact that

Albania and Greece were technically at war with each other, a peace treaty never having been signed at the end of World War Two. In the absence of diplomatic relations, the return of the passengers and the aircraft had to be brokered by a third party.

Tsironis did not wish to live in the Stalinist regime which existed in Albania at that time, so eventually moved to Sweden, where he was sentenced to three and a half years in prison on 7 July 1971.

He returned to Greece in 1974, after military rule had ended, where he founded the OEM (Front of Greece) and became the author of the radical *Little Blue Book*. Following the 1977 elections, in which his party secured more than a quarter of a million votes in Athens alone, Tsironis was declared a wanted man by the newly elected government, of which he was openly critical. A warrant was issued for his arrest, but Tsironis took refuge in his apartment and so began a siege. On one occasion, Tsironis opened fire at the police who tried to get into the building, but given the scale of public support that Tsironis had, they elected to back off rather than force the issue.

Tsironis declared his apartment an independent state, albeit one surrounded by Greek snipers 24 hours a day from December 1977 until 11 July 1978. Every evening, between 7 p.m. and 8 p.m., he made public speeches from his balcony and utilised loudspeakers to amplify his political message of the day. The building was eventually stormed on 11 July 1978 and the hijacker-cum-politician was killed.

LEILA'S FIRST HIJACK

Arguably the most famous hijacker of all time, certainly prior to the events of 11 September 2001, was Leila Khaled, regarded by many as the glamour girl of international terrorism. Her first hijacking was on 29 August 1969, when she, and her colleague

Salim Essawi, hijacked a Trans World Airlines (TWA) flight en route from Rome to Athens.

Khaled freely admits that she was nervous before the operation began. While she had rehearsed the hijack routine many times in her mind, it was the interaction with other people in advance of the hijack that she found most challenging: the conversation with the man seated next to her on her flight from Beirut to Rome; the pickup lines uttered by staff at the airport; and the questioning she had to endure by a fellow passenger prior to boarding TWA flight 840.

In her autobiography, she describes one incident, which occurred while she was at the departure gate, in detail.

> All was going smoothly when suddenly the human element threatened our careful planning. A few seats away there was a little girl with a button on her dress cheerfully proclaiming 'Make Friends'. That message brought me up short, forced me to remind myself, as I watched her playing with her little sister, that this child had committed no crime against me or my people. It would be cruel to imperil her life by hijacking a plane, the symbolic meaning of which she had no conception — a plane that could explode during our attempted seizure or be blown up by Israeli anti-aircraft fire when we entered Israeli airspace.

Once airborne, it was Essawi who acted first, taking the opportunity to enter the flight deck when the flight attendants opened the door to serve lunch to the pilots.

On the flight deck, Captain Dean Carter was powerless to argue with the armed hijackers. Their first demand was to make an announcement using the PA system. The terrified passengers were to hear the words:

> ❝ Ladies and gentlemen, please kindly fasten your seatbelts. This is your new captain speaking. The Che Guevara Commando Unit of the PFLP, which has taken command of TWA flight 840, requests all passengers to adhere to the following instructions. Remain seated and be calm. For your own safety, place your hands behind your heads. ❞

They had selected the flight because they believed (although Khaled later denied this) that the then Israeli ambassador to the United States, General Yitzhak Rabin, would be a passenger on board, hence the announcement continued:

> ❝ Among you is a passenger responsible for the death and misery of a number of Palestinian men, women and children, on behalf of whom we are carrying out this operation to bring this assassin before a revolutionary Palestinian court. The rest of you will be honourable guests of the heroic Palestinian people in a hospitable, friendly country. Every one of you, regardless of religion or nationality, is guaranteed freedom to go wherever he pleases as soon as the plane is safely landed. ❞

That was not completely true.

The hijackers instructed Captain Carter to plot a course for Lydda (Lod Airport) in Israel. As the aircraft approached the Israeli shoreline over the eastern Mediterranean, Khaled spoke to the air traffic control tower demanding the aircraft be given permission to land. All communication was in English, but Khaled told the Israelis, and Captain Carter, that, instead of commencing each transmission with the words 'TWA 840', they had to say 'Popular Front. Free Arab Palestine' instead. They complied.

As Leila had grown up in Haifa, and had not seen her homeland for over 20 years, her next demand was that the captain fly low over Haifa so that she could view the city of her birth. She then forced the plane to overfly Lebanon, before entering Syrian airspace. Before the aircraft eventually landed, low on fuel, in Damascus, Khaled told the passengers to 'evacuate immediately on landing' and to 'have a happy holiday in Syria.' Having released all of the passengers and the crew, she and Essawi proceeded to attempt to destroy the aircraft with an explosive charge. Their first attempt failed and Essawi actually had to reboard the aircraft to reset it. Second time lucky... but the blast only caused damage to the cockpit, not the aircraft's entire destruction.

While the Popular Front for the Liberation of Palestine (PFLP) felt it had made its point, the Syrian government, albeit sympathetic to the Palestinian cause, saw the hijack as an opportunity to secure the release of Syrian prisoners held in Israel. Only six of the 101 passengers on board the TWA flight had been Israeli (most Israelis preferred to fly El Al if they could), so Syria decided that while the 95 non-Israelis were free to leave Syria, the others would be held as bargaining chips. Syria did eventually agree to the women and children being released, but they held on to Saleh Muallem and Shlomo Samueloff until 5 December, only releasing them after Israel released 13 prisoners it was holding. Twice, hijacks had resulted in the release of prisoners from Israeli prisons – it was proving an effective tactic.

Khaled and Essawi were kept under house arrest in Syria for 45 days, being continuously moved to avoid any rescue attempt. Eventually they were released and Khaled made her way, via Lebanon, to Jordan, while Essawi remained in Syria as his parents lived in Homs.

Khaled's actions secured front page news for the PFLP, not only because of the destruction of the airliner but because the act had been perpetrated by a young, good-looking Palestinian woman. Khaled was none too pleased with the international coverage of her involvement as she was keen to carry out further missions on behalf of the PFLP. Such was her commitment to the Palestinian cause, and so famous was her face, that she underwent cosmetic surgery to fundamentally alter her facial appearance prior to carrying out her next action. Today, when we consider the possibility of terrorists undergoing surgical procedures in order to infiltrate devices into secure areas, we should remember that almost half a century ago Khaled was prepared to do likewise.

ATTACKING EL AL ON THE GROUND

On 26 December 1968, an El Al flight was preparing to depart Athens for New York, when members of the PFLP attacked the aircraft with a sub-machine gun and hand grenades, killing one of the passengers in his seat.

Three months later, in February 1969, another El Al flight was attacked on the ground, this time at Zurich Airport, whereupon the Israeli first officer was killed and another eight were wounded. Mordechai Rachamim, a sky marshal on board the aircraft, opened fire from the aircraft's door and managed to kill one of the terrorists. However, despite his having helped the Swiss police in their initial response to the attack, Rachamim was arrested. After all, who was this plain-clothed, armed man shooting from the doorway of a commercial airliner? Indeed, it only became officially known, as a result of the trial which resulted in Rachamim's acquittal, that El Al was carrying armed sky marshals on board its aircraft.

In both the Athens and the Zurich incidents, terrorists were arrested, but in both cases the subsequent hijackings of Olympic Airways and Swissair flights within the year resulted in the release of all those arrested for the perpetration of the original airport attacks.

'OPERATION HO CHI MINH'

The advent of targeting multiple aircraft on the same day for terroristic purposes was on 6 September 1969. This time it was the turn of South American revolutionaries, protesting the deaths of students during anti-government riots at the University of Guayaquil in Ecuador earlier in the year. In 'Operation Ho Chi Minh' (named after Ho Chi Minh, the president of North Vietnam, who had died four days earlier), two Ecuadorian air force transport planes were hijacked – one by six men and the other by six men and one woman – while on domestic flights from Quito to Guayaquil.

The hijackers, who were students from Quito University, were armed with sub-machine guns and demanded that the aircraft fly to Cuba but, with insufficient fuel, both planes had to land in Tumaco, Colombia. On the ground, the co-pilot of one of the aircraft tried to overpower the hijackers, but he was outnumbered and paid the ultimate price: the resulting firefight resulted in his death and the aircraft being seriously damaged. With the plane out of commission, all the hijackers transferred to the other plane, using passengers and crew as human shields as they exited one aircraft and boarded the other. The surviving aircraft then departed and flew, via Panama and Jamaica, to Cuba.

6 September 1969 may have been the date on which Ecuadorian revolutionaries initiated multi-hijacking, with two

aircraft being seized; a year to the day later, on 6 September 1970, Palestinian revolutionaries tried to seize four aircraft.

ANOTHER VIETNAM CASUALTY

Many people today are keen to classify certain types of passengers as 'trusted' individuals; this is especially true in the United States, where war veterans are regarded as national heroes. Yet it was a Purple Heart veteran of the Vietnam War who, in 1969, became responsible for the longest (in terms of distance flown) hijacking in history. The perpetrator was Italian-born US Marine Raffaele Minichiello.

Minichiello was due to be court-martialled on 31 October 1969, for having carried out a burglary at a store within Camp Pendelton. He was a principled robber who had stolen goods valued at exactly $200, being the sum which he felt he had been underpaid by the military for combat duties. Rather than face the court-martial, he opted to hijack a TWA flight, scheduled to fly from Los Angeles to San Francisco, and, armed with an M-1 Carbine, ordered the crew to head for New York. The aircraft had to land and refuel and, at its stop in Denver, all the passengers and flight attendants were released except for one flight attendant, Tracey Coleman, who voluntarily remained on board. In New York, Minichiello fired a single shot when he thought the aircraft was going to be stormed and the captain was immediately told to depart for a trans-Atlantic journey.

Once in Rome, and after a number of stops en route, the aircraft was met by the authorities and the crew were released, but only after the airport's police chief, Pietro Guli, had boarded the aircraft, unarmed, to become the official hostage during the negotiations. Eventually, Guli was taken down the steps to his car and ordered, at gunpoint, to drive Minichiello away from the airport and into the woods. Minichiello was later arrested in a church, the Sanctuary of Divine Love, after a priest had notified the police about a suspicious, short-sleeved man attending Mass there.

The hijacker was sentenced to seven and a half years in prison, but released after 18 months for good behaviour. Italy regarded Minichiello, who was considered exceptionally good looking (and even later posed nude for *Playmen* magazine), as a national hero and a victim of the Vietnam War. There was no way that they were going to extradite him to face hijacking charges in the United States.

Minichiello eventually married a woman called Cinzia, but during the birth of his second child, she was to die due to a blood clot. A distraught Minichiello now planned a different kind of criminal attack, this time against the doctors who, he felt, had failed to save Cinzia. His intent was to effect the bombing of a medical conference taking place in Fiuggi, but during the planning phase he found religion and never carried out his mission. He married again (although his second wife, Teresa, was to die due to stomach cancer in 2002), was officially pardoned by the US in 1999 and has, since, even joined his marine platoon for various subsequent reunions.

The colourful character, who at one point even owned a restaurant in Italy called *Hijacking*, is said to have inspired the creation of Sylvester Stallone's character *Rambo*.

A CHAMPAGNE RECEPTION

The value of having armed guards on board aircraft was proven on an Ethiopian Airlines aircraft en route from Madrid to Addis Ababa on 12 December 1969. Members of the Eritrean Liberation Front attempted to hijack the aircraft to Aden in South Yemen and wanted to effect a propaganda mission highlighting atrocities allegedly committed by the Ethiopian military; they were also the world's first hijackers to be killed by sky marshals in-flight.

One of the hijackers, Hamed Shenen, had actually been sitting next to one of the sky marshals in the First Class section of the aircraft and was shot dead before he even reached the cockpit door. The other hijacker, Mahmoud Suliman, who was armed only with a knife, was also shot and killed by the in-flight security team. As for the passengers, well, with the hijackers dead, there was obvious cause for celebration; they were all given champagne.

TREFOR OWEN WILLIAMS: EXEMPLIFYING THAT RACIAL PROFILING DOES NOT WORK

At some point between 2 and 6 December 1969, retired British Army Captain Trefor Owen Williams was arrested for possession of 11.5 oz of gelignite, two detonators and a timing mechanism with which he intended to construct an IED in order to destroy an El Al aircraft departing Heathrow. Williams, who pleaded innocent to the charges, was actually betrayed by his accomplice, neo-Nazi Ronald Hannan.

The court was told, in January 1970, that Williams had been offered $72,000 to carry out the attack and was in the process of discussing much more lucrative projects with Fatah, including a plot to kidnap some prominent British Jews and ship them to Jordan in refrigerated boxes. Williams and Hannan had both been taken to Egypt and Jordan to undergo explosives training under the instruction of a man named Omar Sharif. It was following their return that Hannan decided to report the plot, as he did not wish to see innocent people lose their lives.

While the plot was unsuccessful, it is pertinent because it illustrated the links between terrorist organisations and the criminal world, and the desire for Arab groups, such as Fatah, to employ people who did not look Arabic to perpetrate attacks in their name; an early example of the perils of relying on racial profiling.

The 40-year-old Williams had succumbed to Fatah advances off the back of his having used his military expertise as a mercenary in the Congo and, once back on British shores, having set up a construction company which had declared bankruptcy. He needed money, but received a 10-year prison sentence instead.

HIJACKED FROM ASUNCION

As the 1960s drew to a close, Cuba remained the preferred destination for many a would-be hijacker. On 19 December 1969, 23-year-old Patricio Alarcon Herrera hijacked a LAN Chile aircraft after its departure from Asuncion, Paraguay. The sole assailant, a member of the Leftist Revolutionary Movement, achieved his goal of reaching Havana, maintaining control of the aircraft and all on board, despite having to make refuelling stops in Arica and Guayaquil. The arrival of these unexpected flights was beginning to become costly – and Cuba felt that the costs should be passed on to the carriers concerned! Accordingly, the aircraft was only released by the Cuban authorities after LAN Chile paid them $20,000 in landing fees.

Patricio Alarcon Herrera reappeared on the scene back in Chile on 5 July 1977, when, accompanied by his two brothers and a female 'friend', he hijacked a Ladeco Airlines flight to Lima, Peru, this time demanding the release of Chilean socialists imprisoned in Santiago. They did not achieve their objective, but the Peruvians did grant them the opportunity to exit the country and make their way back to Cuba, where they were granted asylum.

SIMULTANEOUS BOMBINGS À LA PFLP-GC; HIJACKINGS À LA PFLP

The advent of multiple aircraft being bombed on the same day was on 21 February 1970, when two aircraft were targeted by the Popular Front for the Liberation of Palestine – General Command (PFLP-GC). The PFLP-GC was an off-shoot of the PFLP formed by Ahmed Jibril, who promulgated a more aggressive approach to tackling the Palestinian question. Sabotage was one course of action.

A Swissair aircraft was operating from Zurich to Tel Aviv, when, shortly after take off, they requested permission to land following what they suspected to be an explosion in the cargo hold. The aircraft crashed 15 miles away from the airport killing all 47 people on board. The subsequent investigation showed an IED with a barometric control mechanism had detonated in the main cargo hold.

On the same day, and only two hours prior to the Swissair disaster, an Austrian Airlines flight en route from Frankfurt to Vienna was also forced to land following an explosion on board; the IED, seemingly contained within a package being sent to Israel by airmail, was also triggered by a barometric mechanism.

While the PFLP-GC was engaging in sabotage, the PFLP continued to exploit traditional hijacking as a tactic to secure the release of prisoners held both in Israel and overseas.

Two of the terrorists who had attacked the El Al aircraft on the ground in Athens in December 1968 were to stand trial on 24 July 1970. And so it was that the PFLP decided to hijack an Olympic Airways flight en route from Athens to Beirut – their demand was the release of their two colleagues, and five other PFLP members held in Greek prisons. The aircraft returned to Athens, where the Greek government was adamant that the terrorists' trial should proceed, but they also struck a deal whereby they would release all seven PFLP members held in Greek prisons within one month of the release of the hostages.

Andre Rochat, a representative of the International Red Cross, brokered the deal, an action which was heavily criticised by Israel, which felt that the organisation should not have become embroiled in hostage negotiation. The hostages were released, the trial proceeded and hefty sentences passed; yet on 13 August, the seven members of the PFLP were released by Greece.

The PFLP-GC could see the tactic was working and so set about planning the greatest terrorist spectacular of all time involving civil aviation – until, of course, 11 September 2001.

THE STASI AND THE INTERFLUG HIJACK COVER-UP

East Germany is renowned for having had one of the most repressive regimes of the Cold War era, perhaps due to the country being literally on the frontline between East and West. Erich Honecker was, apart from being East Germany's leader from 1971, the Berlin Wall's political architect. Following its construction in 1961, he advocated the so-called 'order to fire', thus legitimising the use of lethal force to prevent the wall being scaled, burrowed under or otherwise penetrated. Many died in their attempts to breach the wall, but there were also a few brave souls who chanced their luck by hijacking their way to freedom... most notably newlyweds Eckhard Wehage and Christel Zinke.

Wehage had a track record when it came to attempted escapes from East Germany. As a teenager, he had twice been arrested in the process of doing so: at age 15 he attempted to escape by boat across the Black Sea with a friend, and at 16 he opted for rail as a mode of transport.

Wehage was even placed in protective custody following his second attempt at fleeing the Republic. According to the website *Chronik der Mauer* (which tells the story of the wall and those who died trying to cross it), Wehage was sentenced to 'eight months' probation on October 18, 1963'. It goes on to report that a:

> Protective chaperone was also assigned because of the considerable errors in his upbringing by his parents and that the court explained that he should have realised that, 'it is in his own interest that the worker and peasant state not allow him to cross over from a socialist state to an exploiter state.'

Wehage seemingly learned the error of his ways and even joined the East German Marines and served his country for three years, during which time he was to meet and marry Christel Zinke.

Life in East Germany in the late 1960s was not easy, and for an ambitious young couple who wanted to have the right to choose how they lived their lives, it was a worthwhile gamble to try transportation mode number three – air!

Wehage requested leave from his base and stole two Makarov pistols and ammunition from the armoury, before heading to East Berlin to meet Zinke for their 9 March 1970 Interflug flight to Dresden. They wrote letters to their families, explaining the rationale for their flight to the West:

> All we want is to live our own lives the way we would like [...]. Should our plan fail, Christel and I are going to depart this life. [...] Death is then the best solution.

Their plans were disrupted from the outset, starting with the fact that their Interflug flight on 9 March was cancelled and they were forced to book on to another flight on 10 March; this time they chose a flight from East Berlin to Leipzig.

Once airborne, Wehage acted quickly. Threatening the flight attendant with one of the stolen pistols, he told her to instruct the pilots to divert to Hanover. When there was no response from the flight deck, Wehage fired a shot at the lock and opened the door, only to find a seondary barrier blocking his way. The flight attendant tried to reassure Wehage that the crew were complying but that they would need to refuel at Berlin Tempelhof – in the West German sector. Wanting to believe her, the newlyweds took their seats for landing, but as soon as they realised that the captain had actually landed at Berlin Schönefeld in East Germany – where they had boarded the flight – they opted to commit suicide and shot themselves.

The East German authorities were keen to cover up the hijack attempt, despite the failure of Wehage and Zinke to reach their intended destination; they did not want the young couple's idealism to become infectious. Meanwhile, their parents were also paying the price for their offsprings' unpatriotic actions and were held partially culpable, as recipients of their farewell letters *before* their Interflug flight had departed (because of the cancellation on 9 March) and, with the couple dead, the Stasi needed scapegoats who they felt must have known of Wehage and Zinke's intentions. Accordingly, the family were pressurised to explain their children's deaths as being the result of a car crash while the couple were on their way to Rostock to look at an apartment they could share. The *Chronik Der Mauer* states:

> In response to any possible curious enquiries, both
> [sets of parents] [agreed to] explain that the accident
> was the result of driving at too high a speed along icy
> roads and that there were not any witnesses.

The irony of the official version would have been laughable were the consequences not so tragic – it was the fact that the couple were not being offered any accommodation together that they had opted to hijack the flight to the West.

On 26 March 1970, the crew of the hijacked Interflug flight was granted the NVA Gold Medal of Merit, awarded to them personally by Stasi Minister Erich Mielke. The minister also gave the pilot a radio, the co-pilot a tape recorder, the mechanic a rug and the stewardess a knitting machine.

TAKE ME EAST

While deaths in-flight as a result of aircraft hijackings had occurred around the globe, it was not until 17 March 1970 that an individual died in US airspace. The incident took place on board an Eastern Airlines flight from Newark to Boston.

In those days, it was customary for flight attendants on board shuttle flights to collect the fare en route but, when air hostess Christine Peterson asked John DiVivo for his $15.75 fare, he removed a .38-calibre revolver rather than a wallet from his bag and told her to 'take me east'.

DiVivo got up from his seat and made his way towards the flight deck. Another flight attendant, Sandra Saltzer, tried to notify Captain Robert Wilbur Jr that an armed passenger wanted to gain access to the cockpit, but the flight deck personnel could not understand what Saltzer was trying to say and opened the door anyway. Once inside, DiVivo continued with his demands to fly in an easterly direction.

As the aircraft started to run low on fuel, the pilots tried to convince DiVivo that they had to land. Thinking that he had agreed, they turned the aircraft towards Boston; the movement unsettled DiVivo, who fired a shot into the First Officer James Hartley's chest and two shots at Captain Wilbur, one into each arm. The aircraft was in a critical stage of flight, on its final approach into Boston Logan Airport, and yet Hartley, despite his injury, still managed to disarm DiVivo and use the .38 revolver to fire three shots into the assailant.

Captain Wilbur landed the aircraft but the first officer died of his injuries. Both pilots are regarded as some of the greatest heroes in aviation history as nobody else, except for the hijacker, was injured. DiVivo was charged with murder but committed suicide in prison prior to his trial.

DRESSING UP LIKE PYONGYANG

One of the most dramatic hijacks of all time occurred on 31 March 1970, perpetrated by nine samurai-sword-brandishing members of the Japanese Red Army on board a Japan Airlines flight operating a domestic route between Tokyo and Fukuoka. The initial demand by the Samurai Nine, as the hijackers later became known, was that the aircraft head to Pyongyang in North Korea.

The crew convinced the hijackers that it would be necessary to refuel the aircraft before flying to Pyongyang, as the North Korean capital was twice as far away as Fukuoka. Consequently, the aircraft landed at the air force base in Itazuke, where the Japanese negotiators tried and failed to convince the hijackers to surrender. The aircraft's departure was initially prevented by cars blocking the runway, but the authorities conceded when some of the hostages released in Itazuke confirmed that, in addition to samurai swords, the hijackers also had explosives and might well be willing to commit suicide, killing all on board, if they were not granted passage to North Korea.

In Seoul, the South Korean government was monitoring the situation and was keen to prevent Western airliners being hijacked to their North Korean neighbour. Once the Japan Airlines flight had taken off and was heading west across the South China Sea, they unilaterally hatched a plan to dupe all parties – including the captain, who had zero experience of flying international routes and who was navigating using a school atlas provided to him by the hijackers – into believing that the South Korean airport of Kimpo was in fact Pyongyang's airport.

First Officer Teiichi Ezaki later reported that, when they tried to communicate with the North Korean authorities via the international emergency frequency, they were told to communicate on the Pyongyang frequency, which just happened to be Kimpo's. Meanwhile, intercept aircraft escorted the aircraft into Kimpo, which, in the interim, had been converted to look like Pyongyang. North Korean flags were flown in place of South Korean flags, soldiers on the ground wore North Korean uniforms and even the name on the building bore the name Pyongyang. All signs in English had also been removed.

Safely on the ground in pseudo-North Korea, the lead hijacker, Takamaro Tamiya, announced that the passengers were to be released, their goal having been reached. However, when the other members of the Samurai Nine saw both a US Air Force aircraft and an American Northwest Airlines aircraft on one of the runways they became suspicious; they were further perturbed by the absence of portraits of Kim Il Sung. Eventually the South Koreans were forced to concede the failed hoax.

Japan's Deputy Minister for Transport, Shinjiro Yamamura, flew to Kimpo and offered to trade himself for the lives of all the hostages, believing that they would value a high-profile member of the government's life as being equal to that of numerous members of the Japanese proletariat. The hijack was well into its third day before the deal was struck, delayed in part because the hijackers required confirmation that Mr Yamamura was indeed Mr Yamamura (achieved by their agreeing to have Sukeyoshi Abi, a socialist member of the Japanese parliament, fly in from Japan to attest to the minister's identity).

Eventually, the swap was done and the aircraft continued to the real Pyongyang… except nobody, it would seem, had told the North Koreans! The pilots, exhausted and still reliant on a school atlas as their guide, found themselves visually searching for Pyongyang and ultimately landed at a disused airfield, where it took more than an hour for the North Koreans to meet them.

Yamamura was released two days later, along with the crew. The hijackers were granted asylum, although most reports indicate that the North Korean government had not been particularly impressed by their actions.

'OPERATION WEDDING'

Although the Soviet Union was one of the first states to recognise Israel as an independent country, it was also one of the first to break off relations with Israel after the Six-Day War of 1967. Thereafter, it became increasingly difficult for Soviet Jews (often referred to as Refuseniks, albeit that not all Refuseniks were Jewish) to obtain exit visas from the USSR to make their way to Israel.

On 15 June 1970, 12 Refuseniks, ten of whom were Jewish, devised a plan to escape the USSR by commandeering an aircraft to Sweden. The plan, authored by Edward Kuznetsov, was called 'Operation Wedding' as it involved purchasing all of the seats on a flight from Leningrad to Priozerzk, supposedly to attend a wedding there. One of the group, Mark Dymshits, was a trained pilot and planned to replace the pilot of the Antonov AN-2 aircraft. The real crew were to be left on the runway while the 12 wedding guests flew on to Sweden.

However, their plan failed. The entire group were arrested; Dymshits and Kuznetsov were later sentenced to death and the others to prison sentences of up to 15 years. The sentences were so severe that the incident drew international attention to the plight of Soviet Jews and resulted in protests taking place in cities around the world. So extreme was the global public outcry, led by Israel and Jews in the diaspora, that the Soviet Union actually capitulated and reduced the death sentences to life imprisonment.

Kuznetsov was eventually freed in 1979, in a deal brokered by the United States, in which he and four other Soviet dissidents were exchanged for two Russian spies. Kuznetsov then emigrated to Israel. Alexei Murzhenk and Yuri Fedorov were the last to be released and were the two non-Jewish 'wedding guests'. Dymshits died in Israel in 2015.

XHAFERI, THE ALBANIAN LONE WOLF

Haxhi Hasan Xhaferi (also known as Haxhi Hasan Xyaert) is an example of a 'lone wolf', the individual who is sympathetic to a particular cause but not officially a member of a terrorist organisation.

Xhaferi was regarded as a freelance activist, who operated on behalf of the Palestinian cause and was also an opponent of American involvement in Vietnam. On 22 June 1970, he boarded a Pan American Airways flight in Beirut bound for

Rome and, armed with a .22-calibre pistol and a flash gun, which he claimed was a bomb, he ordered the crew to divert to Cairo.

He had gained access to the flight deck by showing flight attendant Veronica Ballman that he had a gun, albeit keeping the firearm out of sight of the rest of the passengers, and ordering her to take her to the captain. Once inside the cockpit, according to Captain John Burn, Xhaferi told him:

> Tell Nixon to get out of Vietnam and Cambodia. Tell Nixon do not sell Phantoms to Israel.

Once in Cairo, Ballman said Xhaferi became very nervous as the police approached the aircraft. He fired a single shot in the air to show that the firearm was genuine, but political point made, he quickly surrendered. Xhaferi was released without charge.

Albeit Albanian-born, Xhaferi was also an American citizen and so he did eventually return to live in the United States; he was arrested in Los Angeles and sentenced to 15 years in prison on 8 June 1973 for the hijacking.

CHOCOLATE SURPRISE

While anti-American sentiment may have been high in certain quarters, the early 1970s was also a period during which many of those who felt trapped in Eastern Europe were dreaming of a life in the West, and ideally in the United States. On 26 August 1970, Rudolf Olma, a Polish citizen with a German father, boarded a LOT Polish Airlines flight from Katowice to Warsaw with an IED concealed within a chocolate cake; he claimed the device consisted of 400 g of TNT. Shortly after departure he ordered the cabin crew to tell the pilots to fly to Vienna. However, due to sudden movement of the aircraft, the IED detonated, splattering the cabin with chocolate, and causing some of the passengers permanent damage to their hearing and sight. Olma lost an eye and a hand in the explosion, but the pilots managed to land the aircraft. Olma was sentenced to 25 years in prison, but released after 18 years; he later settled in Hamburg.

AMERICAN HYPOCRISY?

On 15 October 1970, Pranas Brazinskas hijacked an Aeroflot flight, operating a then domestic flight from Batumi to Sukhumi (both cities now in Georgia), with the support of his 13-year-old son Algirdas. Their mission was to escape to the West.

Having decided to escape the Soviet Union, the Lithuanian father and son flew first to Vilnius to say goodbye to relatives. On 13 October, they flew to Batumi, and the following day purchased tickets for their flight to Sukhumi, reserving seats in the first row of the Antonov aircraft.

Ten minutes after take off Pranas gave Nadezhda Kurchenko, the 19-year-old flight attendant, an envelope and ordered her to give it to the captain. The written instructions to the crew were clear, but the hijack did not go according to plan. Kurchenko screamed out that the flight was being hijacked, and Pranas was forced to open fire when challenged by sky marshals on board; Kurchenko was killed in the crossfire and three other crew members on the flight deck were seriously injured.

The aircraft landed in Trabazon, Turkey, where the hijackers surrendered and were imprisoned for four years. On their release, they moved to Italy, then Venezuela, and later to the United States, where they were granted asylum. The Soviet Union made numerous attempts to secure their extradition, but all to no avail, prompting an accusation of American governmental hypocrisy in the handling of hijackers responsible for deaths on commercial passenger flights.

The story of the Brazinkas family was not, however, to have a happy ending. On 5 January 2002, the two men became involved in a heated domestic argument which resulted in Algirdas – by then known as Albert Victor White – bludgeoning Pranas to death with some dumb-bells.

WHEN ALBANIA SAID 'NO'

There was one final hijack prior to the dramatic events on 'Hijack Sunday', 6 September 1970. On 30 August 1970, three Algerians hijacked an Air Algerie aircraft operating a domestic route between Annaba and Algiers, and demanded it be flown to Albania. Initially, the aircraft landed in Sardinia, where eleven of the passengers were released, and the captain requested maps for Albania's Vlorë Air Base. The next stop was Brindisi, Italy, where bottles of mineral water were provided for those still on board.

The hijackers, armed with pistols, a Molotov cocktail and, according to the press, 'a curved eight-inch knife', were demanding that the captain fly them to Tirana, Albania, but the Albanian authorities refused permission for the aircraft to land and, therefore, the aircraft diverted to Dubrovnik in what was then Yugoslavia, where the hijackers claimed asylum.

The hijacking ended the following day at which point, according to the *Chicago Tribune*, Captain Dagubert Dacosta-Rios told that waiting media that:

> I'm utterly exhausted. I've been in that plane since 6 a.m. Sunday, a good deal of the time with a dagger at my neck.

One of the flight attendants, who had been tied up for much of the time, confirmed that one hijacker had kept the knife at Dacosta-Rios' throat throughout the hijacking.

DAWSON'S FIELD SPAWNS BLACK SEPTEMBER

Until 11 September 2001, the most significant attack against civil aviation took place on 6 September 1970, when members of the PFLP-GC, under the control of Wadi Hadad, tried to hijack four planes on one day. The aim was to release prisoners held in Swiss prisons (as a result of the Zurich Airport attack of 1969), prisoners in German prisons (as a result of an attack perpetrated at Munich Airport in February 1970), and many more held in Israel.

Two PFLP-GC members hijacked a TWA flight while it was en route from Frankfurt to New York, but which was carrying Israeli passengers as the flight had originated in Tel Aviv. Two hijacked a Swissair flight from Zurich to New York, and, in Amsterdam, four members of the PFLP-GC attempted to board an El Al flight operating from Amsterdam to New York. Two of those who attempted boarding in Amsterdam were rejected by Israeli security agents (within the industry often referred to as 'profilers') at the check-in and they simply crossed the airport terminal concourse and purchased tickets for a Pan Am flight from Amsterdam to New York instead. Two of PFLP-GC hijackers successfully boarded the El Al flight without being intercepted by profilers, as they were transit passengers who had arrived from Germany. One of them was Patrick Arguello and the other was Leila Khaled (see p.55), now on her second hijack mission.

Both the TWA and Swissair flights were successfully hijacked to Zarqa airstrip in Jordan. Zarqa was known by the British as 'Dawson's Field' as it had previously been a Royal Air Force base. For the PFLP-GC, Zarqa airstrip was to be renamed 'Revolution Airstrip'.

The Pan Am hijacking, which was never part of the original plan, was very close to being prevented in Amsterdam. The two hijackers, who had been denied boarding by El Al, were Senegalese passport holders by the names of Sémou Pathé Guèye and Sanghoné Diap. In a subsequent television interview with the Pan Am crew, John Ferruggio, the flight engineer, said, 'We were ready for take off in Amsterdam, and the airplane came to an abrupt stop in the middle of the runway. And Captain Priddy called me up into the cockpit and says, "I'd like to have a word with you." I went up to the cockpit, and he says, "We have two passengers by the name of Diop [sic] and Gueye." He says, "Go down and try to find them in the manifest, because I would like to have a word with them."'

Co-pilot Pat Lavix reported, 'Captain Priddy said to them, "I apologise for asking but I am going to have to search you." And they said, "Search us."'

Ferrugio continued, 'So Captain Priddy sat them down... He gave them a pretty good pat. They had a Styrofoam container in their groin area, where they carried the grenade, and the 25-mm pistols. But this we found out much later.' The flight took off for New York.

The Pan Am flight was taken first to Beirut, where it refuelled, and then to Cairo, in part because the hijackers didn't know whether the Boeing 747 would be able to land on the Jordanian airstrip, given that the plan had never been to hijack this aircraft type in the first place. As soon as it was on the ground, the passengers and crew were told to evacuate the aircraft. With the last of the passengers fleeing the aircraft, Diap and Guèye destroyed it by detonating the charges they had wired up on board.

On board the El Al flight, when Patrick Arguello and Leila Khaled had sprung into action and shot flight attendant Shlomo Vider, a sky marshal – Mordechai Bar-Levav – on board the aircraft managed to neutralise them both, while Captain Uri Bar Lev performed an aggressive manoeuvre with the aircraft itself. Miraculously, the hand grenades carried by Arguello and Khaled failed to detonate, even though the pins had been pulled, and both hijackers were subdued. The aircraft diverted to London where Arguello died in an ambulance en route to hospital. Khaled survived and was taken to Ealing police station.

On the ground at Heathrow, Bar-Levav and Avihu Kol, the second of the sky marshals on board the El Al flight, were faced with a dilemma. Cognisant of the trial that their colleague Rachamim had to endure in Zurich following his action there in February 1969 (see p.59), they did not wish to be interviewed by the British authorities or open themselves to the risk of being charged in relation to the shooting of Arguello. Accordingly, rather than disembark with the rest of the El Al crew and make their way to the airport's police station, as they had been directed to do, they seized the opportunity to simply board another El Al aircraft preparing to depart for its scheduled flight to Tel Aviv. Albeit irked by their escape, and despite realising the sky marshals location prior to the flight's departure, the British authorities did not force the issue and, to a certain extent, may have been relieved that Bar-Levav and Kol were not on British soil and, hence, there was no need to even consider a prosecution.

At Zarqa, the PFLP-GC commenced its negotiations with the international community and with their Jordanian 'hosts', who had only recently agreed a ceasefire with Israel and were none too pleased at their becoming the arena for the latest attack against civil aviation. Within 24 hours it was agreed that the Jordanian army should withdraw in exchange for the transfer of all non-Israeli women and children on the TWA and Swissair flights to hotels in Amman while their menfolk and their travel documents remained on board the aircraft.

As Khaled was in custody in London, but there were no British hostages on the TWA or Swissair flights, the PFLP-GC was keen to secure her release, and accordingly hijacked a British Overseas Airways Corporation (BOAC) aircraft en route from Bahrain to London and took that to Jordan, where it joined the TWA and Swissair planes on the ground. The passengers included 21 schoolchildren, who were returning, unaccompanied, to the UK for the start of the autumn term. In exchange for their safe return, the PFLP-GC demanded the release of Leila Khaled.

Negotiations were protracted, as groups of passengers and crew were removed from the aircraft and transferred to a variety of locations in and around Amman. A rescue mission was completely out of the question. Germany, Switzerland and the United Kingdom all agreed to prisoner swaps.

On 12 September, the media were summoned to watch the three aircraft being blown up as a media spectacle. The extensive negotiations had concluded and all hostages, barring the 38 who were held as surety pending the release of the prisoners in European prisons, were released.

In 2000, *Aviation Security International* was granted an exclusive interview with Leila Khaled, which provides an interesting perspective of the hijacking of the El Al flight. Khaled claims that when she and Patrick Arguello were interviewed by security in Amsterdam, during the search of their bags, she asked the security agent, 'Why all these measures? I have never been through such measures.'

According to Khaled, the response was: 'Because of these terrorists who hijack planes.'

Khaled describes their boarding of the flight and their attempts to hijack it.

❝ I had two grenades and Patrick had a pistol and a grenade. Our comrades [who later hijacked the Pan Am flight] didn't show up. So Patrick asked, 'What shall we do?' I said, 'We'll do it.' We were waiting and then we went to the underground and there were soldiers having their guns with them. The man who searched us at the airport was waiting at the door of the plane. When all passengers went in they told us to go in and we went in. We sat – there were two seats and they said, 'You sit here.' It was only just the second row. We expected to sit at the back. So we sat there and it was good for us. So I told Patrick that nobody knew. So he said, 'Are you Queen Elizabeth?' I said, 'No, I have an experience before.' Although he saw me before he didn't realise my face. So I told him, 'I'm Leila Khaled.' So half an hour [after take off] we had to move. We stood up. I had my two hand grenades and I showed everybody I was taking the pins out with my teeth. Patrick stood up. We heard shooting just the same minute and when we crossed [into] First Class, people were shouting but I didn't see who was shooting because it was behind us. So Patrick told me, 'Go forward, I protect your back.' So I went and then he found a hostess and she was going to catch me round the legs. So I rushed, reached to the cockpit, it was closed. So I was screaming[,] 'Open the door.' Then the hostess came; she said, 'She has two hand grenades,' but they did not open [the cockpit door,] and suddenly I was threatening to blow up the plane. I was saying[,] 'I will count and if you don't open I will blow up the plane.' **"**

While the hijacking of the El Al flight failed, Khaled herself views their actions as a success.

" To help to take all the planes at one time, you know it was very big mess in the world. I once saw some drawings and caricatures of planes flying around the globe and it was written 'PFLP Airspace'. Of course there was a very big discussion in the world about such acts and we were described as terrorists, [but] we didn't have any other means except to do something that drives the Israelis crazy. **"**

At the time of the interview, Khaled lived in Amman with her husband and two teenage sons, who knew of their mother's involvement in the hijacking.

" When they grew up they knew about it, but at the first time my child, the first one, was angry in the garden. One day I was coming back home, he was there, and the minute I opened the door he said, 'Mum, are you a thief?' I said[,] 'I couldn't be a thief. Why do you say that?' He said it was the teachers in the kindergarten were saying that 'I'm the boy of a woman who stole a plane['.] I said, 'No, I didn't steal a plane.' Then he said[,] 'OK, where is it? I want to go to see it.' He thought that it was a model. And afterwards I told him what I was doing and I told him the whole thing. It was, you know, a story for him the first time, but afterwards he began to understand. 🙶

Aviation Security International asked her whether she would be proud of her children if they were to commit similar criminal acts in the name of the Palestinian cause:

🙶 You know, all the time I was asking this question to myself. Sometimes my children ask me 'if we want to fight for Palestine?' I say 'any time, when you're convinced, when you have the opportunity, don't hesitate to do that.' The younger one always says 'and if I die?' I say 'I will be proud of you because you're fighting for your people and for your land.' 🙶

September 1970 was a highlight for those who embraced hijacking as a terrorist tactic, yet it was also the beginning of the end for many of the Middle East's central figures. Jordan's King Hussein was livid about the negative impact that having three airliners ceremoniously destroyed on his soil had on his country's reputation, and commenced a military operation to oust the Palestinian paramilitary groups from Jordanian soil. By 15 September, the country was involved in a civil war which resulted in the PLO moving its base to Beirut – a black day for the Palestinian cause – and the origin of a new group, Black September. And a new target appeared for them: Royal Jordanian Airlines. One year on, the airline was a regular target for acts of aerial piracy; the carrier was quick to learn from the experience of their estranged Israeli neighbours and commence the deployment of sky marshals on all flights.

In Egypt, President Gamal Abdel Nasser died in the midst of the conflict, possibly due to the stress the situation had placed on those leaders keen to explore diplomatic solutions to the region's many problems.

Hijacking had again achieved its goals. Leila Khaled, despite her involvement in two high profile incidents and the destruction of multiple aircraft, has to this day never served any time for her involvement in attacks against civil aviation. She became an active member of the Palestinian National Council and remains wholly committed to the Palestinian cause, although she has been keen to distance herself from organisations associated with terrorism today, such as Islamic State.

Khaled has become part of modern day popular culture: the TV character Leela in the TV series *Doctor Who* is allegedly based on her; pop group The Teardrop Explodes has a song called 'Leila Khaled Said', which lead singer Julian Cope claims was a love song dedicated to her. Indeed, such was his infatuation, that he called disc two of his solo album *Phase of Leila Khaled* (2012).

Strangely enough, the hijacking of aircraft has been a subject of a number of popular songs, including 'Him' by Lily Allen. In this case, however, rather than revere the perpetrators, Allen mocks those who target aviation in the name of religion, citing September 2001 as the moment in which God himself may well have lost faith in his own creation.

CHAPTER V
1971–1975

INTRODUCING THE PARAJACKER

Paul Joseph Cini hijacked Air Canada flight 812 operating from Vancouver to Toronto on 13 November 1971, and his reason was the desire for fame. He boarded the aircraft in Calgary and was carrying a parachute. The delusional individual, assisted by alcohol, claimed to be a member of the Irish Republican Army (IRA) and demanded that the aircraft fly to Ireland and that he be given US$1,500,000 in cash. The aircraft landed in Great Falls, Montana, where $50,000 – significantly less than Cini's demand – was brought on to the aircraft.

As the aircraft continued in an easterly direction, Cini asked one of the crew to open the doors as he planned on parachuting from the aircraft with his ill-gotten gains. Unfortunately for Cini, he couldn't actually release the parachute and had to ask the crew for a knife. As Cini tried to cut through the parachute, he put down his gun, which was then seized by the captain and the first officer took the crash axe and hit Cini on the head with it, fracturing his skull. Cini survived and was sent to prison for life for his attempted hijack. He had, however, initiated a new style of hijacking. 'Parajacking' – hijacking a plane and then using a parachute to escape – was to become famous following the actions of D. B. Cooper, 11 days later. Cooper achieved what Cini wanted. Fame!

THE LEGENDARY MR D. B. COOPER

While the events of 6 September 1970 in Jordan may have been the most significant attack against aviation until that time, there is little doubt the hijacking that took place on 24 November 1971 was the most mysterious and saw the first successful act of 'parajacking'.

D. B. Cooper, a school teacher, hijacked a Northwest Orient Airlines flight en route from Portland to Seattle. Mid-flight he placed a note into a flight attendant's bag that read:

> **❝** I have a bomb in my briefcase, I will use it if necessary, I want you to sit next to me. You are being hijacked. **❞**

The flight attendant, Florence Schaffner, asked to see the device and Cooper did open his briefcase which revealed a suspicious item. He demanded US$200,000 in cash, four parachutes and that a fuel truck meet the aircraft when it arrived in Seattle. They agreed to provide him with the money and the parachutes, and landed at Seattle, where he released all the passengers and flight attendants. He then ordered the captain to take off and fly to Mexico City at an altitude of 10,000 ft, with the landing gear down, and with the door open and staircase (in the tail cone) extended. Cooper jumped out of the aircraft with the cash and has never been seen since. The case remains the only unsolved hijacking in American aviation history.

Numerous theories of widely varying plausibility have been proposed by experts, reporters, and amateur enthusiasts. While FBI investigators have always postulated that Cooper probably did not survive his jump, the agency maintains an active case file.

THE *GANGA* AFFAIR

In the early 1970s, hijacking was a regular feature on the news, as more and more groups exploited the oxygen of publicity afforded them by the mass media. The increased usage of television, accompanied by the general upward trend in the number of people taking to the skies for leisure purposes, made the regional conflicts everybody's business.

The *Ganga* Affair involved the hijacking of an Indian Airlines Fokker Friendship (named *Ganga*) flight, on 30 January 1971, and was perpetrated by members of the Kashmiri Liberation Front, Mohammed Ashraf and Hashim Quirshi. The aircraft was diverted to Lahore in Pakistan, where the hijackers made demands for the release of 36 prisoners held in Indian jails. In Pakistan, Quirshi and Ashraf were initially regarded as heroes. India refused the release of the prisoners and the hijackers set fire to the aircraft, injuring themselves in the process. The men were eventually arrested, as they were suspected of being Indian agents who had intentionally brought Pakistan into disrepute and the Pakistani government has claimed to this day that the *Ganga* Affair was orchestrated by the Indian government.

PEPPED UP TO PIRATE

On 2 July 1971, a Braniff flight departed Acapulco for Mexico City, San Antonio, Dallas, Washington and New York. It was a long trip but one that was to become far longer than planned as, while the aircraft was flying over the US/Mexican border, US Navy deserter Robert Lee Jackson and his Guatemalan girlfriend, Ligia Lucrezia Sanchez Archila, both armed with pistols, seized the aircraft and demanded that the pilots divert to Monterey.

Braniff was quick to give in to the hijackers' initial demands – US$100,000 for the release of the passengers and all but five of the crew. The newly wealthy hijackers instructed that the aircraft depart for Lima, Peru, where the hijackers released the original crew and replaced them with a volunteer crew consisting of three pilots, a flight engineer and two Peruvian stewardesses. No further demands were made except for the delivery of pep pills, which were duly provided to Jackson.

Jackson requested that the aircraft refuel in preparation for a trans-Atlantic flight to Algeria, where the government had agreed to provide asylum to the young couple. However, even with a full fuel load the B-707 did not have the range for such a journey, so Jackson agreed to an additional refuelling stop in Rio de Janeiro.

On the ground, the Brazilian government opted to prevent the aircraft from continuing on to Algeria and when the police tried and failed to board the aircraft, Jackson ordered the captain to take off immediately, despite the fact the aircraft had not been fully refuelled and that the runway was partially blocked. Once airborne, the crew and hijackers had to select a destination, Algeria still being beyond reach. Asuncion in Paraguay, Montevideo in Uruguay and Buenos Aires in Argentina were the only options and they opted for the latter, even though it was the furthest away from Algeria; it was the only one in which there was both a Braniff operation and Algerian diplomatic representation.

On the ground, Braniff sought to refuel the aircraft, as they felt that permitting the aircraft passage to Algeria was the safest bet, but the Argentinians had a different opinion and so commenced a lengthy period of negotiation. A SWAT team considered various options, including introducing a nausea-inducing gas into the plane through the air conditioning system, sending in policemen dressed as mechanics and policewomen dressed as stewardesses to overpower the duo, and, of course, a full-on assault.

The stand-off continued. Braniff looked at sending in a new aircraft with a longer range and yet another fresh crew. The Argentinians drew up various plans to ensure that Jackson and Co. never left Buenos Aires. And the negotiators negotiated! Eventually, Captain Schroeder was allowed to leave the aircraft to mediate between the hijacker and the authorities, and he took the opportunity to give the police a detailed analysis of the situation on board the aircraft and of Jackson's state of mind. When he returned to the aircraft, he took some beers with him and shared them with Jackson. The general rule when dealing with hijackers is to try to prevent them consuming alcohol, but the medical team in Buenos Aires felt that the opposite would be effective in this case, suggesting that drinking the beer on top of the pep pills Jackson had taken earlier would act as a depressive and help bring the situation to a conclusion.

Jackson realised that Algeria was no longer an option, so started questioning the authorities about what would happen should he surrender. He asked about the extradition treaty which existed between Argentina and the United States, how he could guarantee that his girlfriend did not face charges, whether he could use the money he had obtained from Braniff to fund his legal defence, and whether he could use any remaining funds for charitable donations. The discussions were simply delaying the inevitable and so it was that 43 hours after Jackson and Sanchez Archila initiated the hijack, Jackson handed himself over to the Argentine authorities and the saga concluded.

NAÏVE WOMEN

The use of a duped passenger, or 'mule', whereby a completely innocent individual (which the aviation industry terms as a 'naïve') is tricked into transporting an improvised explosive device onto an aircraft, is exemplified by the 1986 incident in which Ann-Marie Murphy was found to be carrying a bomb as she attempted to board an El Al flight to Israel at London Heathrow (see p.165). However, the phenomenon, and even the target, were nothing new. Fifteen years earlier, Ann-Marie's predecessors had even closer calls with death – they had boarded flights with devices which had either failed to detonate or had actually detonated but not destroyed the aircraft, whereas Ann-Marie's bomb was found during pre-flight screening by El Al profilers.

In the latter part of the summer of 1971, there were two attempts to destroy El Al flights in European skies. In both cases, naïve young women, fooled by love, had been tricked into carrying packages with them on flights to Israel – one was a Dutch girl flying from Rome to Tel Aviv on 28 July; the other was a Peruvian flying from London to Tel Aviv on 1 September.

Later in September 1971, in what might well have been a test of El Al's security procedures, an attempt to infiltrate a toy pistol onto another El Al flight operating from London to Tel Aviv was foiled. The gun had been concealed inside a cake which was being carried by a girl who claimed she received the cake as a gift from an unknown person.

It was Jayanti van der Meer (born as Jetty van der Meer) who was manipulated in the first incident; she now goes by the name of Catharina Windmeijer. Aged 19 at the time, and very much a hippie, Jayanti left home to backpack her way around Europe. In an age of free love, hedonism and easy access to psychedelic drugs, Jayanti visited Belgrade, where she encountered a Lebanese man, who she later named as George, and who was able to supply her with marijuana.

Their friendship blossomed and George realised that she might be just the vehicle he needed to infiltrate an IED onto an El Al flight. Jayanti was told that George wanted to move to America but that he needed to send some things back home to Bethlehem first. He asked her if she would take a letter and some presents to Israel for him, a request she did not even question (possibly because she was in a continuously stoned state). He was paying, and the proposed three-day trip would just be another great experience... or so she thought.

The unlikely couple travelled to Rome from where Jayanti would fly to Tel Aviv. George asked her to take a suitcase with his belongings back to his home, as he was headed to the US. Again she agreed, even packing her own belongings and his presents in the case herself.

She boarded the El Al flight and being the young, chatty individual that she was, she was quick to strike up a conversation with the passenger seated next to her. He gave her his contact details and said she should call him if she needed anything. On arrival in Israel, she headed straight to Bethlehem to deliver the suitcase, the letter and the presents to George's parents. The only problem was that she couldn't find the address. This was quite understandable since it didn't actually exist.

With nowhere to stay and no money, seeing that she had expected to be staying with George's family, she went to a police station, where she was questioned and provided overnight accommodation. Her bags were not searched.

As she was quite sober, she became increasingly aware of her surroundings and increasingly perturbed about the strange sequence of events that had brought her to the city of Jesus' birth. That said, she had the telephone number of the passenger she had been seated next to on her flight to Israel from Rome. She called him and they met up; she confided in him that she was somewhat suspicious of the suitcase she had been given by George. Together they searched the bag and uncovered a false bottom and there they discovered an IED comprising several bricks of TNT and detonating cord.

The police were called and the subsequent investigation showed that the IED was equipped with a barometric device designed to detonate at altitude. However, it had not functioned as planned, as the cargo bay in which the bag had been transported had been pressurised.

On 1 September, 21-year-old Delia experienced a similar situation. Delia was originally from Peru and had become friendly with a dark-haired man named Roberto Yusef Antonio, who had convinced her to transport a suitcase from London to Tel Aviv on board an El Al aircraft.

Upon her arrival in Tel Aviv, she checked in at a hotel, where she tried, without success, to open the locked bag. Eventually, she asked a hotel bell boy to help her; they were to discover a large IED, using Semtex as its main charge, concealed beneath a false lining in the base of the case.

On 9 September, Jayanti and Delia appeared together at a press conference in Tel Aviv, to warn other young women of the perils of falling in love with Middle Eastern men, especially those who ask for favours!

A year later, on 16 August 1972, despite Jayanti and Delia's warnings, Audrey Walton and Ruth Watkins were duped into transporting an IED onto an El Al flight, once again leaving Rome. The two 18-year-old British girls had become romantically involved with Adnam Ali Hasham and Ahmed Zaid who, the girls believed, were Persian. They had met when Walton and Watkins stopped the men in the streets of Rome and asked for directions; they had ended up staying with the men for ten days.

This time, the device itself was concealed inside a portable record player. It detonated when the aircraft was at 12,000 ft, triggered by a barometric device. However, the 200 g of explosives were insufficient to penetrate the fuselage of the El Al aircraft and the plane was able to land safely back in Rome with Captain Yehuda Fux at the controls.

The girls' partners were arrested and identified as an Iraqi and a Jordanian. While they were given prison sentences, the Italian authorities released them in February 1973 on the grounds that the IED had not been of sufficient size to destroy an aircraft.

THE AIR HOSTESS WHO FELL TO EARTH

In the aftermath of the 1988 Lockerbie disaster, there was much speculation over whether any of the victims were aware of their impending fate. Dr William Eckert of Wichita State University believes that many might have lost consciousness because of a lack of oxygen when Pan Am 103 exploded at 31,000 ft, but would likely have revived at about 15,000 to 10,000 ft, and may well have been aware of what was happening for the final third of their fall. There are indeed numerous reports of bodies having moved on the ground and one rescuer claims to have found a weak pulse in one of the bodies. Many are quick to ridicule such speculation as being little more than scaremongering. They have probably not heard of Vesna Vulovic.

On 26 January 1972, a JAT Airways DC-9 en route from Copenhagen to Zagreb and Belgrade exploded 33,000 ft over Srbska-Kamenice in Czechoslovakia. Ustashe, otherwise known as the Croatian National Movement, later admitted their responsibility for the bombing that should have killed all 29 passengers and crew. Miraculously, however, there was a survivor. The body of flight attendant Vesna Vulovic was recovered from the wreckage and thirty years later she was interviewed by *Aviation Security International*. She remembers nothing of the flight itself; her last memory was 'boarding the plane by the rear door and seeing a few women cleaning the plane'. Her recollections of the incident begin a month later:

> The first thing I can remember is seeing my parents in the hospital. I was talking to them and asking them why they were with me in Slovenia. I thought I was in Slovenia as I had just visited Ljubljana before going to Copenhagen.
>
> The biggest injury was to my brain. I had broken my skull and then haemorrhaged. I had broken three vertebrae, one of which was crushed completely and had stopped me from being able to move my legs. After an operation I could move my left leg. I could not move my right leg for another month. Now I can walk.

Vulovic was in a Prague hospital until 12 March, and then transported by plane to Belgrade.

> They told me that they would give me injections to help me sleep on the flight. I refused. I was looking forward to flying again. You must remember that I had no memories of the accident. To this day I enjoy travelling and have no fear of flying.

On the day of the bombing, Vulovic believes that she had seen a man behaving strangely in Copenhagen while she, and her fellow crew members, were waiting to board. The aircraft had arrived from Stockholm and the new crew had been watching the passengers disembark; she is convinced that one suspicious character had brought the bomb on board in Stockholm and then disembarked in Copenhagen.

> The police were worried about me after the accident as I had seen the man who may have put the bomb on the plane in Copenhagen. So, when I was in the hospital I had a police guard at my door. Every six hours they changed shift. Nobody could come in my room except my parents and doctors. Maybe they [Ustashe] wanted to kill me as the only witness.

Vulovic was asked how she thought she survived and whether she regarded herself as having been lucky.

> Nobody knows that. One of them [doctors] said that I had very low blood pressure. I should never have been an air hostess in fact. I had a lot of coffee to drink before my interview, so that when I had my medical exam I passed. Maybe my low blood pressure saved me. I lost consciousness quickly and my heart did not burst.
>
> The man who found me told me that I was in the middle part of the plane. I was found with my head down and my colleague on top of me. One part of my body with my leg was in the plane and my head was out of the plane. A catering trolley was pinned against my spine and kept me in the plane. The man who found me, says I was very lucky. He was with Hitler's troops as a medic during the war. He was German. He knew how to treat me at the site of the accident.
>
> I'm not lucky. Everybody thinks I am lucky, but they are mistaken. If I were lucky I would never had this

accident and my mother and father would be alive. The accident ruined their lives too. Maybe I was born in the wrong place. Maybe it was a bad place. 🟥🟥

In retirement, Vesna campaigned against Slobdan Milosovic and was regularly seen demonstrating in the streets of Belgrade. While the police often made arrests, Vesna remained untouchable – she had become a national hero. When the Milosovic regime finally tumbled, Vesna was on the balcony at the city hall as one of the celebrities making victory addresses that were the entrée to a night of partying for the Serbian people.

Nobody knows how Vesna survived the accident. Some have said it was due to the fuselage hitting the side of the hill at an angle rather than hitting the ground directly. In practical terms, the figure of 33,000 ft is somewhat irrelevant because, according to the *Guinness Book of Records* it is estimated that 'the human body reaches 99 per cent of its low-level terminal velocity after falling 573 m (1,880 ft), which takes 13–14 seconds'.

At normal atmospheric pressure, and in a random posture, a body would fall at a rate of 117–125 mph. Others have survived falls above 1,880 ft. In 1942 a Russian bailed out of his Ilyushin at 22,000 ft when being attacked by German Messerschmitts. He landed in thick snow and made a speedy recovery. In another war story, RAF gunner Nick Alkemande fell 18,000 ft and suffered only sprained a leg. The branches of pine trees and the snow on the ground saved him.

Vesna thinks that her story gives people hope that such incidents are survivable. The question is whether we want that hope...

There are many who doubt that the JAT flight crashed as a result of a bomb and who are convinced that this was merely a politically expedient explanation put forward to cover up the fact that the aircraft had in fact been shot down by mistake by MiG planes from the Czechoslovak air force. The reason postulated is that the aircraft had been experiencing technical problems that resulted in it making a rapid descent during which it strayed from its assigned route, prompting the MiGs to perceive it as an enemy aircraft on the attack. The Czechoslovak air force was reported to have been on high alert at the time as Leonid Brezhnev, then leader of the Soviet Union, had just concluded a meeting with East Germany's Erich Honecker in Prague and Brezhnev's aircraft was reported to be airborne at the time.

THE CURSE OF THE KENNEDYS

In February 1972, a Lufthansa flight was hijacked en route from New Delhi to Athens. On board was Joseph Kennedy, the son of the late senator Robert Kennedy, who had been assassinated by a Palestinian, Sirhan Sirhan, in 1968. The incident ended in Aden in Yemen within 48 hours, but only after a $5 million ransom had been paid – yet another German capitulation to the demands of terrorist groups.

ANOTHER RANSOM, ANOTHER PARAJACKER

On 7 April 1972, a United Airlines flight was operating from Newark to Los Angeles via Denver, when Richard Floyd McCoy Jr was seen to be holding a hand grenade while seated in the passenger cabin. A pilot on board approached McCoy, who gave him a sealed envelope labelled 'Hijack Instructions'. He asked the pilot to get the flight attendant to deliver the envelope to the flight deck. As the whole incident played out in such a calm manner, most of the people on the flight were oblivious to the fact a hijack was in progress. The captain decided to land at Grand Junction in Colorado, explaining to the passengers that it was due to a mechanical problem with the aircraft.

The instructions were accompanied by the pin from a hand grenade and a bullet, thereby causing the crew to take the threat very seriously. The instructions dictated that the aircraft fly to San Francisco and that, once there, McCoy be given $500,000 in cash and four parachutes. The aircraft took off from Grand Junction, with the captain explaining to the passengers that the small regional airport couldn't deal with the repairs needed and that they would be going to San Francisco instead.

In San Francisco, the money and parachutes were delivered and many of the passengers were released. The captain was ordered to take off and fly at 16,000 ft at a speed of 200 mph over Utah. All the instructions were sent to the flight deck from McCoy, who remained at the rear of the aircraft during the incident, via one of the flight attendants. McCoy then put on a parachute and a helmet and jumped from the aircraft, which later landed in Salt Lake City. The authorities searching for the parajacker had no idea as to his identity, but eventually received a telephone call from somebody citing McCoy's name and saying that he was a Vietnam veteran, helicopter pilot and qualified skydiver. McCoy was located, but denied any involvement in the incident; his fingerprints, left on board the plane, proved otherwise. He was sentenced to 45 years in prison. He escaped in 1974 and was killed when police officers tracked him down three months later.

ISRAELI PRIME MINISTERS STORMING PLANES

On 8 May 1972, a Sabena flight to Tel Aviv was hijacked by Black September. The lead hijacker was Ali Shafik Ahmed Taha, better known as Captain Rafat, whose CV would indicate that he had been one of the hijackers on board the El Al flight to Algiers in 1968. The team of four hijackers – two men and two women – had only met for the first time the day before the attack, and yet posed as two young couples. Believing that Israeli passports would be regarded as a positive indicator for a flight to Tel Aviv, they used forged Israeli passports to board the flight in Brussels. The hijack was initiated 20 minutes after its departure from its transit stop in Vienna.

The aircraft landed in Tel Aviv and negotiations for the release of 315 Palestinian prisoners commenced. Israeli Minister of Defence Moshe Dayan was unequivocal in his view that if one gave in to terrorist demands, more acts of terrorism would be perpetrated. And the evidence, as it pertained to hijacking, was on his side.

Dayan also decided that now that the plane was on the ground, that was where it was going to stay. In order to achieve this, he instructed mechanics to deflate the aircraft's tyres and to drain the hydraulic fluid. This act of self-sabotage also gave Dayan reason to justify sending out mechanics to 'repair' the aircraft, which, in turn, prompted a whole series of excuses for extending the deadline.

The International Red Cross arrived in Tel Aviv and became intermediaries, on the condition that neither the Israelis nor the terrorists used force while negotiations were in progress.

On board, the situation deteriorated and the captain of the Belgian airliner – a British Jew – became increasingly convinced that the hijackers would indeed blow up the aircraft. At one point, the two female hijackers, Therese Halsa, 19, and Rima Tannous, 21, were instructed to detonate the devices, prompting Captain Reginald Levy to try to grab the gun from Rafat.

The stand-off continued through the night and, early in the morning of 9 May, Levy was allowed to disembark, in order to prove to the Israeli authorities that they really did have explosives – he was sent with samples. In actual fact, each of the hijackers was armed with two handguns, two hand grenades, and two explosive belts with 2.5 kg charges. Levy returned to the aircraft out of both a sense of duty and because, unbeknownst to the hijackers, his wife was a passenger; she had joined him for the trip as the flight was on his fiftieth birthday and they had planned on celebrating the event over dinner in Tel Aviv.

Eventually, Moshe Dayan ordered the aircraft to be stormed – in 'Operation Isotope' – and Sayeret Matkal (special forces) managed to get close to the aircraft by waving the Red Cross flag as they approached. The Sayeret Matkal SWAT team included two men who were later to become Prime Ministers of Israel: Benjamin Netanyahu and Ehud Barak. While the raid was successful, the male hijackers killed and the female hijackers arrested, Israel was criticised by the Red Cross for its abuse of their flag. Israel did apologise and guaranteed it would never again use the flag in this way.

That said, Israel had made it abundantly clear that it was not going to be held hostage by guerrillas prepared to imperil the lives of the innocent. Considering that aircraft were not being stormed by SWAT teams, it was impressive that only one passenger – Miriam Holtzberg, 22 – was killed during the assault and one commando, Benjamin Netanyahu, slightly injured.

The two female terrorists who survived the assault were sentenced to life imprisonment, but were released by Israel in a subsequent prisoner swap.

QUITO REPLICATES TEL AVIV

The Sabena incident was the first example of a commando force storming a hijacked aircraft. However, the tactic was to be repeated two weeks later on 22 May 1972 in Quito, Ecuador. An Ecuadorian man named Lomas had hijacked an Ecuatoriana De Aviacion flight, ten minutes after its departure from Quito to Guayaquil. Lomas had demanded $40,000 and a parachute. The aircraft landed back in Quito and while negotiations took place, a commando team managed to access the luggage hold and, from there, the aircraft cabin itself, where they shot Lomas dead.

THE JAPANESE ATTACK TEL AVIV

Back in Tel Aviv, on 30 May 1972, Lod Airport became the scene of a massacre perpetrated by three members of the Japanese Red Army in an action conducted as a demonstration of sympathy with the Palestinian cause and in coordination with the PFLP. The terrorists did not arouse suspicion when they disembarked an Air France flight, which had arrived from Rome, in part because they were Japanese: since the El Al hijack to Algiers in 1968, the Israelis had been focusing their attention on passengers of Arabic origin.

One of the terrorists was Kozo Okamoto, the brother of one of the Samurai Nine who had hijacked the JAL to Pyongyang in 1970 (see p.70). The three terrorists entered the baggage reclaim hall and collected three violin cases, which they then proceeded to open and from which they extracted Czech VZ. 58 assault rifles and grenades. They opened fire indiscriminately, killing 16 Puerto Rican pilgrims about to start a tour of the Holy Land, eight Israelis and a Canadian; 81 other people were injured.

Kozo Okamoto was the sole surviving terrorist and was sentenced to life imprisonment. In jail, it is claimed that he tried to convert to Judaism and that he even attempted to circumcise himself with nail clippers. He was actually released in 1985 as part of a prisoner exchange negotiated with the Palestinians in exchange for the release of Israeli soldiers being held hostage. The Lod Airport massacre demonstrated to the global aviation security community that there was a need to screen checked luggage, previously deemed unnecessary as the focus had been on the prevention of hijacks in which weapons would be required on flight; it was a lesson that few governments or airlines learned, and it was another 13 years before there was any global impetus for comprehensive baggage screening. The massacre did, however, prompt the Israeli authorities to re-evaluate their excessive focus on Arabic passengers; racial profiling was not only unethical, but had been proven to be devoid of security logic.

While the PFLP and the Japanese Red Army had orchestrated and perpetrated the Lod Airport massacre, behind the scenes North Korea was held responsible for providing the necessary training and financing for the mission; PFLP leader George Habash had even visited Pyongyang in the run up to the attacks.

In June 2010, North Korea was sued for its role in the massacre in a San Juan federal court and was found liable for the murder and maiming of the victims. The Puerto Rican court ruled that North Korea should pay $378 million in compensation and punitive damages to the Puerto Ricans who had been injured, or who had lost relatives, in Israel back in 1972. No money has been paid.

THE MUNICH OLYMPICS AND THE QUESTIONABLE LUFTHANSA HIJACK

The year 1972 was certainly the peak of the attacks against Israelis perpetrated by Palestinians. While many of these incidents took place on commercial airliners, probably the most significant attack took place at the Munich Olympics when, in the early hours of 5 September, eight members of Black September entered the Olympic village and took nine members of the Israeli Olympic team hostage; two other Israelis were killed as they fought back.

This action went against all Olympic ideals of sportsmanship, unity and camaraderie. To make matters worse for the Olympic hosts, the act of terrorism was being played out on German soil against the Jewish state less than 30 years after the Holocaust. For a country desperate to cleanse itself of its Nazi past, and wishing to dispel the imagery of Hitler's Olympics in 1936, the impact was immense.

Black September demanded the release of 234 prisoners held in Israeli prisons and freedom for Rote Armee Fraktion members Andreas Baader and Ulrike Meinhof. And so began a long day of negotiations which culminated in an agreement to fly the terrorists and their hostages to Cairo. The first leg of their journey was to be by helicopter from nearby Fürstenfeldbruck (a NATO airfield) to the international airport, where a B-727 was waiting for them. Yet the German government was keen to ensure that the terrorist act would be unsuccessful and hence launched a mission to rescue the hostages in Fürstenfeldbruck. It ended in disaster: all nine Israeli hostages, one German policeman and five of the terrorists were killed in the ensuing firefight. Three members of Black September – Jamal al-Gashey, Adnan al-Gashey and Mohammed Safady – survived and were arrested. Their time in jail was foreshortened, despite the depravity of the crime they had committed.

On 29 October 1972, two fellow members of Black September hijacked a Lufthansa jet operating from Damascus to Frankfurt, via Beirut and Ankara. No passengers boarded the flight that day in Damascus, although it is believed that the weapons used in the subsequent hijack were loaded there. At the transit stop in Beirut, 13 passengers joined, two of whom effected the hijack shortly after the aircraft took off for Ankara. All the other passengers on board were male and most of them were from Arab states.

The first demand issued was that the aircraft fly to Munich and that, once there, the three surviving members of the Munich Olympic attacks be released. The Lufthansa jet initially landed in Nicosia to refuel, then continued to Zagreb and from there to Tripoli. Once in Libya, all the Arab passengers were released and allowed to fly home.

The hijack had started at around 7.15 a.m. By 2 p.m., the West German government had already agreed to the release of the al-Gasheys and Safady. By the end of the day, the Lufthansa hijackers and Munich murderers were celebrating together in the Libyan capital. Whether this was the result of German capitulation to terrorism, carried out in a desperate attempt to avoid yet another disaster to befall Germany at the hands of Palestinian terrorists, or whether it was actually part of a plan hatched between the German authorities and Black September – in order that the Munich terrorists not remain in Germany – has been the subject of much speculation.

The suggestion that Germany had been complicit in the hijacking of the Lufthansa jet, however, is not a social-media-orchestrated conspiracy theory; it is supported by the sole surviving hijacker, Jamal al-Gashey (Adnan al-Gashey and Mohammed Safady have since been killed as part of Mossad's 'Operation Wrath of God', launched by Golda Meir as a response to the success of the Lufthansa hijacking). It is also a view held by Ulrich Wegener, the founder of the GSG 9 SWAT unit.

IN A TOWN CALLED ALICE

'This is a hijack' were the first words Miloslav Hrabinec uttered to a flight attendant on board an Ansett Airlines flight as it was about to land in Alice Springs, Australia, on 15 November 1972. He persuaded the flight attendants to let him into the cockpit, where the captain continued to land the aircraft. Hrabinec demanded a parachute, a jump suit and a light aircraft, and according to flight attendant Kaye McLachlan, in an interview with the *The Australian*, he said that money was not his objective:

> He told us over the four hours we were held captive that he wanted to commit suicide in a spectacular way. He intended to parachute out over the desert and survive as long as he could and then commit suicide.

On the ground in Alice Springs, a Cessna aircraft was brought alongside the Ansett aircraft, which Hrabinec then exited. The Cessna was being piloted by Ossie Watts and what appeared to be a flight navigator, but who was in reality police officer Paul Sandeman. As Hrabinec made his way to the Cessna, Sandeman tried to grab his gun but failed to disarm him and ended up being shot in the hand and stomach. Other police officers started shooting but Hrabinec escaped before shooting himself in the head, thereby achieving his goal of a spectacular suicide.

QUEBECAIR IN THE CROSS HAIRS

Quebecair flight 321 was the target of Larry Maxwell Stanford's actions on 14 December 1972, when the 21-year-old student actually pulled out a .22-calibre rifle during the boarding process. Initially he instructed the crew to fly to Montreal, where the passengers were released before continuing to Ottawa. Stanford seemingly lacked any plan or rationale for his actions as, once the aircraft was in Ottawa, he ordered the captain to fly back to Montreal, where he permitted his father and a psychiatrist to board the aircraft; the two men negotiated his surrender. He spent ten years in jail but, within a year of his release, was re-arrested for the attempted murder of his sister, for which he was sentenced to a further 20 years in jail. He was released in 2008.

SHOT DOWN OVER SINAI

The threat posed to individuals on board aircraft straying off course was exemplified on 21 February 1973, when a Libyan Arab Airlines Boeing 727 operating from Benghazi to Cairo strayed off course due to adverse weather conditions. Lost in the skies over the Sinai Peninsula, having missed Cairo, the aircraft was intercepted by two Phantom II aircraft from the Israeli air force.

Using hand signals, they tried to indicate to the aircraft's captain that he should land at an air force base and initially the B-727 did lower its wheels as if preparing for landing but then suddenly raised them again and tried to escape. The Israelis, fearing that this commercial airliner was going to be used as a weapon to target Tel Aviv, opened fire, and the Libyan aircraft caught fire and crashed. Only one of the nine crew members and four of the 104 passengers were to survive. Israel was forced to apologise and paid compensation amounting to $3,000,000.

A TALL ORDER

On 18 May 1973, a Venezuelan aircraft, AVENSA flight 523, was hijacked by three armed men and one woman, while en route from Valera to Barquismeto. The pilot was ordered to fly to Panama City for refuelling, and then Merida for further refuelling, and then to Mexico City, where the hijackers made it clear that if 79 political prisoners in Venezuela were not released the aircraft would be destroyed.

The hijackers were told that the Venezuelan government would not negotiate with them but that they were willing to provide them with food and fuel for a flight to Cuba. They were joined on that flight by the sub-director of the Federal Security Police of Mexico. On arrival in Cuba, the hijackers surrendered and the remaining passengers and crew returned to Venezuela.

DISAPPEARING HIJACKERS

Oscar Borjas Gonzales and Francisco Lopez Dominguez achieved their place in history by hijacking an aircraft on 30 May 1973 and managing to escape from it without anybody noticing. The two men hijacked a SAM Colombia flight from Cali to Bogota via Pereira and demanded to be flown to Lima, Peru. They also wanted money and the release of 140 prisoners held in Colombian jails. However, the aircraft developed technical problems and had to divert to Aruba. When it was repaired, it took off for San Salvador, but the hijackers, fearing they were being duped by the authorities, then demanded that the aircraft return to Aruba. The airline arranged for the delivery of $50,000 to the aircraft before it again departed Aruba and landed at Guayaquil in Ecuador to refuel before continuing to Lima. The hijackers then released 14 more passengers before the aircraft took off, heading towards Argentina, initially landing in Mendoza, where all the remaining passengers were released.

Still fearing arrest, the hijackers then ordered the crew to fly to Resistencia and then Asuncion in Paraguay before landing for the final time in Buenos Aires. It was only once they reached Buenos Aires that the crew realised the hijackers were no longer on the aircraft! They had probably escaped when the aircraft had stopped at the Paraguayan capital of Asuncion, given that Lopes Dominguez was a Paraguayan citizen.

Lopes Dominguez was eventually arrested in Paraguay and extradited to Colombia to stand trial in 1975.

PRIME MINISTERS WHO HIJACK PLANES

Not many people can claim to have both hijacked an aircraft and to have been democratically elected as a prime minister of a country. One who can is Girija Prasad Koirala, often referred to as GPK, the founder of the Nepal Mazdoor Congress (NMC). GPK was not only a leading trade unionist and the acting head of state of Nepal between January 2007 and July 2008, as the country transitioned from a monarchy to a republic, he also served four separate terms as prime minister of Nepal.

However, back in 1973, he participated in a plot to hijack a Royal Nepal Airlines flight and steal money, being transferred by the Nepal Rastra Bank from Biratnagar to Kathmandu, in order to finance the armed revolution designed to bring about a multi-party democracy. GPK's revolutionary colleagues carried out research to find out on what days money was being transported, as they only wanted to hijack a flight if it was worthwhile to do so!

The hijackers chosen to perform the heist on 13 July 1973 were Durga Subedi, Basant Bhattarai and Nagendra Dhungel, but on the day in question there were only two seats available on the flight. As all three men needed to be on board the aircraft, Subedi persuaded one of the other passengers to give up his seat by pretending to be sick, saying that he needed to get to the Nepalese capital as quickly as possible for medical treatment. During the flight, they entered the cockpit and ordered the captain to fly towards Forbesganj, where they located a small landing strip, identifiable by a red flag flying in a tree; it had been placed there as a marker by GPK himself.

GPK and a fellow activist met the aircraft and escaped with INR3,000,000. The Indian currency was particularly useful because many of the activists were actually living in exile in India.

MASSACRE IN ROME

In one of many attacks perpetrated against aviation during the pre-Christmas period, the events in Rome on 17 December 1973 managed to combine a front-of-house airport attack with an assault on an aircraft and a hijack. It is one of the most audacious terrorist attacks of all time, yet strangely it is rarely referred to.

The incident started when the five terrorists, arriving off a flight from Madrid, opened their hand baggage and pulled out machine guns and grenades. Their first act was to take six police officers hostage; some of the team stayed with them, while the rest made their way towards the tarmac, brandishing their weapons and firing indiscriminately.

At the same time, a Pan Am Boeing 747 was preparing for departure. From the cockpit, Captain Erbeck noticed the armed assault taking place inside the terminal. He ordered passengers and crew to get their heads down.

The stairs were still attached to his aircraft and the doors were open, when two of the terrorists, now on the tarmac, threw phosphorus grenades into the Pan Am jet, setting the aircraft on fire. Thirty people died due to either smoke inhalation or the burns caused by the phosphorus; Captain Erbeck's wife was one of the dead. The aircraft itself went down as a total hull loss.

The second team of hijackers, who had been holding the police officers hostage, now made their way towards a Lufthansa Boeing 737, where they took a further two members of ground personnel hostage. Antonio Zara, a customs officer, made a heroic attempt to stop the attack and opened fire himself. Zara was shot and killed.

Once the assailants of the Pan Am jet had joined their colleagues and the hostages on the B-737, the Lufthansa crew were instructed to depart for Athens. The hijackers demanded the release of Black September activists held in Greek prisons, but the Greek government did not submit to the request; an Italian hostage was killed on board and the aircraft departed for Beirut.

The Lebanese denied the Lufthansa jet permission to land, but Syria allowed it to refuel in Damascus before it continued to Kuwait, where the hijackers were finally arrested.

By the end of the day, 32 people had lost their lives.

THE MAD ADVENTURES OF RABBI JACOB

The vast majority of hijackings relating to the Arab-Israeli conflict in the early 1970s were perpetrated by Palestinian groups and their western European revolutionary friends. The 16 August 1973 was an exception to the rule. It was on board a Middle Eastern Airlines B-707 en route from Benghazi to Beirut that a 37-year-old Libyan by the name of Toumi entered the cockpit holding two guns and ordered the captain to divert to Tel Aviv.

The aircraft landed in Israel with an Israeli fighter jet shadowing it. At a press conference, Toumi stated that the cause of the hijack was 'to show that not all Arabs want to throw the Jews into the ocean'. Despite the fact that he was offered financial support from around the world from people keen to ensure that Toumi was not sent to jail, he was found to be mentally ill and committed to an Israeli psychiatric hospital.

In a similar vein, it was Daniele Cravenne who hijacked an Air France B-727, en route from Paris to Nice, on 18 October 1973. Daniele's husband Georg Cravenne was a film producer who had just launched a comedy entitled *The Mad Adventures of Rabbi Jacob*, a film that she felt was anti-Palestinian. Accordingly, she hijacked the flight in order to prevent the film's release.

On board the aircraft, armed with a .22 calibre pistol, she declared herself to be a member of the Solidarity Movement for French–Israeli–Arab Reconciliation. The aircraft landed in Marseilles, where French police disguised as maintenance workers boarded the plane and shot and killed Cravenne. *The Mad Adventures of Rabbi Jacob* was still released.

CURDS AWAY

The Provisional Irish Republican Army (IRA) may well be associated with numerous acts of terrorism. Attacking aviation is not regarded as one of the group's primary modus operandi; however, there have been a number of exceptions.

On 24 January 1974, Rose Dugdale (ironically the wealthy daughter of an airline magnate) and a number of her IRA compatriots hijacked a helicopter in County Donegal and used the aircraft to drop bombs housed in milk churns on a Royal Ulster Constabulary barracks in Northern Ireland. None of the bombs detonated.

TARGET: THE WHITE HOUSE

The events of 11 September 2001 brought home the relative ease with which an aircraft could be hijacked and utilised as a weapon to target prominent landmarks. One would have thought that the actions of Mohamed Atta would have been the first such plot to target US cities. However, way back in 1974 Samuel Joseph Byck had also devised a plan whereby he would hijack a Delta Air Lines flight and fly it into the White House with the aim of assassinating President Richard Nixon.

One would expect anyone intent on hijacking an airliner to maintain a low profile – but not Byck. Armed with a Smith & Wesson .22-calibre gun and 40 rounds of ammunition, Byck went to Baltimore International Washington Airport on 22 February 1974 and, once inside the terminal, shot and killed a police officer, George Neal Ramsburg. Despite the (albeit limited) access control hurdles in place in 1974, he made it as far as a Delta aircraft. He was chased by another officer, Charles Troyer, but not before Byck had got into the cockpit and had executed First Officer Fred Jones. Captain Reese Loftin tried to reassure Byck that he would comply with his requests. Byck left the flight deck when Loftin had told him the doors of the aircraft needed to be closed for departure and Loftin used the opportunity to summon police assistance. Byck returned to the flight deck and shot Loftin a total of three times before Troyer managed to neutralise him.

Three days after the bizarre hijack event, the *Miami News* received a written explanation for his actions in which he said:

> It has become evident to me that this government that I love, dearly, will not respond to the needs of the majority of the American citizens. The majority of the people in government, so-called public servants, are financed by special-interest groups and if they are servants, they are servants to these groups. Now is the time! Independent-minded citizens must take back the government before their government takes complete control of them all. I, for one, will not live in a controlled society and I would rather die as a free man than live like a sheep. Power to the people.

CARLOS THE JACKAL

One of the most infamous names in the history of terrorist atrocities is that of Venezuelan-born Ilich Ramirez Sanchez. He was better known as 'Carlos' or 'Carlos the Jackal'.

Born into a wealthy family, Carlos had a fairly international upbringing, which included being educated at the exclusive Stafford House College in London, where he completed his A-levels. Although he was known to have leftist leanings and to empathise with the revolutionary groups in Europe and Latin America, Carlos also became renowned for living a playboy lifestyle.

After university, Carlos soon hooked up with the PFLP and, starting in 1972, commenced a flurry of terrorist attacks that resulted in his being on many countries' 'most-wanted' lists. He tried to assassinate the president of Marks & Spencer, Joseph Sieff, in his home in 1973; in 1974, he participated in the organisation of an attack against the French Embassy in the Netherlands in conjunction with the Japanese Red Army and personally threw a grenade into a café in Paris in order to ensure that the JRA's demands were met – and they were.

But Carlos' attacks against civil aviation, while still creative and no doubt causing further fear in the minds of passengers keen to travel to foreign shores, were less successful.

On 13 January 1975, acting on behalf of the PFLP-GC, but in concert with Johannes Weinrich of the Revolutionären Zellen, Carlos attempted to destroy an El Al aircraft on the ground at Paris' Orly Airport using a Soviet RPG-7 rocket-propelled grenade launcher. The two men drove up to the perimeter fence and Weinrich fired two grenades, both missing the El Al aircraft they were targeting. One hit a Yugoslav Air Transport (JAT) airliner, where the shrapnel injured a steward on board, as well as an airport porter and a policeman; the second hit an airport building. On their escape, Carlos and Weinrich ditched the RPG-7 launcher.

El Al was still the target and Carlos had the audacity to return to the same airport on 19 January. However, without the rocket launcher and with a heightened state of security at the airport, the three-man team decided not to attack from the perimeter but rather from the observation balcony within the terminal itself. They still had a less sophisticated launcher, but the failure of their plan was more as a result of poor planning than lack of weaponry: they arrived late!

Their target, an El Al aircraft, was already on the move when Carlos and Co. took to the balcony armed with their RPG-2. The police immediately opened fire, prompting the terrorists to take ten people hostage inside the terminal's toilets, one of whom was a four-year-old girl.

The siege lasted for 17 hours, during which the police chief, Pierre Ottavioli, even considered piping sleeping gas into the lavatory to sedate both the terrorists and their hostages. They opted to exercise patience. None of the hostages were killed, primarily due to Carlos not wishing to target French citizens unconnected with the El Al flight. The drama was brought to an end when the French government agreed to fly the terrorists out of Paris to Baghdad, on an Air France aircraft with a volunteer crew, in exchange for the lives of the innocent hostages.

Carlos was to re-emerge from Iraq onto European soil later in the year. On 21 December 1975, he was to storm the Organisation of Petroleum Exporting Countries (OPEC) convention in Vienna, taking many of the leaders hostage; three Austrian police were killed in the attack. The terrorists and their hostages were to leave Vienna the next day on an Austrian Airlines aircraft specifically chartered to take them to Algiers... but that's another story.

11 KILLED AT LAGUARDIA

1975 was to end with a significant, yet often overlooked, attack against aviation on American soil. It was at New York's LaGuardia Airport that, on 29 December, a bomb exploded killing 11 people and injuring 74 others. The device had been placed in a left-luggage locker in the TWA baggage reclaim area and the huge blast, with an estimated force of 20 to 25 sticks of dynamite, caused a 4x6-ft hole in the reinforced concrete ceiling above the lockers and further damaged the ceiling of the floor above that!

There were initially reports that a man telephoned the authorities the same day and claimed responsibility for the Palestine Liberation Organisation, but the PLO later disclaimed responsibility. Many believe it was the work of OTPOR, the resistance group campaigning for a free

VIOLENCE IN THE SKIES

Croatia, and the subsequent hijacking, in 1976, of a TWA flight departing LaGuardia by Zvonko Busic and his OTPOR team (see p.124) added credence to the speculation, especially as they had also secreted a device in a luggage locker. Zvonko Busic, however, denied responsibility until his dying day. The crime remains unsolved.

CHAPTER VI
1976—1980

GERMANS AND PALESTINIANS BECOME PARTNERS IN CRIME

The close relationship between West German and Palestinian terrorist groups became increasingly apparent in the mid-1970s. On 25 January 1976, a plot was foiled to shoot down an El Al aircraft in Nairobi. Armed with SAM-7 heat-seeking missiles, the three Palestinian and two German terrorists, associated with the PFLP and Baader-Meinhof Gang respectively, were captured and spirited out of Kenya to Israel. The group languished in prison without trial, as the Kenyan authorities had not wished to publicise their cooperation with the Israeli security services.

It was only in March 1977 that Israel announced that Brigitte Schultz, aged 23, and Thomas Reuter, aged 24, were being held and they were only officially put on trial and sentenced in 1979; they returned to Germany in December 1980.

On 25 May 1976, Bernard Hausmann was stopped by an Israeli customs officer, Marguerite Ben Yishy, after his arrival in Tel Aviv off an Austrian Airlines flight from Vienna. Ben Yishy was concerned about Hausmann's behaviour and, believing him to be a drug smuggler, requested to inspect his documents and his three suitcases.

Hausmann was actually a 25-year-old German member of the Baader-Meinhof Gang and was travelling on false documents.

His forged Dutch passport indicated that his name was Hugo Müller. He was taken to an inspection room and asked to open the first of his suitcases; upon doing so, there was an explosion which killed both Hausmann and Ben Yishy. Six other people were injured by the blast as the room's glass wall shattered, spraying shards of glass in all directions.

The subsequent investigation revealed that one of Hausmann's other bags also contained an IED.

Both suitcases were made of fibreglass and had been packed with plastic explosives. Earlier in the day it is believed that the suitcases were opened in Vienna, and that the process may have armed the devices. Nobody questioned how Hausmann could be travelling 13 kg overweight, despite the cases only containing old underwear, shoes and toiletries. The check-in agent did suggest that he send some of his luggage by airfreight, but Hausmann refused and paid US$800 for the overweight in cash.

It is not known whether or not Hausmann knew the contents of his baggage. He certainly knew he was part of a mission and that his role was to deliver a case to Israel. Hausmann had travelled to Amsterdam earlier in the month, where he had been given his false documentation by a Dutch student, later named as Rudy M. From there he went to Vienna and stayed in the Wolf Hotel on the night of 24 May; he had been accompanied by a man bearing a Kuwaiti passport under the name Khaled Mohammed Al-Katami.

Also on 24 May, Hausmann visited the Südring travel agency to buy a ticket routed Vienna–Tel Aviv–Tehran–Athens. He tried to pay by traveller's cheques, but they were not accepted; Hausmann left the agency and returned less than five minutes later to pay 18,000 schillings for his ticket in cash.

A month later the German-Palestinian combo effected the legendary Entebbe hijacking.

ENTEBBE: 'OPERATION YONATAN'

For a few years the number of hijackings of airliners for terroristic purposes subsided but the dramatic events during the eight days commencing 27 June 1976 reminded governments and passengers of the threat posed to civil aviation by terrorist groups.

On 27 June 1976 members of the Revolutionäre Zellen cooperated with the PFLP-SOG (Special Operations Group) and took control of an Air France flight which was en route from Tel Aviv to Paris via Athens.

The hijackers had arrived in Athens on a Singapore Airlines flight, which they had boarded at a transit stop in Bahrain. The team consisted of Fayez Abdul Rachim Jaber, Jayel Naji al-Arjam – representing the PFLP-SOG – and Wilfried Bose and Brigitte Kuhlmann – representing the Revolutionäre Zellen.

At Athens Airport, the X-ray machines were not fully operational and the security staff were forced to perform cursory, and obviously less effective, baggage inspections by hand. Seven minutes after taking off for Paris, the hijack commenced. Bose took control of the flight deck, the PFLP-SOG members the Economy cabin and Kuhlmann made the announcement that the aircraft was now under the control of 'The Che Guevara Group and Gaza Unit of the Popular Front for the Liberation of Palestine'. The aircraft's new call sign was 'Haifa One'.

Kuhlmann is reported to have been vicious from the onset, hitting passengers who showed any sign of resistance and issuing a litany of anti-Semitic comments.

Bose instructed Captain Michel Bacos to fly to Benghazi in Libya. On the ground, a British passenger, Patricia Martel, feigned pregnancy and pretended to be having a miscarriage by cutting herself. The hijack team permitted a Libyan doctor to board the aircraft and he confirmed that Martel was miscarrying; she was allowed to disembark and was flown to London the same evening. It was Martel who was able to give the authorities the first description of the make-up of the hijack team.

The Air France jet was refuelled and departed for Entebbe International Airport, serving the Ugandan capital of Kampala. It took nine hours of negotiation before the hijackers and the hostages were allowed to disembark and set up camp in what was the old terminal of the airport. The conditions inside the disused building were appalling.

The four hijackers were joined by four colleagues and the team of eight hijackers could also rely on the support of the Ugandan military. Understandably, ensconced in the heart of East Africa and held hostage by heavily armed militants, the hostages were somewhat pessimistic about being rescued. After all, the last time Sayeret Matkal had resolved a hijack situation, it had been in their own backyard in Tel Aviv.

On the afternoon of 28 June, Idi Amin, the charismatic president of Uganda, arrived at the airport, accompanied by his son; this was the first of a number of visits by the head of state, during which he exploited every opportunity to blame Israel for the plight of the hostages.

In Israel, the government was already evaluating the possibility of embarking upon a rescue mission. The fact that the hostages were being held in the airport's old terminal building proved favourable in the pre-mission risk assessment. In 1971, an Israeli company, Solel Boneh, had been called upon to quote on the construction of a new terminal building in Entebbe and had copies of the plans of airport's old buildings.

In Nairobi, Mossad hooked up with Bruce Mackenzie, Kenya's Minister for Agriculture. He was known to have a light aircraft and was willing to assist both the British and the Israeli intelligence communities. Mackenzie used his aircraft to overfly Entebbe in order to photograph the airfield and terminal buildings, providing the Israelis with valuable data that would be utilised in the subsequent raid.

On the third day, the specific demands of the hijackers were made clear – once again the release of prisoners held in Israel, West Germany, Kenya, Switzerland and France. The various governments were given until 1 July to transport the prisoners to Entebbe.

At the same time, the Israeli and overtly Jewish passengers were separated from the other passengers. The process was orchestrated by Brigitte Kuhlmann; her German accent barking out Hebraic names was a terrifying ordeal for those selected, as well as for those observing their fate.

On the fourth day, 47 of the non-Jewish hostages were released and flown back to Paris. Aside from the relief for them personally, and for their families, this also provided another opportunity at intelligence-gathering for the Israelis, who were still working out whether a rescue mission was doable. The next morning, the remaining non-Jewish hostages were also released. So too were the Air France crew, but Captain Michel Bacos and his entire crew opted to stay with the 94 Jews that were held back, even though the deadline and their possible execution was fast approaching.

It was just over an hour before the deadline expired that the Israeli government notified Idi Amin they would agree to the hijackers' demands. Amin, in turn, persuaded the hijackers to extend the deadline until 2 p.m. on Sunday 4 July. In the interim, Amin was going to be out of the country chairing a meeting of the Organisation of African Unity. The Israelis, however, had no intention of capitulating to the demands of terrorists; they were in the midst of planning 'Operation Thunderbolt' and needed as much time as possible.

Inside the old terminal at Entebbe, Dora Bloch, a 74-year-old dual national of the United Kingdom and Israel, choked on some food. In a rare moment of sympathy shown, the hijackers permitted her to be taken to hospital for treatment. Her son, Ilan Hartuv – who was acting as English/Hebrew translator for Idi Amin during his visits – remained behind.

On Saturday 3 July, the Jewish Sabbath, the Israeli military were rehearsing their plan and getting the mission underway, while the politicians lead by Prime Minister Yitzhak Rabin were meeting in cabinet to deliberate the potential political fallout of the mission. In Entebbe, the hostages were dehydrated, and suffering from food poisoning and low morale.

The mission was eventually given the green light and, by that time, the Hercules aircraft were well on their way to Uganda, led by Lt. Col. Yonatan Netanyahu – Benjamin Netanyahu's brother. Two B-707 aircraft were also en route; one to land in Nairobi and serve as a field hospital if the Kenyans would allow the Hercules aircraft to land there on their return flight to Israel. Kenya had no idea that 'Operation Thunderbolt' was underway and could have refused to be part of a mission that would have undermined their African neighbour, however much they detested the Amin regime. Bruce Mackenzie was contacted and the wheels were put in motion to try to influence the Kenyan authorities to assist when push came to shove.

The first Hercules landed, undetected, in Entebbe just before midnight. As it ground silently to a halt, a black Mercedes bearing a Ugandan number plate and two Ugandan flags emerged from the bowels of the aircraft, followed by two Land Rovers. The plan was for the motorcade to approach the terminal slowly, pretending to be bringing Idi Amin on another of his visits to greet the hostages and their captors. 29 members of Sayeret Matkal were inside the three vehicles.

Another two Hercules aircraft were then to land, each bringing in armoured vehicles and paratroopers.

The plan did not go without a hitch. The silent approach to the old terminal was broken when Ugandan troops exchanged fire with the rescue mission. One of the hijackers, Bose, heard the shots but seemed to think that they were being attacked by Ugandan soldiers rather than the Israeli military.

Sayeret Matkal troops stormed the terminal building, killing Jaber, Bose and Kuhlmann as they did so. Jaber was able to fire a number of shots – one of them mortally wounding Netanyahu – before succumbing himself.

Two of the Air France hostages were killed in the hail of bullets between the Israeli troops and the terrorists – Ida Borochovitch, 56, and Pasco Cohen, 52. Another hostage, 19-year-old Jean-Jacques Maimoni, died due to friendly fire when he stood up as soon as the gunfire subsided. The entire terminal operation was completed within 45 seconds, and less than four minutes had passed since the Hercules had first touched down.

Given the response from the Ugandan troops, it was some time before the hostages could be flown out of Uganda. Kenya, to everybody's relief, granted permission for the aircraft to refuel in Nairobi and then they made their way back to Israel and into the annals of history. 'Operation Thunderbolt' was renamed 'Operation Yonatan' (Mivtza Yonatan) in Yonatan Netanyahu's memory.

Left behind in a hospital in Uganda was Dora Bloch. In an act of retribution by Idi Amin, she was taken from her bed and executed. Many Ugandans who Amin felt had failed him were also to lose their lives. One victim that is rarely mentioned is Bruce Mackenzie, Kenya's Minister for Agriculture.

Bruce Mackenzie visited Uganda on 24 May 1978, almost two years after Entebbe. He was flown there by Paul Lennox and accompanied by two business colleagues, Keith Savage and Gavin Whitelaw. The group left their Piper Aztec 23 at Entebbe Airport and went into Kampala to attend a series of business meetings. On their return, Idi Amin came to the airport to bid them farewell. One of his aides gave Mackenzie a stuffed lion's head as a gift, which Mackenzie reportedly tried to respectfully decline. Amin persuaded him to accept the offering and the group departed. The timing device inside the lion's head triggered an explosion as the Piper Aztec was on its approach to Nairobi's Wilson Airport. The aircraft crashed into the Ngong Hills, killing all on board. Idi Amin had now not only facilitated an act of aviation terrorism, but effected an act of aerial sabotage himself.

ZVONKO AND JULIENNE'S VISIT TO ICELAND ON 9/11

Not all terrorists and freedom fighters were fighting for the Palestinian cause. On 10 September 1976, five separatists associated with OTPOR (Croatian National Resistance), led by Zvonko Busic and his American-born wife, Julienne, hijacked a TWA flight after its departure from New York. They were somewhat poorly prepared, as they demanded that the B-727 aircraft fly to Yugoslavia; the aircraft did not have that range.

In order to convince the authorities that they were not only armed but also in the possession of real explosives, the hijackers had placed an IED in a baggage locker at Grand Central Station in New York. They told the authorities where the device was and claimed to have provided the authorities with instructions on how to disarm it. However, one member of the bomb squad, Brian Murray, was killed and another blinded in their attempts to do so. The authorities were thus left in no doubt that the hijackers did have real explosives on the aircraft which, in fact, they did not.

The aircraft landed in Montreal and demands were made that a letter written by Zvonko Busic, highlighting the Croatian national cause, appear on the front page of Canadian newspapers. They then continued their flight to Gander and from there to Reykjavik in Iceland, where it landed on 11 September. Throughout the incident both the crew and the passengers later reported that the hijackers seemed to be extremely concerned for their well-being and, despite their use of a bomb in New York, were very attentive towards passengers who were frightened. The aircraft continued to Paris, where they demanded fuel again in order to continue their journey to Yugoslavia, but the French authorities shot out the tyres, forcing the hijackers to surrender. Given that the terrorists' goal was publicity for their cause, which they had achieved, they willingly gave up their arms and were sent back to America to stand trial. They were sentenced to life imprisonment for the murder of the member of the bomb squad.

In order to gain some insight into the mind and motivation of a hijacker, *Aviation Security International* met with Julienne Busic some years after her release. The naïve nature of the planning process shone through.

 There were only a few months of planning, consisting mainly of my xeroxing pages about airplanes from the public library. Even that information provided little help, since I was not capable of interpreting it correctly, and that's why the plane had to stop several times along the way to refuel. It wasn't equipped to fly the entire route to Europe otherwise. And then leaflets had to be written and translated, of course. Those were the parts I was involved in.

TWA was one of the international lines and we thought, incorrectly, that it could fly non-stop to Europe. As for the route, that also was arbitrarily chosen.

Julienne explains that she felt 'as though it were happening in somebody else's life. You have to bear in mind that I was the average, all-American girl, brought up to respect the law and live a productive life'. By 1976, and passionately in love with Zvonko, Julienne had become aware of the repression the Croatian people faced during Tito's reign:

and so [I] had to choose whether to violate man-made law in the service of a higher law, a natural law. I was acting this time on the basis of a fear that my husband would soon be murdered and also deep political beliefs that the criminality of the Tito regime had to be publicised and stopped before it was too late.

The pre-flight security checks revealed nothing of concern. As Julienne puts it:

[W]e had no weapons, only a metal pot and some clay, which would later be used to fashion something that looked like a bomb. This was 28 years ago and things were a lot different then. Today I'm sure this would have been highly suspicious. But we were adamant about not having any weapons on the plane because we wanted to be sure nobody could possibly be hurt.

My husband simply went into the cockpit and handed a note to the pilot, saying the plane was hijacked, and that the only demand was the printing of the leaflets in the major newspapers. At that time he also gave detailed instructions about the device in the locker at Grand Central Station so it could be found right away and rendered harmless. Detailed deactivation instructions were also left along with the explosives in the actual locker.

The real explosives' [at Grand Central Station] only purpose was to convince the authorities there were real weapons on the plane so that the leaflets would be printed.

At first, there was some panic until the passengers realised we were not 'lunatics' as they themselves expressed it. Of course we knew the explosives we had on board were not real, but they did not, so they felt great fear in the beginning. After they got to know us better, they said they became more relaxed. Then they read the leaflets and most told us they supported the Croatian cause for independence based on what they'd read, and wondered why they knew nothing about this issue. At various stops, approximately 40 passengers were released, those who had medical problems, pressing engagements, weddings, graduations, etc. And some of the passengers who could have left actually said they wanted to stay on the plane until the end, that they considered it an 'adventure'. After our arrest, many of them wrote letters to our trial judge asking for leniency, and for years afterwards, several corresponded with me directly and even visited me in prison. One told me he could envisage one of his own daughters getting involved in something similar. It was a human situation, and people who can identify with the heart and not just the mind were the ones who kept in touch, wrote to the judge, visited me, and so forth. This didn't mean they approved, it only meant they could identify with us on a human level. That's a rare quality, especially in these current times when everyone and everything tends to be lumped together and stereotyped. 🔒

Julienne claims to have been shocked when she heard the news of the death of the police officer in New York.

At first, I thought it was a trick to force us to surrender... I simply refused to believe it, didn't want to believe it. We'd taken so many steps to ensure nobody could possibly get hurt, and then the worst happened. It was little comfort that the policeman's widow eventually filed a gross negligence suit against the police department, because it was our actions that set things in motion. We even set up a trust fund for the policeman's children through a Croatian businessman, but that ended when he passed away, so later, while I was still in prison, I donated money to the fund that I earned doing translations and various other jobs. Of course in retrospect I know how naïve and ridiculous it was to assume nothing could go wrong. But we were young and idealistic and thought that good intentions were enough. Now I know that things can always go wrong and usually do. And we'll have to live with that knowledge, that guilt, for the rest of our lives.

You have to bear in mind that the hijacking took place during revolutionary years, Vietnam, the civil and human rights movement. We were young idealists who thought we should and could change the world. Like most of the rest of our generation. But we never advocated violence, and ironically didn't consider the hijacking to be an act of violence then, since no weapons were on the plane. We were sure the explosives left behind would be detonated safely by the experts, using our instructions.

The reaction of the passengers towards the hijackers was unusual, perhaps illustrative of a degree of Stockholm Syndrome having set in. 'Several corresponded with me for years, and some even visited me in prison in California. [One] even appeared as my representative at the parole board hearings in support of my release.'

Despite the fact that Croatia was granted independence in the interim, Zvonko Busic remained in jail for 34 years, before being released in 2008 and deported to Croatia, where he was greeted as a hero. Zvonko couldn't deal with freedom after so many years in captivity and committed suicide on 1 September 2013. He had shot himself at home, leaving a suicide note for Julienne.

THE DEATH OF THE CUBAN FENCERS

Fencing, as defined by the Oxford English Dictionary, is 'the action or art of using the sword scientifically as a weapon of offence or defence'. It is often described as being a noble art and the fencer's skill and dexterity has, historically, been considered an indication of manliness. In Europe, in the Middle Ages, matters of honour were often settled by a duel between two opponents; the non-judicial process was agreed upon by the concerned parties, with a refusal to accept a challenge being regarded as an act of cowardice. How ironic it is that acts of terror perpetrated alongside international sporting competitions have twice claimed the lives of innocent fencers, where no gauntlet was thrown down and where there had been no agreement to engage in duels.

In 1972, Israeli fencing coach Andre Spitzer was one of the 11 Israeli athletes massacred at the Munich Olympiad, killed by gunfire rather than the sword. But, on 6 October 1976, it was the entire Cuban fencing team that died on their way home from the fourth Central American and Caribbean Championships, held in Venezuela, having won all the gold medals; their sporting prowess with foils, epées, and sabres was to be no match for the unannounced detonation of two C4-based IEDs infiltrated on board Cubana flight 455.

The destruction of the Cubana aircraft, which killed all 73 souls on board (57 Cubans, 11 Guyanese and five North Koreans), marked the first terrorist bombing of an aircraft in the western hemisphere. It also marked the start of an investigation which, to this day, seriously calls into question the United States' commitment to fighting terrorism and, according to some, actually implicates the Central Intelligence Agency, at best, in ensuring the perpetrators were never brought to justice, or, at worst, being actively involved in supporting the masterminds' actions.

The Cubana de Aviación flight was to start its fateful journey in Timehri Airport in Guyana, where the flight's departure was delayed 27 minutes due to the late arrival of the North Korean passengers, who were part of an official delegation. The aircraft then stopped in Port of Spain in Trinidad and Tobago, where two Venezuelan passengers, Hernán Ricardo and Freddy Lugo, joined the flight, along with the 24 members of the Cuban fencing team; all had flown into Port of Spain on a Pan Am flight from Caracas.

The next stop was Barbados, where Ricardo and Lugo were two of the 18 passengers who disembarked. They, however, had not taken all their belongings with them. They had left two IEDs on board, one concealed in a Nikon camera beneath a seat, somewhere between rows 7 and 11, in the mid-section of the aircraft, and the other in one of the toilets at the rear. Some of the reports indicate that, in addition to C4 explosives, a chemical was also used in the bombs, and that it had been infiltrated on board in tubes of Colgate toothpaste.

Cubana flight 455 departed for Jamaica, its last intended stop before its planned final destination of Havana. It reached neither. As the aircraft climbed through 18,000 ft, the IED beneath the passenger seat, activated by a timer, detonated, filling the cabin with fire and smoke. The pilots notified air traffic control, 'We have a blast and we are descending immediately. We have fire on board!' and were granted permission to make an emergency landing. However, four minutes later, when the crew seemed to have control of the aircraft and had managed to lower the landing gear, the second device detonated. The crew now all but lost control of the doomed jet. Captain Wilfredo Perez's final act was to turn the aircraft away from the shoreline, thereby avoiding any casualties on Barbados' beaches.

Ricardo and Lugo immediately telephoned their paymasters to notify them of the success of their mission. Indeed, it was these calls which helped prove that this was a terrorist attack organised by an anti-Castro group known as the Coordination of United Revolutionary Organisations (CORU), headed up by Luis Posada Carriles and Orlando Bosch. The bombers never got through to Carriles, but when they told Bosch of their 'success', he responded, 'Friend, we have a problem here in Caracas. You never blow up a plane while it is in the air.' The implication was that CORU would have preferred the bombing to have taken place on the ground, presumably, as there would be a lower death toll.

Ricardo and Lugo then headed back to Trinidad, but the authorities were already on to them and they were quickly arrested. Initially they denied any involvement in the bombing, but as hours of interrogation became days, the men realised the game was up and admitted to the crime. They further claimed that they were in the pay of the CIA and reported to Luis Posada Carriles. Between them, they had been paid $25,000 for their mission.

Ricardo attempted to commit suicide while in custody, perhaps sensing that he would either be executed once deported back to Venezuela or, if not, killed by fellow inmates. He and Lugo were eventually sent to Caracas, where both Luis Posada Carriles and Orlando Bosch had also been arrested. The bombers were sentenced to 20 years in prison; the paymasters, albeit after a very lengthy judicial process, walked free. In the case of Bosch, there was apparently a 'lack of evidence', despite the testimony of Ricardo and Lugo; Carriles was convicted, but somehow managed to escape from prison before he was sentenced.

It would seem that Carriles and Bosch had friends in high places. There was tremendous pressure on the judges to acquit the men. The first judge withdrew from the case following death threats. Whether payments were made or not is unclear. What is known is that Carriles and Bosch were able to enter the United States and live there as free men, despite the depravity of the crimes they were responsible for. Not surprisingly, this has resulted in the American government being accused of having dual standards when it comes to the handling of terrorists. Bosch wound up in Florida in 1988, dying there in 2011.

Carriles, however, was far from ready to retire after the Cubana bombing – and its fallout – and he decided to assist the United States with another of their enemies. In Nicaragua, the Sandinista government was viewed by Washington as posing a similar threat to regional peace as Castro's Cuba. Consequently, America offered support to the Contras, a group which used terrorist tactics in its attempts to overthrow the Sandinistas; Carriles became the go-between.

Fidel Castro, however, remained his number one target. In Panama, Carriles was arrested and charged with attempting his assassination during a presidential visit in 2000. Despite this, or perhaps because of it, on his release, Carriles managed to enter the United States. He was charged with a series of visa-related offences, but never convicted of any act of terrorism. He lives in Florida, where he is regarded by many of the local population as a national hero. To many overseas, he is no better than Osama bin Laden.

Recently released documents further illustrate American complicity in the Cubana bombing. Carriles had apparently spoken of his intent to target a Cubana flight a few days before the demise of flight 455. While the CIA reportedly informed the powers that be in Washington, nobody felt it to be actionable intelligence and, accordingly, Cuba was left in the dark.

MOGADISHU

In terms of high profile incidents and drama, Middle Eastern terrorists remained the most active throughout this period. On 13 October 1977, a Lufthansa flight was operating from Majorca to Frankfurt and, in addition to the 75 tourists, most of whom were German, and 11 beauty queens on board, there were four members of the PFLP.

The team was led by Zohair Youssif Akache, who called himself Captain Martyr Mahmud. He had undergone pilot training and was familiar with avionics and aviation terminology. He was supported by his fiancée, Hind Alameh, Wabil Harb and another female hijacker, Suhaila Sayeh. They had travelled to Majorca a week before their attack and started their final preparations. They bought their tickets – two in First Class and two in Economy – in cash at a travel agency in Palma.

Security at Palma Airport was certainly ineffective. On the day of the hijack, they managed to infiltrate automatic pistols – a .357 Magnum, a Russian 7.62-mm Tokarev and a 9-mm Makarov – as well as six grenades and 1.5 kg of explosives in the form of pentaerythritol tetranitrate (PETN). It was the female hijackers who brought the cache on board, concealed in the false bottom of a vanity case and inside a cassette recorder.

Once the aircraft was at cruising altitude, the two hijackers seated in First Class swung into action and headed towards the cockpit. Simultaneously, the two hijackers in the Economy cabin stood up and commanded the passengers to hold their hands above their heads and maintain silence.

Inside the cockpit, Akache forced First Officer Jurgen Vietor from his seat and placed him in the passenger cabin. Akache replaced him in the right-hand seat and announced that the aircraft was now under the control of the PFLP. His first demand was that Captain Jurgen Schumann fly to Rome instead of Frankfurt; Schumann, alone on the flight deck with an armed hijacker, complied.

The hijacking took place little more than a month after the Rote Armee Fraktion (RAF) had kidnapped the German industrialist, Hans Martin Schleyer. Schleyer was both the president of the Federal Association of German Industries and the president of the Federal Employers Association; he epitomised German capitalism. The RAF had demanded the release of 11 RAF prisoners in exchange for Schleyer, but the German government had not made any concessions. The hijacking of Lufthansa flight 181 was, in part, designed to increase the pressure on the government.

Indeed, on the ground at Fiumicino, Akache made it clear that this was a joint operation of the PFLP and the Rote Armee Fraktion (RAF) – and for this mission they were operating under the name of the Commando Martyr Halimeh unit of the Struggle Against World Imperialism Organisation (SAWIO). Halimeh was the name afforded Brigitte Kuhlmann, the member of Revolutionäre Zellen who had been killed at Entebbe the year before. The only demand, at this stage, was to refuel. The Italians agreed and the aircraft departed for Cyprus. Some of the incident reports indicate that, before take off, Captain Schumann was able to leave the authorities with a vital clue regarding the hijackers: he dropped four cigars from the cockpit window, two of which were broken in half. This was supposedly a pre-arranged code which would indicate the number and gender of the hijackers.

Flight 181 was not on the ground in Larnaca for long, as the hijackers were keen to head eastwards to countries supposedly friendly to their cause. The next stop was supposed to be Beirut, but the Lebanese authorities denied the aircraft permission to land. So too did the Syrians, Jordanians and Kuwaitis. In the early hours of 14 October, the aircraft landed in Bahrain.

At this point, the link between the abduction of Hans-Martin Schleyer and the hijacking of the Lufthansa flight became abundantly clear with the release of what came to be known as the 'SAWIO Ultimatum':

> To the Chancellor of the Federal Republic of West Germany
>
> This is to inform you that the passengers and the crew of the lh 737 plane, flight no. 181 leaving from Palma to Frankfurt, are under our complete control and responsibility. The lives of the passengers and the crew of the plane as well as the life of Mr. Hanns-Martin Schleyer depends on your fulfilling the following –
>
> 1. Release of the following comrades of the raf from prisons in West Germany – Andreas Baader, Gudrun Ensslin, Jan-Carl Raspe, Verena Becker, Werner Hoppe, Karl-Heinz Dellwo, Hanna Krabbe, Bernd Roessner, Ingrid Schubert, Irmgard Moeller, Guenter Sonnenberg – and with each the amount of DM100,000.
> 2. Release of the following Palestinian comrades of pflp from prison in Istanbul – Mahdi and Hussein.
> 3. The payment of the sum of US$15 million according to accompanying instructions.
> 4. Arrange with any one of the following countries to accept to receive all the comrades released from prison:
>   i) Democratic Republic of Vietnam
>   ii) Republic of Somalia
>   iii) People's Democratic Republic of Yemen
> 5. The German prisoners should be transported by plane, which you should provide, to their point of

destination. They should fly via Istanbul to take in the two Palestinian comrades released from Istanbul prison.

6. The Turkish government is well informed about our demands.

7. The prisoners should all together reach their point of destination before Sunday 16 October 1977, 8 a.m. GMT.

8. The money should be delivered according to accompanying instructions within the same period of time.

9. If all the prisoners are not released and do not reach their point of destination, and the money is not delivered according to instructions, within the specified time, then Mr Hanns-Martin Schleyer, and all the passengers and the crew of the lh737 plane flight no. 181 will be killed immediately.

10. If you comply with our instructions all of them will be released.

11. We shall not contact you again. This is our last contact with you. You are completely to blame for any error or faults in the release of the above mentioned comrades in prison or in the delivery of the specified ransom according to the specified instructions.

12. Any try on your part to delay or deceive us will mean immediate ending of the ultimatum and execution of Mr. Hanns-Martin Schleyer and all the passengers and the crew of the plane.

S.A.W.I.O.

13 October 1977

Next stop Dubai. The aircraft was now on the ground, but the heat of the Middle East made conditions on board almost intolerable. The Emiratis were trying in vain to persuade the hijackers to release any women and children. However, the hijackers were awaiting news of their demands being met. The Germans were preparing their SWAT team, the GSG 9, to carry out an assault of the aircraft with the reluctant support of officers of the Dubai Defence Force and, by invitation, two members of the British SAS who had specific experience with and, more importantly, a stock of G60 stun grenades.

The hijackers were following media reports regarding the situation and became aware that the GSG 9 were on their way to Dubai. They demanded the aircraft be refuelled; once they had enough fuel on board for the short flight to Oman, they departed.

The Omanis had a different idea and, like many of the other Arab states, they denied the flight permission to land. Captain Schumann headed for Aden, but there too the Yeminis had blocked the runway. The aircraft was now exceptionally low on fuel and there was no alternative airport to divert to, so the Lufthansa crew did the only thing they could – they landed on one of the sand-covered, uneven, taxiways alongside the main runway in Aden.

The Lufthansa flight was told that they would be supplied with fuel and to depart as quickly as possible. Yemen did not want the hijacked aircraft on its soil. Captain Schumann was not so confident that the aircraft could depart; he was concerned that, having landed on a taxiway, the undercarriage had sustained damage. Akache told Schumann that he could disembark the aircraft to carry out an inspection.

Inspection completed, Schumann seized the opportunity to speak with the Yemini authorities, and then in full view made his way to the airport's control tower; it was a move that would later cost him his life. Akache was incensed by Schumann's excursion and threatened to destroy the aircraft; the Yemini authorities did not wish to get involved and told Schumann to return to the aircraft. On doing so, he was taken to the First Class cabin and told to get down on his knees. Schumann obeyed, placing his hands over his head. According to an article in *Der Spiegel*, Akache then said, 'This is a revolutionary tribunal. You betrayed me already once. This second time I will not forgive you. Are you guilty or not guilty?' Schumann is reported to have responded, 'Captain [the title which Akache insisted upon being called] there were difficulties in returning to the plane.' Akache hit him with his left hand in the face and again said, 'Guilty or not guilty?' Akache did not wait for a response and shot Schumann in the face, in front of the passengers.

Co-pilot Jurgen Vietor was ordered to take off single-handed and plot a course for Mogadishu. Akache was his co-pilot.

On the ground at the Somali airport, Vietor was offered the opportunity to leave the aircraft by a grateful Akache; he, like the heroic Air France crew in Entebbe a year before, opted to stay with the passengers and crew in what were by now horrendous conditions. Four days after the hijack had commenced, the toilets were overflowing and the stench of urine, faeces, and sweat was overpowering; to make matters worse, there was now the decomposing body of the murdered captain lying in the aircraft aisle.

Another Lufthansa jet, which Akache believed was carrying the German negotiating team, landed in Mogadishu. In fact, on board were members of the GSG 9, accompanied by their two British colleagues from the SAS.

Passengers, crew and hijackers were increasingly desperate for a swift, negotiated resolution to the crisis. In a subsequent interview, Vietor said, 'With ladies stockings, we were handcuffed, restrained to seats, buckled up and doused with duty-free liquor so that we would burn better. Then plastic explosives were attached to the partition between First Class and Economy.'

At one point the body of Captain Schumann was thrown off the aircraft.

As tempers frayed, one of the flight attendants, Gabriele Dillmann, made an impassioned appeal over the radio on behalf of all on board – she was later called 'the Angel of Mogadishu'. She spoke in English, saying:

> I want to say we're going to die because the German government has failed us. And we are going to die. They've tied us up already. Theirs is what we'd call a suicide mission in Germany. They don't care about their lives or the lives of any other human beings. The German government doesn't care about our lives at all either. We're going to die now. I've tried to bear it as well as possible, but the fear is too much. All the same, we'd like you to know that the German government did nothing to save our lives. They could have done everything, everything. We just can't understand it.

Dillmann ended her speech by stating her name and sending her love to her parents and her fiancée, Rüdiger von Lutzau. As it happens, Rüdiger was not only a Lufthansa pilot but the very same co-pilot who was flying the GSG 9 into Mogadishu; he was far closer to Dillmann than she thought.

Akache was assured that a deal was on the table and that prisoners were in the process of being released and would be on their way to Somalia. However, a decision had been made to storm the aircraft. And so it was that, in the early hours of 18 October, while the Germans were still talking about the logistics relating to money transfers, operation *Feuerzauber* (Fire Magic) commenced.

At 2.07 a.m., Somali officers set fire to a fuel truck situated a safe distance in front of the aircraft; it exploded with a huge bang that lit up the night sky. This diversionary tactic worked, as it drew both Akache and one of the other hijackers into the cockpit. At the same time, the GSG 9 stormed the aircraft. By the end of the operation, all the hostages were released, and three of the four hijackers were dead.

It was in Germany itself, where the casualty rate was highest. By the following morning, upon hearing that the Lufthansa hijack had ended in failure, three Rote Armee Fraktion activists committed suicide in their Stammheim prison cells – Andreas Baader and Jan-Carl Raspe allegedly shot themselves and Gudrun Ensslin hanged herself. A fourth RAF member, Irmgard Möller, also tried to commit suicide, but survived; she later claimed that the others had not committed suicide but had been killed by the German government.

Upon her release from prison, Suhaila Sayeh, the sole surviving hijacker, moved to Norway, where she still lives as a free woman. In a subsequent television programme, Suhaila Sayeh, Monika Schumann - the widow of the murdered captain - and Barry Davis, one of the SAS commandos, met to discuss the impact the event had on their lives.

Vietor continued to fly for Lufthansa until 1999. Dillmann married Rüdiger von Lutzau. As for Hans-Martin Schleyer, once those holding him hostage had heard of the deaths of their comrades in Mogadishu and Stammheim prison, he was executed and left in the boot of a green Audi car in Mulhouse, France.

THE FIRST MALAYSIAN MYSTERY

The loss of MH370 (see p.296) in 2014 was not the only Malaysian aircraft to disappear in mysterious circumstances. On 4 December 1977, a Malaysia Airline System flight en route from Penang to Kuala Lumpur crashed shortly after the crew had told air traffic control that an unidentified hijacker was ordering them to divert to Singapore. The cockpit voice recorder showed that two shots were then fired in the flight deck, presumably killing the captain and first officer.

There were no survivors and nobody actually knows how many hijackers were on the plane or what the cause was, although the Japanese Red Army is suspected of being behind the incident. One of those killed on board was the Cuban ambassador to Malaysia.

IN THE GENES

Certain families, it would seem, have an affinity with hijacking. Garrett Trapnell hijacked a TWA flight in 1972 and demanded $306,800, the amount he'd lost in a court case. While serving his prison sentence, Barbara Ann Oswald had started communicating with Trapnell and, on 24 May 1978, she hijacked a helicopter and ordered the pilot to fly her to the prison where Trapnell was being held. She instructed the pilot to land inside the perimeter fence but, as he did so, he grabbed Barbara's gun and shot her dead. That was not the end of the story.

Seven months later, on 21 December 1978, Robyn Oswald, Barbara Ann's 17-year-old daughter, hijacked a TWA flight en route from Louisville to Kansas City ordering the crew to fly to Williamson County Airport and to bring Garrett Trapnell to the aircraft from the prison. She showed the crew what she claimed to be three sticks of dynamite strapped to her body. FBI negotiators successfully secured the release of all passengers and crew.

Robyn's rationale for the hijacking is the subject of debate; her family claim that she believed that Trapnell was actually her real father, whilst others think that she simply regarded Trapnell as the father figure she had never had.

AEROLINEE ITAVIA AND THE GADDAFI ASSASSINATION PLOT

The skies were no safer in the 1980s, although the first significant incident officially remained a mystery until 2008.

It was on 27 June 1980 that an Aerolinee Itavia flight crashed near the island of Ustica while en route from Bologna to Palermo. As was the case with TWA flight TW800 in 1996, Malaysia Airlines flight MH17 in 2014 and Metrojet flight KGL9268 in October 2015, the flight disappeared suddenly off the radar without any warning. All the scenarios that caused those flights' destruction – fuel tank explosion, missile and bomb (probably) respectively – were considered distinct possibilities. For years, the theory that it had been downed by a missile was deemed the most likely, yet the investigation was hampered by a disturbing sequence of incidents, which included witnesses meeting untimely deaths and evidence disappearing.

When the truth did finally emerge, it was shocking. Not only had the Aerolinee Itavia flight been shot down, but it wasn't an accident. A French air force pilot intentionally fired at the aircraft, believing it to be the private jet on which Colonel Gaddafi was travelling home from Europe – this state-sponsored assassination attempt went wildly wrong, in part because Gaddafi got wind of the plot (from Italian inside sources) and opted not to fly.

When Gaddafi did not arrive back in Tripoli as planned, his own air force went in search of him, but stray Libyan fighter jets were not exactly welcomed in European skies, and both the American and Italian military sent their own aircraft to intercept the intruder. A Libyan pilot, for reasons which are still not 100 per cent clear, flew towards the Aerolinee Itavia flight (perhaps thinking it was Gaddafi's aircraft, or maybe opting to stay near a commercial flight as he knew he was being chased and believing that neither American nor Italian forces would fire upon a commercial aircraft). The French Mirage pilot, however, assumed that the Libyan pilot was escorting Gaddafi's jet back to Libya, so fired a missile, resulting in the deaths of all 81 souls on board.

In 2011, the Italian government was ordered to pay $127 million to the families of the victims for its role in the cover up and its failure to protect the aircraft and all on board. France, seemingly, got away scot-free.

CHAPTER VII
1981–1985

A STORM IN BANGKOK

The Western world's media tended to focus on terrorist attacks perpetrated in the European arena and on flights from the USA to Cuba. As demonstrated by the Malaysian incident in 1977 (see p.142), hijacking was alive and well on the Asian continent. On the 28 March 1981, a Garuda Indonesian Airlines aircraft was operating a domestic flight from Palembang to Medan when two of the passengers arose from their seats and commandeered the aircraft. Three of their colleagues were also on board and together these members of the Jihad Commando Group had complete control of the aircraft and it was flown to Don Mueang International Airport in Bangkok, Thailand.

While the Indonesian government was immediately keen to use military force to resolve the crisis, the Thai government opted for extended negotiations. This was, in part, because, back in 1972, they had managed to bring a siege of the Israeli Embassy in Bangkok – conducted by members of Black September – to an end without loss of life. However, eventually military force was authorised and the aircraft was stormed on the 30 March by members of the Royal Thai Air Force and Indonesia's Kopassandha commandos. One of the commandos and the captain of the aircraft were killed, as were two of the hijackers. The terrorist leader, Imran Bin Muhammad Zein, was sentenced to death a few weeks later in Indonesia.

While the storming of the Garuda flight was a significant achievement, the key reason it did not get much publicity globally was the fact that Ronald Reagan was shot in the USA on the same day.

Some events get publicity due not to their severity but to the colourful nature of the story; one occurred in May 1981.

WHEN TRAPPIST MONKS HIJACK PLANES

Trappist monks may not be the stereotypical image of the hijacker, but it was one such individual who, on 2 May 1981, hijacked an Aer Lingus flight while it was en route from Dublin to London Heathrow.

Australian-born Laurence Downey visited the toilets after departure, poured water – which he claimed to be petrol – over himself and re-entered the cabin demanding that the aircraft divert to Tehran and that, if it didn't, he would set fire to himself and the aircraft. He had, he claimed, drafted a new constitution for the people of Iran and wished to deliver it personally!

The crew managed to convince Downey that a B-737 planning to go from Ireland to London would not have enough fuel to reach Iran. Downey agreed to the aircraft landing in Le Touquet, France, to refuel. On the ground, Downey announced that what he really wanted was for Pope John Paul II to reveal the 'Third Secret of Fatima'.

The 'Three Secrets of Fatima' were apocalyptic visions given to three Portuguese shepherdesses by an apparition of the Virgin Mary back in 1917. The first two of the prophecies were made public in 1941 – and related to Hell, and World Wars One and Two – but the third prophecy was regarded as being so sensitive that Lucia Santos, one of the recipients, was told to write it down and keep it secret. Downey wanted to know why the Vatican wished, in 1981, not to make public the Virgin Mary's prophecy.

Downey did allow a few of the passengers to deplane at Le Touquet while negotiations with the French and Irish authorities continued. Eventually the siege was brought to an end, when French police stormed the aircraft and arrested Downey. He was later sentenced to five years in prison, released 16 months later and deported back to Australia.

Pope John Paul II did reveal the third prophecy to the public on 26 June 2000, when he claimed that it related to the assassination attempt made on his life by Mehmet Ali Ağca on 13 May 1981 – the original apparition had first appeared to the Portuguese shepherdesses on 13 May 1917. However, there are many who feel that the Vatican is still withholding the actual prophecy as an assassination attempt on the pope, while tragic and highly significant, is hardly comparable to world wars; there is a sense that if the third prophecy is about the 'end of days' or some other apocalyptic vision, then withholding details of the 'Third Secret' might be more justifiable.

XI'AN: THE ORIGINAL 'LET'S ROLL'

A CAAC flight departing Xi'an on 25 July 1982 became the first hijacking of a Chinese airliner to be officially acknowledged in China. The flight was scheduled to operate to Shanghai but shortly before landing, somewhere over Wuxi, five men – Sun Yunping, Yang Feng, Gao Keli, Xei Zhimin and Wei Xeuli – brandishing knives, and carrying a large brown cylinder which they claimed to be an IED, demanded to be flown to Taipei. Two of the team took control of the flight deck, while the others maintained order in the cabin. The captain convinced the hijackers that he had insufficient fuel to reach Taiwan, so they agreed to Hong Kong as an alternative destination.

The captain remained alone on the flight deck while the first officer and navigator were permitted to exit the cockpit as they had been injured in the initial takeover of the aircraft and required medical attention. Once in the cabin they discreetly organised passengers into teams as they planned to overpower the hijackers. The captain, meanwhile, was simply circling rather than flying to Hong Kong; the hijackers on the flight deck did not realise they were being duped as they were unfamiliar with avionics, the electronic systems that control communication and navigation.

Eventually, the passengers in the cabin, accompanied by the technical crew and flight attendants, attacked the hijackers, one of whom threw a grenade which detonated and created a hole about 3 ft^2 in the wall of the toilet compartment. Fortuitously, the cabin did not depressurise, but as the aircraft was desperately short of fuel, the two port engines already cut out, and a full-scale fight going on in the cabin, the captain had to land. Powered only by the starboard engines, the aircraft hit the runway in Shanghai so hard that two of the tyres blew.

While the Xinhua News Agency reported that the hijackers, later identified as being factory workers from Xi'an, had been captured alive, some of the witnesses on board thought that a few of them had been killed in the fight. An American passenger, Ronald D. Roth, said that

> they were dragged off by their feet through the aisles. Some of the Chinese spat on them as they went by.

Regardless, by 19 August they were all dead as Radio Peking reported that they had been executed.

LOCKERBIE PRECURSORS

The early 1980s saw an increase in the use of explosives and two incidents in August 1982, wherein Pan Am was the target, indicated a concerted effort to undermine the public's faith in civil aviation security, a resolve that would be realised six years later with the destruction of Pan Am flight 103 over Lockerbie.

On 11 August 1982, a Pan Am jet was preparing to land in Honolulu, having completed a trans-Pacific flight from Tokyo, when an IED, using sheet explosives as a charge, detonated beneath seat 10F. One Japanese passenger was killed but the aircraft withstood the blast, even though a hole was made in the cabin floor and rivets in the fuselage skin were popped. Two weeks later, another Pan Am airliner landed in Rio de Janeiro and, while it was being serviced for its return flight, a ground maintenance employee found an IED in the cabin, once again beneath seat 10F. The device's construction was similar to that which had detonated in Honolulu.

THE UNHAPPY REFUSENIK

Seeking asylum, or pastures greener, was not only a cause of hijackings from and to Cuba. In September 1982, Igor Shkuro, a Soviet Jew who had been allowed to leave his home in Leningrad in 1977, decided that life in the West was not quite as good as he thought it would be. In 1981, he was deported from Australia, despite having been granted Australian nationality, for having expressed anti-Western sentiments, and so it was that in September 1982 he boarded a flight from Rome to Algiers in the hope of finding a way to return to the Soviet Union.

He was denied entry to Algeria and placed on the same aircraft to return to Rome. During his return flight, he produced an eight-inch knife and demanded to be flown to Libya instead. The Libyan authorities denied the aircraft permission to land and the pilot was forced to land at Catania on the island of Sicily, where Shkuro released the passengers. He then demanded to be flown to Moscow but the captain and first officer managed to overpower him and he was arrested.

GULF AIR

One tends to think that if a group successfully bombs an aircraft, it would claim responsibility. Otherwise, what's the point? The evidence, however, points otherwise. No group claimed responsibility for Pan Am 103 over Lockerbie in 1988 and, indeed, there was no immediate *mea culpa* for the actions that took place in the United States on 11 September 2001. The same is true in respect of the bombing of Gulf Air flight 771 en route from Karachi, Pakistan to Abu Dhabi on 23 September 1983.

As the aircraft was on its final approach to Abu Dhabi International Airport, it abruptly lost altitude and crashed killing all 110 passengers and crew on board. The crew had little time to react, although Captain Saoud Al Kindy, from Oman, reportedly prayed as he realised his fate.

A subsequent investigation proved that a bomb had detonated in a suitcase belonging to a passenger who had checked in for the flight in Karachi but never boarded. As to who he worked for, well, it remains a subject of debate. The Abu Nidal Organisation (ANO) was the prime suspect, despite it being an attack on an Arab carrier.

Under the leadership of Sabri Khalil al-Banna (aka Abu Nidal), the ANO was a ruthless organisation which opposed compromise at any price. As a result, while it attacked Israeli targets, it also targeted those which it regarded as 'soft', including members of the Palestine Liberation Organisation leadership who intimated that a negotiated settlement with Israel might be reached. (Later attacks against airports in Rome and Vienna in 1985 were allegedly planned by Abu Nidal due to Italy and Austria putting themselves forward as peace-brokers for the Middle East.) The ANO also needed money and Abu Nidal had no qualms about extorting it from states he felt should be supporting his war against the Zionists. Some reports indicate that Saudi Arabia and Kuwait ultimately succumbed to Abu Nidal's demands and hence no attacks were perpetrated by the ANO on their soil.

It was against this backdrop that the Gulf Air flight was targeted, as the United Arab Emirates had previously refused to make 'charitable donations' to the cause. This was confirmed by Atef Abu Bakr, a former member of Abu Nidal's Fatah-Revolutionary Council, in an August 2002 interview with the London-based newspaper *Al-Hayat*, in the days following Abu Nidal's suicide/assassination (which of the two is a moot point!). This was the same interview in which Abu Bakr claimed that the ANO had been responsible for the bombing of Pan Am 103 over Lockerbie in 1988 and that the wrong men had been convicted.

SOME WEDDING PARTY

Most people conducting hijacks in any way related to the Soviet Union in the 1980s were trying to move from the East to the West. On 18 November 1983, seven Georgian intellectuals hijacked an Aeroflot flight while en route from Tbilisi in Georgia to Leningrad. All the hijackers were pretending to be part of a wedding party and demanded that the aircraft divert to Turkey. The captain used an aggressive manoeuvre to throw the hijackers off balance and managed to land the aircraft back in Tbilisi. On 19 November, the Alpha Group stormed the aircraft, during which three crew members, two passengers and three hijackers were killed. The surviving hijackers and an orthodox priest, who had not been on board the aircraft but who had been their confessor, and had thus known about the incident, were sentenced to death.

WHEN TESTRAKE AND DERICKSON BECAME HEROES

In Europe, the Palestinians continued to threaten civil aviation and so it was on 14 June 1985 that one of the longest hijackings on record commenced; the Islamic Jihad hijacking of Trans World Airlines flight 847 en route from Athens to Rome.

The hijackers had purchased their tickets at the Gesinor travel agency in Beirut and flew with Middle East Airlines to Athens. Hasan Izz-Al-Din and Mohammed Ali Hammadi, who were both Shiite Lebanese, forced their way into the TWA cockpit shortly after the B-727 aircraft departed for Rome. They were supposed to have been accompanied by Ali Atwa, but he had been denied boarding to the flight in Athens and was arrested by the Greek authorities after the TWA flight was hijacked.

The hijackers demanded that the aircraft divert to Algiers, but with insufficient fuel on board, and not wishing to go to Cairo, Captain John Testrake suggested they opt for Beirut. The hijackers agreed, but Lebanon refused the aircraft permission to land. It was only when Testrake pleaded that they relented. His words have gone down in hijack history:

> He has pulled a hand grenade pin and is ready to blow up the aircraft if he has to. We must, I repeat, we must land at Beirut. We must land at Beirut. No alternative.

They did.

On the ground, the hijackers made their demands clear: the release of 700 Shiite prisoners held in Israel prisons, along with others held in Kuwait, Cyprus and Spain. The flight attendants were ordered to collect all the passports and to identify Jewish passengers and anyone travelling on military ID.

Initially, 19 women and one child were released. The hijackers had, however, also identified five US Navy divers and Kurt Carlson, a major in the US Army Reserves, as the ideal scapegoats and targets of their aggression; they became the subject of regular beatings. At one point, Carlson slipped in and out of consciousness as he was beaten for hours.

As negotiations stalled, the hijackers were keen to keep the aircraft on the move. Testrake was ordered to depart for Algiers. On arrival there a further 23 passengers were released, while the six American military personnel continued to be beaten.

The hijackers demanded fuel which was not readily provided: the ground personnel demanded payment first. While the pilots argued with them, explaining that pilots of aeroplanes did not pay for petrol in the same way that a driver does for his car, Uli Derickson, the flight purser, asked the hijackers for permission to go to her handbag. She pulled out her Shell credit card and put $5,500 worth of jet fuel – 6,000 gallons – on her own account. TWA did refund her later!

TWA 847 was only on the ground in Algeria for five hours before the hijackers opted to return to Beirut. They needed reinforcements and were keen to have the support of the Amal militia – a Shi'a group and competitor of Hezbollah – based in Beirut; so, in addition to their demands for prisoner releases, they demanded manpower to support their efforts. Frustrated by the delays, they shouted, 'One American must die,' and, eventually, after having subjected him to further beatings, a US marine by the name of Robert Stethem was executed with a shot to the temple; his body was unceremoniously dumped on the tarmac. Seven passengers, bearing Jewish surnames, were then taken off the aircraft and handed over to Hezbollah.

The Amal militia still had not boarded the aircraft and the hijackers selected Clinton Suggs, a friend of Stethem, to be executed next. It was Derickson who intervened and saved him; having refused to identify Jewish and military passengers, paid for the fuel and prevented an execution, Derickson became one of the heroes of the incident. One of the hijackers spoke German and was able to communicate with Derickson, who also spoke a little Arabic, and he responded positively to her shout of 'Enough' and to her rationale that, with the death of Stethem, they had already made their point.

A group of approximately 12 members of the Amal militia did eventually board the aircraft – dashing any thoughts that the passengers and crew had of overpowering the two hijackers – and the hijackers ordered that the aircraft be refuelled and depart, yet again, for Algiers. They also made it clear that they expected Ali Atwa, who had been arrested in Athens having failed to board the flight, to be released by Greece and flown to Algiers to meet them. He did. On arrival, 53 passengers and the female flight attendants, including Derrickson, were released; TWA flight 847 then returned to Beirut with Atwa on board!

Back in Beirut, on 16 June, TWA's flight engineer managed to simulate mechanical problems with the aircraft so effectively that both the hijackers and his fellow crew members believed that the Boeing 727 could no longer fly. The Amal militia, who were now making their own demands, removed all the passengers from the aircraft and, as had happened to the hostages at Dawson's Field in 1970, the hijacked aircraft passengers now found themselves secreted in the city, thereby negating the possibility of an Entebbe or Mogadishu-style rescue mission.

Over the next couple of days, more passengers were released, including Robert Peel Sr, who had been taken sick, and the larger-than-life Greek pop star Demis Roussos. Behind the scenes, a settlement was being negotiated by the Amal's leader, Nabih Berri. Compared to the brutality of the first few hours of the hijack, the last few days were more civil. The International Red Cross was invited to meet the hostages and, on 28 June, they were taken to Damascus, where they were afforded a farewell dinner at the Sheraton Hotel. On 30 June, following their release, the remaining 39 hostages were flown to Frankfurt, West Germany.

By the mid-1980s, it was becoming increasingly apparent that, despite the number of hijacks perpetrated in the name of the Palestinian cause, there seemed to be no prospect on the horizon of a Palestinian state being created. Additionally, the leftist groups that had been so active in Europe in the preceding decade seemed to be hanging up their arms. That, however, did not mean that the threat to aviation had in any way diminished. The tactics and even the causes changed.

LLOYD AEREO BOLIVIANO SURVIVES A BLAST

Of course, one thing that didn't change were the incidents involving people with psychological problems targeting the industry. On 23 January 1985, a passenger on board a Lloyd Aereo Boliviano flight en route from La Paz in Bolivia to Asuncion in Paraguay seemingly detonated an IED while inside the toilets at the front of the Boeing 727. The passenger had taken out a significant life insurance policy but failed in his attempt to destroy the airliner; his body absorbed the blast rather than the aircraft.

'THE STORY IS WRITTEN'

It was the result of one of the greatest misjudgements of a pre-existing security threat in history and an incident that exemplifies a litany of poor security decision making. Then again, it is easy to criticise in hindsight. The end result, however, remains to date the highest toll of passengers and crew perishing in-flight as the result of a terrorist attack against civil aviation.

It was on 23 June 1985 that Air India flight 182 operating from Montreal to London Heathrow, exploded off the coast of Ireland. 329 people died following an explosion in the forward cargo hold. The aircraft was named *Kanishka*, after a Kushan emperor ironically renowned for his military, political, and spiritual accomplishments.

Kanishka actually commenced its journey in Toronto, where some of those boarding had transferred from a CP Air flight which had arrived from Vancouver. It was subsequently determined that the bomb that destroyed flight 182 had been checked-in in Vancouver.

On the same day, another explosion took place at Narita Airport in Tokyo when the bomb inside a suitcase being transferred from a CP Air flight, also arriving from Vancouver, detonated prior to being loaded onto an Air India flight bound for Bangkok.

The subsequent investigation into the two explosions revealed that reservations had been made for two men with the same surname – Mohinderbel Singh and Jaswand Singh – on both flights. The names on both tickets were changed two days after the reservations were made, but the surnames remained the same. Their tickets were for one-way trips and paid for in cash. Both Singhs checked in with the same check-in agent, Jeanne Adams; the men never boarded their flights, yet their baggage was permitted to travel, despite, even at that time, it being a standard security procedure to offload baggage of passengers who were 'no shows' at the gate. CP Air also failed to notify anyone in Toronto and Tokyo respectively that two passengers who were supposed to be connecting onto Air India flights had not embarked on the first leg of their journeys in Vancouver.

For some time prior to the attacks, the Canadian authorities were extremely concerned about certain elements within the large Canadian Sikh community, specifically the activities of members who were believed to be associated with Babbar Khalsa International, widely considered a terrorist organisation. On 1 June 1985, three weeks before the attack, Air India's head office in Bombay had sent a telex to Air India stations around the world, specifically warning them of the possibility of time-delayed explosive devices being placed aboard Air India aircraft or in checked baggage.

Babbar Khalsa International were, in part, fighting for Khalistan's independence from India, believing that their community in India's Punjab was being actively discriminated against by the nation's Hindu majority. It was a struggle that may have been headline news within India itself, but failed to attract international attention. Certainly, for the Canadian security services, it was a much easier sell to request resources to combat Palestinian terrorism than to surveil the Sikh community.

In the year leading up to the Air India attack, tensions were certainly on the increase. On 6 June 1984, a massacre had taken place at the Golden Temple in Amritsar, in which over 250 Sikh activists, many of whom were heavily armed, were killed by the Indian military in their attempt to end a three-month siege. The Sikh's leader, Jarnail Singh Bhindranwale, was one of those killed in the attack – a key objective of 'Operation Blue Star'. At the end of October 1984, India's prime minister, Indira Gandhi, was assassinated in New Delhi and her son Rajiv Gandhi was elected prime minister that December.

Rajiv Gandhi planned a visit to the United States in June 1985, on the anniversary of the Amritsar massacre. Tensions were high and security around the new Indian prime minister was very visible. Across the border in Canada, the security services were keeping some key players under surveillance, most notably Talwinder Singh Parmar.

Parmar was a wanted man in India, but Canada had resisted calls for his extradition, as he was a naturalised Canadian citizen. He was also the leader of Babbar Khalsa International and, as such, there were concerns that he might have been orchestrating an assassination attempt of Rajiv Gandhi. But Gandhi's visit to the United States passed without incident. Parmar had another plan in mind.

According to a Canadian Broadcasting Corporation (CBC) docudrama in 2008, there were some concerns in the security services over a series of bugged telephone conversations between Talwinder Singh Parmar and Ripudaman Singh Malik, a wealthy businessman associated with Babbar Khalsa. In the aftermath of the bombing, it would appear that Parmar's question, 'Have you written the story yet?' and Malik's response, 'The story is written,' were coded messages to initiate the bombing of two Air India flights by loading the devices, contained in checked luggage, onto CP Air flights departing

Vancouver. The bomb-maker was a Babbar Khalsar member, Inderjit Singh Reyat.

On the day in question, fortune favoured the bombers. There was no requirement for Canadian airports to screen checked luggage at that time; consequently, neither of the bomb bags were examined in Vancouver. Air India, however, did contract Burns Security to X-ray baggage going onto their flights in Toronto – the departure point for Air India flight 182. The X-ray machine in the baggage make-up area was not functioning, so the contract security personnel were given a Graseby Dynamics PD4-C hand-held explosive-vapour detection devices; however, they had next to no training in the use of the technology.

22 June was also the day that the Royal Canadian Mounted Police had selected as a training day for its canine explosive detection teams; all of the RCMP bomb dogs were in Vancouver! For one day only, there was no canine team on duty in Toronto – the one day that a bomb was to pass through the airport.

Air India flight 182 disintegrated at 31,000 ft off the coast of Ireland, shortly before it was to commence its descent into London Heathrow. All 329 people on board died, yet only 131 bodies were ever recovered.

One hour earlier, the other suitcase bomb detonated prematurely at Tokyo's Narita Airport, saving the passengers and crew of Air India's flight 301 to Bangkok from certain death. Less fortunate were the baggage handlers in Tokyo; Hindeharu Koda and Hideo Asano were killed when the device detonated as they were processing baggage from the incoming CP Air flight.

The fact that the bomb exploded on the ground was a blessing, not only for those who should have been on board but also for the accident investigation team. They discovered a metal fragment from a Sanyo FMT 611K tuner in which Reyat had concealed the bomb. This prompted the RCMP to start visiting all retail outlets which sold the product.

Meanwhile, the Canadian Center for Strategic and International Studies (CSIS) also confirmed that Parmar, who had been under their surveillance anyway, had telephoned Reyat on several occasions prior to the bombings and had been seen meeting with him in a town called Duncan, where there was a Woolworths outlet that just happened to sell Sanyo FMT 611K tuners. A sales assistant at the store confirmed that she had sold one such Sanyo tuner to an East Indian man on 5 June 1985, the day after Parmar had visited Reyat in Duncan.

Back in Tokyo, the Japanese investigators determined that the Narita bomb – and, most likely, the *Kanishka* bomb as well – used a Micronta car clock as a timing device, an electrical relay as a switch, an Eveready 12-volt battery as a power source, a can of Liquid Fire starting fluid, smokeless gunpowder, a blasting cap as the igniter and a high-explosive charge. Neither the starting fluid nor the gunpowder were requisite components of the IED, but may have been included as Reyat's signature.

Officially, nobody claimed responsibility for the bombings. CSIS were, however, convinced that Babbar Khalsar International was behind the attacks. Reyat was eventually arrested and charged – but only for possession of explosives. Although he was convicted, he received only a nominal fine and decided to emigrate to the United Kingdom, where he managed to get a job with Jaguar. He was, later, to be extradited back to Canada and charged with the bombings; he eventually confessed and is the only person to have actually been convicted in relation to the incident. Reyat was released on 27 January 2016 after having served 20 years in prison.

The main reason for the failure to convict anybody else was an absence of evidence. For all CSIS' phone-tapping, which implicated Parmar, Malik and others, in an amazing lack of foresight, CSIS had transcribed the translated versions of the various phone conversations but had erased the original tapes!

Parmar returned to India, but was arrested there in 1992. Following his interrogation, in which he allegedly confessed to masterminding the Air India bombings, he died – how remains a mystery. Some attest that there was a shootout between his supporters and the Indian authorities, others are convinced that he was murdered following his confession.

Babbar Khalsar financiers Ripudaman Singh Malik and Ajaib Singh Bagri were also charged but the cases against them were never proven, although the judicial process did result in their spending four and a half years in prison. Following his acquittal, Malik was reappointed director of the Khalsa Credit Union – the most financially prosperous Sikh commercial entity in the world – of which he was a founder and long-time president. He was later removed from his post by Canadian government regulators in 2005 due to his terrorist connections. Overall, in both Canada and India, there is a sense that justice has not yet been done.

The infiltration of IEDs onto the CP Air flights by means of checked luggage heralded the commencement of a global initiative to introduce hold baggage screening for all baggage being loaded onto international flights – an initiative that was accelerated following the subsequent destruction of Pan Am flight 103 over Lockerbie in 1988.

Despite the obvious need for baggage to be screened, it was still not until after 1993, when the British Airports Authority actually demonstrated a hold-baggage screening system that was operationally viable, that such a fundamental security methodology was rolled out in Europe and parts of Asia; in the United States it took a further decade, and the attacks of 11 September 2001 (albeit unrelated to checked baggage), for the initiative to be adopted. While the threat of aircraft sabotage became the prime concern for the industry, traditional hijackings were still perpetrated.

MASSACRE AT LUQA

In a truly bad year for aviation, 1985 was also the year in which three members of the Abu Nidal Organisation hijacked an Egyptair flight en route from Athens to Cairo. As the hijackers started to collect identity documents from the passengers, an Egyptian sky marshal opened fire and killed one of the terrorists. However, he and two flight attendants were injured in the exchange of fire, and the aircraft's fuselage was perforated causing rapid depressurisation.

While the intended destination for the hijackers was Libya, the aircraft had to land at Luqa Airport in Malta due to the condition of the aircraft and injuries to passengers. The prime minister of Malta became the chief negotiator and refused to allow the refuelling of the aircraft until the passengers were released. 11 Filipino passengers and the two injured flight attendants were allowed to deplane.

The lead hijacker, Omar Rezaq, was one of the most ruthless in aviation history. For him a deadline was a deadline. In order to convince the authorities of his seriousness, he called Tamar Artzi, an Israeli passenger, to the front of the aircraft. He shot her in the back of the head and the force of the shot caused her to topple out of the aircraft and down the steps. To her surprise, she lived and, conscious, was able to simply roll under the aircraft. Rezaq then said he would execute a passenger every 15 minutes.

Indeed, 15 minutes later he called Natan Mendelson, another Israeli woman on board, to the front of the plane. Knowing what had happened to Artzi, she refused to identify herself but was eventually dragged to the front of the aircraft and executed. There being no more Israeli passengers on board, Rezaq then started executing American passengers, one every 15 minutes. Starting with Patrick Scott Baker, followed by Scarlett Marie Rogenkamp and then Jackie Nink Pflug. Miraculously, of the five passengers Rezaq shot at point-blank range, three survived.

The Maltese government had excellent relations with Arab states on the Mediterranean, and therefore was not keen to initiate military intervention, but equally they were concerned that an American, or worse, an Israeli commando unit, might arrive to take control of the situation. With the aircraft belonging to Egyptair, Malta's preference was that an Egyptian counterterrorist force be permitted to end the hijack and they were reassured by the fact that Egypt's Thunderbolt unit had actually received training by US Delta Force. The assault itself was one of the least successful: 54 of the 87 passengers were killed by gunshot, the explosion of the hijackers' grenades or the fire that engulfed the aircraft.

The subsequent investigation also showed that four of the passengers had been shot by the commandos. The sole surviving hijacker was Rezaq, who pretended to be one of the injured passengers. He was identified at St Luke's Hospital by other surviving passengers. He was later sentenced to 25 years in prison, but released after eight. Rezaq was then deported to Nigeria, where he was again arrested, and later extradited to the United States, where, in 1996, he was sentenced to life imprisonment.

SYNCHRONISED ATTACKS IN ROME AND VIENNA

The end of 1985 was also a bloody affair and the association of the Christmas holiday season with terrorist extravaganzas commenced. On 27 December 1985, a coordinated attack was initiated at both Rome and Vienna airports when the Abu Nidal Organisation launched simultaneous attacks on TWA and El Al check-in counters at both airports.

19 people were killed and more than 100 injured before El Al security guards patrolling the airport terminals managed to neutralise the terrorists. In Rome, 16 people were killed, plus three of the four gunmen. In Vienna, three people were killed, plus one of the terrorists. Before escaping by car, those who had attacked Vienna Airport had thrown hand grenades into the crowds of passengers who were checking into a flight to Tel Aviv. The Austrian police managed to capture two of the terrorists.

CHAPTER VIII
1986–1987

THE DISAPPEARING ACT OF MAY ELIAS MANSOUR

The year 1986 was no better than the end of the previous one. On 1 April, May Elias Mansour flew from Cairo to Athens on board TWA flight 840, leaving an IED beneath her seat, number 10F (as in the Pan Am bombing attempts of August 1982 – see p.149), as she deplaned. She continued her journey to Beirut. The plan was allegedly to allow the device to be triggered by somebody sitting in the seat for the subsequent leg – the flight from Athens to Rome. The passengers who flew from Athens to Rome that day were indeed fortunate as no one was seated in the seat Mansour had vacated. Passengers flying from Rome to Athens the next day were less fortunate as the device was triggered, albeit at an altitude of only 15,000 ft. Four American passengers were killed when they were sucked from the aircraft, but the rest arrived safely with the plane in Athens.

The attack against TWA 840 was attributed to the Revolutionary Cells, a group associated with the Abu Nidal Organisation.

ANN-MARIE MURPHY

Amazingly never committed to the silver screen, no one can fail to be moved by the story of Ann-Marie Murphy. Except, perhaps, Nezar Hindawi and his associates in the Syrian government.

On Thursday 17 April 1986, Ann-Marie Murphy, six months pregnant with Hindawi's child, checked in for El Al Israel Airlines flight LY016 to Tel Aviv at London Heathrow Airport in the belief that she was travelling to be married in Israel. In reality, she was an unwitting bomber who had been duped by love and desperation.

Elsewhere, on the very same day, Syria was celebrating the anniversary of its independence; British television journalist John McCarthy was kidnapped in Lebanon; four other Britons were murdered in Beirut; and America was defending its decision to launch air raids against military installations in Libya two days earlier.

The selection of London as the boarding point for Hindawi's bomb is not surprising. Not only did London's large Arab population diminish the possibility of a Middle Eastern terrorist being identified as out of place but it also was regarded as a target by Libya's allies and resident terrorist organisations.

Ever since Qaddafi had become President of Libya, following a coup against King Idris in September 1969, relationships with the West had gone from bad to worse. Britain and America had supported the Idris regime since World War Two and he had managed to remain in power through the 1967 Arab-Israeli conflict. Qaddafi, himself a devout Muslim, was a strong proponent of the Palestinian cause, and he spoke out vehemently against America, branding it an infidel and chief sponsor of the Zionist state. Initial hopes that Libya would become a partner in the Middle East were unsurprisingly dashed when it became apparent that Libyan military strength was to be enhanced through a spirit of cooperation with the Soviet Union. The 'special relationship' between the United States and United Kingdom added to Libyan hostility towards Britain, especially during the Thatcher/Reagan years.

Many Libyan exiles led anti-Qaddafi campaigns throughout the 1970s and early 1980s. These campaigns were to end in the tragic killing of WPC Yvonne Fletcher outside the Libyan People's Bureau in St. James' Square, London on 17 April 1984, two years to the day before another woman, Ann-Marie Murphy, was to become the victim of a cause for which she had no concern. WPC Fletcher's death was as a result of gunshots fired from within the bureau during a siege that lasted ten days. Following the siege's peaceful conclusion through negotiation, the Libyan diplomats were deported rather than charged and diplomatic ties were severed.

Tensions between Libya and the West continued to increase. Unlike his Democrat predecessor Jimmy Carter, President Reagan openly challenged Libyan claims to the Gulf of Sirte, and, in March 1986, the US Sixth Fleet destroyed Libyan gunboats patrolling their self-proclaimed territorial waters. By this stage the Americans were convinced that Libya not only sponsored terrorism but provided refuge to the captains of world terror, including the infamous Abu Nidal. Whether or not the Libyan government was actually privy to the plans for the previously discussed Egyptair hijacking or the attacks at Rome and Vienna airports is debatable. However, Libya's clearly sympathetic stance led to America's controversial decision to teach Qaddafi and his allies a lesson.

American missile attacks on Tripoli and Benghazi resulted in the deaths of 37 people, including Qaddafi's adopted daughter. The American jets were granted permission by British Prime Minister Margaret Thatcher to use British soil as a point of departure on their destructive mission. The United Kingdom's European partners disapproved.

The selection of an El Al flight, operating from London to Tel Aviv, as a target may also have been precipitated by the Israeli interception of an executive jet en route to Damascus from Tripoli on 4 February 1986. In the skies over the Mediterranean, the Israelis instructed the private aircraft to divert to Tel Aviv. Their rationale was intel that Dr George Habash, leader of the Popular Front for the Liberation of Palestine, was on board. They could not have been more mistaken. Having kept the aircraft on the ground for five hours, it was released with all its passengers. Unfortunately for the Israelis, the passenger list included Abdullah Ahmar, Assistant Secretary-General of the Syrian Arab Ba'ath Socialist Party, and President Assad's number two! Syria, not surprisingly, was furious.

Much political rhetoric followed. The very same day, according to former Mossad agent Victor Ostrovsky (in his book *By Way of Deception*), Ahmed Jibril, leader of the Popular Front for the Liberation of Palestine General Command with bases in both Syria and Libya, made it clear that civilian passengers flying on Israeli or American aircraft would be considered legitimate targets.

> We ask you to tell the entire world not to board Israeli or American aircraft. From this day on we will not respect civilians who use them.

In Damascus, Ostrovsky claims that Chief of Staff Major General Hikmat al-Chehabi stated that Syrian forces would 'answer this crime by teaching those who committed it a lesson they will not forget. We will choose the method, the time and the place.'

Had the bomb actually exploded at 39,000 ft over southern Europe as planned, it is a distinct possibility that neither the method of attack nor the perpetrator would ever have been identified. As it was, El Al's security operatives discovered the device by implementing their passenger profiling system. This discovery was to end not only with the arrest of the terrorist who planted the bomb but with the severing of British diplomatic ties with Syria due to their apparent collusion.

Ann-Marie Murphy was typical of many an observant Roman Catholic girl from Dun Laoghaire, a working-class suburb of Dublin. From a large family, where she was one of nine children, she left school aged 14 to start work in a hosiery factory. Her earnings went to supplement the family income and her after-work hours were spent helping her parents care for her siblings. From all accounts, there was little opportunity for Ann-Marie to experience much of a social life. She was not known to have had any boyfriends.

Her life took a dramatic change in October 1984 when, aged 29 and still a virgin, she was made redundant. Like many other young single people seeking employment at that time, the prosperity of England acted as a magnet. She decided to leave Ireland with her close friend Theresa Leonard, and head for the bright lights of London. Shortly after their arrival, the two friends found work as chambermaids at the London Hilton in Park Lane. For young women who were anything but worldly, the Hilton exposed them to a life they had only seen on television and at the cinema. A job as a chambermaid may not be most people's concept of the good life, but this was a major step up the ladder from making ladies' tights and stockings in a factory in Dublin.

This was where the world's wealthy gathered and a significant percentage of the hotel's clientele were Arab. Like any major city's deluxe hotels, the vast majority of guests were businessmen, many of whom would be only too willing to charm their way into an innocent girl's heart. A Jordanian guest named Khalid Hassi achieved this goal and established a relationship with Theresa Leonard. His flatmate was another Jordanian by the name of Nezar Narwas Mansour Hindawi. Theresa introduced Ann-Marie to Nezar and their fateful relationship started.

Nezar Hindawi's family originated from Libya, although in 1922 they moved to Jordan. By all accounts, Nezar came from a prosperous and influential family who were prominent in Jordanian political circles, with two uncles having served as members of the Jordanian cabinet, one of whom chaired the Iraq Solidarity Campaign in Jordan. Following the creation of the State of Israel in 1948, the family settled in Baqura, on the east bank of the River Jordan, where Nezar was born in 1954. At the age of 13, when Jewish boys of a similar age the other side of the border were celebrating their bar mitzvahs, Nezar was to witness the destruction of his village by Israeli jets during the 1967 Six-Day War. Consequently, like many other impressionable youngsters, the appeal of the many post-war guerrilla groups proved irresistible.

Although many of his family had settled in the United Kingdom earlier, Nezar's association with London only really commenced in January 1980 when, aged 25, he embarked on English language courses while pursuing his career as a journalist working for a number of Arabic newspapers.

His various employers all indicated that he was not popular with his peers and that his temper made him incapable of holding down a job. Apparently totally wrapped up in himself, with little care for his colleagues, his behaviour was often a cause of considerable embarrassment to his family. That said, he was obviously capable of charming women.

In 1980, while attending a language class in Kensington, Nezar met Barbara Litwiniec, a 24-year-old Polish girl who had come to London to study English. By Christmas that year

Nezar and Barbara had married. Within a year, Mrs Barbara Hindawi gave birth to a baby girl, Natasha. Barbara returned to her native Poland and settled down near her family in Radzyn Podlaski and Nezar, thereafter, made periodic visits to see his wife and daughter. This somewhat simple Polish girl from a devout Roman Catholic background appeared to have little knowledge of her husband's activities.

Following his arrival in London, Nezar initially earned money on the side by working for the Libyan People's Bureau. Using his journalistic talents he went in search of anti-Gaddafi activists and provided the Libyan authorities with their names and addresses. The lifestyle appealed to him and he idolised many of the notorious terrorist group leaders. He even established his own cell, the Jordanian Revolution Movement for National Salvation, which sought the downfall of King Hussein.

By Christmas 1984, Ann-Marie was pregnant and Nezar mysteriously disappeared. By the time he was back on the scene in February 1985, Ann-Marie had miscarried. Nevertheless, Nezar proposed marriage, although he did tell her there was the small problem of his divorcing his Polish wife, Barbara, to deal with first. Their relationship was further cemented by their moving in to an apartment together in the north London suburb of Kilburn.

Terrorism was in Nezar's blood by now. Even at this stage, he believed that Ann-Marie could be instrumental in his plans. In the somewhat naïve belief that all persons with Irish origins might be IRA sympathisers, he asked Ann-Marie whether she might be able to arrange interviews with IRA leaders to further his journalistic career. Nezar wanted contacts rather than interviews. This should have been apparent to Ann-Marie as he had earlier told her that he had been a terrorist and that he had a hatred of Jews due to their actions in Jordan during his adolescence; however, international politics was a subject alien to Ann-Marie.

Nezar went to visit one of his brothers, Ahmed Nawat Mansur Hazi, in Berlin in March 1985. Hazi lived with a 30-year-old prostitute by the name of Heiderose in the red-light district. He had been married to another German woman for some five years, which secured his German residency. Nezar managed to convince Hazi and another Palestinian resident in Berlin at the time, Farouk Salameh, to join his cause; they returned to London and then visited Tripoli later in the year. The Libyan terror chiefs were not particularly impressed by the Hindawis' curriculum vitae. They based their support upon actions rather than words. Although the brothers were given USD$5,000 to help their cause, Libyan backing appeared to end there.

The Jordanians refused to renew Nezar's passport in 1985 as they already saw him as an opponent of King Hussein. At that stage, Nezar contacted Dr Lutfallah Haidar, the Syrian ambassador in London, who is reported to have advised Syrian intelligence that he might have found a willing recruit in their campaign against Jordan.

Meanwhile, Ann-Marie and Nezar continued their relationship, despite his frequent unexplained absences. By November, Ann-Marie discovered she was pregnant again while Nezar was on his travels. Unmarried, of strict Catholic upbringing, and the victim of one miscarriage already, Ann-Marie felt desperate and alone.

Still working at the Hilton, suffering bouts of morning sickness, Ann-Marie kept news of her pregnancy secret. She never had a contact telephone number for Nezar, but he did periodically call her at work and it was during one such conversation that she told him she was pregnant. Nezar tried to convince her to have an abortion and urged her to contact his other brother, Mahmoud, who lived in West Drayton and was an administrator in the medical section of the Qatar Embassy in London. Abortion was, however, contrary to her religious beliefs; she decided to keep the baby.

In January 1986, Nezar visited Damascus. Syria was already known to sponsor terrorist acts, was a key supporter of the Abu Nidal Organisation and Syrian agents travelled the world disguised as employees of the state flag-carrier, Syrian Arab Airlines, exempting them from intensive security screenings. Many took jobs as clerks in airline ticket offices or as diplomats or officials in Syrian embassies in capital cities around the globe. It was partly such activity that later resulted in Syria being regarded as an international pariah.

Nezar was taken to a training camp and was shown blueprints of suitcase bombs. These were of standard construction and were transported to their desired location on Syrian Arab Airlines, where they could be collected by agents from embassies or crew hotels. A deal was struck. The Jordan Revolution Movement for National Salvation was now in a joint venture with the Syrian government.

On a subsequent trip to Damascus, Nezar was issued with a Syrian service passport under the name Izzam Shara. On 11 February 1986, a messenger was sent to the British Embassy in Damascus requesting a visa for a Syrian government employee, reputedly a mechanic in the Army Supply Office; this application was backed up by a supporting letter from the foreign ministry. Later that day the passport was ready for collection with a single-entry visa numbered 068 stamped onto page 13 and signed by vice-consul Andrew Balfour (a somewhat ironic surname in the context of the Arab-Israeli conflict!). Within 24 hours Nezar was back in London as

Izzam Shara with a permit to remain in the United Kingdom for six months. He did not contact Ann-Marie.

In March, Nezar returned to Damascus again and travelled from there to Lebanon. At a training camp in the Bekaa Valley, he received instruction in the use of the suitcase bomb that had been developed to bring down the El Al flight. Nezar received his down-payment to cover interim expenses; he had been promised a quarter of a million dollars if the attack was successful. The Syrian authorities then applied for a second visa for Izzam Shara from the British Embassy. In order to avoid arousing suspicion, the application was submitted on a day when Balfour was absent from the office, especially because this time the application stated that Shara was travelling as an assistant accountant to the foreign ministry. Seemingly the British Embassy had a Syrian 'mole' on the payroll who ensured the smooth process of the visa application and who vanished following Nezar's subsequent arrest in London, taking with him all records pertaining to Izzam Shara and records of a number of other persons who, no doubt, travelled to Britain illegally or under false pretext.

Over Easter, Ann-Marie visited her family in Ireland. She managed to hide the fact that she was pregnant.

On 5 April, Nezar arrived in London as Izzam Shara and checked in to the Royal Garden Hotel as a member of the Syrian Arab Airlines crew. The next day Syrian agent Adnan Habeb met Nezar in the hotel foyer and gave him the bomb bag. Nezar then checked out of the hotel, took the bag to his father's flat, where it remained for the following ten days, and checked in to the Palace Hotel in Great Cumberland Place, once again as Izzam Shara. Nezar's father even opened the bag in the intervening days, yet found nothing to cause him any alarm.

Over the next few days Nezar led a double life. He is believed to have met up with yet another Syrian agent who issued him with a Browning semi-automatic pistol and ammunition: Nezar, the terrorist. And on 7 April, following a three-month absence, he arrived on Ann-Marie Murphy's doorstep proposing immediate marriage: Nezar, the lover.

The wedding was to be in Israel.

Nezar and Ann-Marie went out for dinner to Julie's Pantry in London's Oxford Street, hardly the most romantic of locations. Over a fast-food meal, Nezar asked Ann-Marie to travel to Israel alone and said that he would meet her there. He explained that he already had a ticket via Jordan, which he was using for journalistic purposes. Considering that she was almost six months pregnant, the offer of marriage was the answer to her prayers and presumably severely clouded her judgement.

Nezar, for so long the absentee partner, transformed himself into the attentive groom. Ann-Marie had no valid passport, so he assisted her in completing the necessary application forms that resulted in her being issued with a new passport at the Irish Embassy on Friday 11 April. That same day, Ann-Marie went for a medical check-up and saw their baby on the scan for the first time.

No bride-to-be would be happy without a wedding dress. For a woman in an advanced stage of pregnancy, white did not seem particularly appropriate, so, with the £100 that Nezar had given her, she purchased a pale blue outfit made of silk. In fact Nezar's generosity knew no bounds; he gave her another £100 to buy more dresses and underwear.

And, throughout this time, Nezar remained contactable; he gave her his telephone number at the Palace Hotel.

On Tuesday 15 April, Ann-Marie bought her flight ticket for £199 from Superstar Travel in Regent Street, Superstar being

El Al's holiday company. She was to travel two days later. Although Nezar went with her to buy the ticket to Tel Aviv, he never entered the agency himself. She made a last-minute plea for him to travel with her, but he said it was out of the question. He said he would meet her in Tel Aviv two to three hours after her arrival. Seemingly blinded by love, she accepted this somewhat implausible story.

That evening, Nezar asked Ann-Marie to change her ticket for Thursday to the Sunday departure instead due to a change in his own travel plans. He also looked at her suitcase and said that it was too big for her to carry as a pregnant woman and that he would buy her a bag on wheels. The following morning she returned to Superstar Travel, where she was told that she could not change her ticket.

At 10 p.m. that night, 16 April, Nezar arrived at Ann-Marie's Kilburn flat with his latest present – a brand new, blue holdall-on-wheels bearing the brand-name 'ACE'. Ann-Marie was not alone; her sister Hyacinth was visiting her with the family's best wishes for her marriage. Later, Nezar let Ann-Marie know that he was extremely upset that she had told anybody of her wedding plans. Ann-Marie still suspected nothing, despite his unreasonable attitude.

Nezar packed the new bag for her, so that she would not have to keep bending down. Into the bag he placed a calculator. Then, perhaps for the first time, Ann-Marie did become concerned about Nezar – not only did he refuse to spend the night with her but he seemed nervous and even told her not to touch or go anywhere near the bag. Concerned she might have been, but she did not act upon her fears.

At 7.20 a.m. on what was supposed to be the last day of her life, Ann-Marie Murphy was collected by Nezar from her home by taxi. She was wearing her wedding dress in order to look her best when meeting her future in-laws for the first time. Many consider that for a groom to see his bride's wedding dress before the wedding ceremony to be tempting fate. For Nezar, it was.

Nezar smoked all the way to the airport, making the pregnant Ann-Marie feel very queasy, yet she said nothing. Neither did she react to him taking the calculator out of the bag, placing a battery in it and returning to the depths of her bag, telling her that he had had it repaired for a friend and that she was to take it with her. Nezar had just armed a bomb that was set to explode five hours, one minute and one second later.

At London Heathrow's Terminal One, Nezar bade farewell to Ann-Marie and said he would see her a few hours later. She did not comment on his lack of baggage. And then, as many pregnant women can attest to, nature called. The somewhat irritated Nezar was left with Ann-Marie's bag while she went in search of the toilets. By 8 a.m., they had kissed goodbye and Ann-Marie went through the British Airports Authority security checks, which included an X-ray of her bag, and through passport control, making her way to Gate 23, the gate set aside as a sterile zone for El Al flights.

El Al's passenger profiling system meant that each passenger had to be assessed by interview in order to determine whether or not they might be a threat to the flight; little reliance is placed on X-ray examination. If they feel there is cause for concern, El Al security agents will ask passengers to open their bags for a hand search. On occasions in which they feel there might actually be a threat, they will subject both the passenger and their baggage to a more thorough examination. The interview with Ann-Marie was regarded as inconclusive and, for El Al, that was not considered sufficient. Furthermore, El Al knew, based on intelligence information received, that an attack somewhere in their system was a strong possibility at that time, especially as it was close to the Jewish festival of Passover.

Ann-Marie's bag was emptied by a security agent and each item, including the bag itself, was individually examined. The sophisticated scientific calculator (in the hands of a hotel chambermaid!) did not arouse suspicion because it was proven to work. Repeat X-rays of the bag showed nothing. Yet, when the security guard picked up the empty bag, he did notice that it was unusually heavy and decided to examine it further.

Around the bottom was a zip that enabled the owner to enlarge the holdall if necessary. In the base was a white plastic sheet affixed to the base of the bag. Upon prising this sheet away from the base, the guard found a flat blue plastic package. The package weighed around 1.5 kg and seemed to be made of a yellowy-orange material with the texture of plasticine, sandwiched in between two pieces of cardboard bearing oil stains. Correctly identifying this as Semtex-H explosive, the security guard called the British police shortly after 9 a.m.

Although El Al had discovered the explosives, there was no trace of any power source, detonator or control mechanism, the other components of a bomb, without which Semtex is about as dangerous as Play-Doh. Peter Gurney, the head of the SO13 Metropolitan Police Bomb Sqaud, attended the call personally and it was he who found that the calculator contained all such components with a minimal amount of explosives. While the miniature calculator-bomb would not have the power to destroy an aircraft or be of sufficient size to warrant further inspection by security staff, it would, if placed at the bottom of the bag, be enough to trigger the main explosive charge situated only millimetres away.

The El Al procedures had just been vindicated. 375 lives and at least one unborn child had been saved, let alone lives in southern Europe which could have been lost had the remnants of El Al Israel Airlines flight LY016 rained down upon them from 39,000 ft.

Ann-Marie was shown the discovery and only then realised how much she had been fooled.

Immediately arrested, she was stripped and led in a white paper boiler suit in handcuffs to an awaiting police car and taken to Paddington Green Police Station.

Ann-Marie gave the police the telephone number that Nezar had given her, which they quickly identified as being a room at the Palace Hotel taken by a Mr Shara. Nezar had been seen twice at the hotel that day, early in the morning when he left in a taxi to pick up Ann-Marie and later when he returned from Heathrow in order to check out. With his picture released, and his alias uncovered, the police quickly knew who they were looking for.

Nezar had left the Palace Hotel and returned to the Royal Garden, where he was to join the crew of a Syrian Arab Airlines flight scheduled to depart Heathrow at 2 p.m. However, the failed attempt to destroy the El Al flight had now been widely publicised in the media, as had Nezar's identity. Syrian agent Mohammed Raja Zidan contacted Nezar and told him to head for the Syrian Embassy in Belgrave Square; he was given a letter to take with him. Arriving at the embassy by taxi around midday, he was met by the ambassador Dr Haidar, who reportedly contacted Damascus for further instructions. Nezar was then taken by two agents, Mounir Mouna and Zaki Oud to 19 Stonor Road in West Kensington, a supposed safe house.

That night, Mouna cut and dyed Nezar's hair and he was given the opportunity to catch up on some sleep. At about 5 a.m., he was awoken and was told that he was being returned to the Embassy. Nezar panicked. He no longer trusted the Syrian agents and feared that he was to be returned to Syria for execution or for his body to be disposed of at some location in England. Although the agents tried to force Nezar into their car, he broke free and ran away. Considering the time of day, the agents also decided to take off before the police could be summoned by local residents whose sleep had been disturbed.

After wandering the streets for a few hours, Nezar made his way to the Visitors Hotel, near Earl's Court. This hotel was owned by a Jordanian acquaintance of Nezar, Niam al-Oran, although he was not on the premises when Nezar arrived. The staff, attuned to the recent media publicity surrounding the attack against El Al, felt that something was amiss when the new guest booked in, in the name of Izzam Shara. They gave him room number 18 and then summoned the owner who subsequently contacted Nezar's brother Mahmoud. Both Niam al-Oran and Mahmoud visited Nezar in his room and tried to persuade him to give himself up to the police, for his own safety. The police, however, had already been tipped off as to his whereabouts and were en route to the hotel to arrest him. Nezar did not resist.

While 'helping the police with their enquiries' Nezar led them to the Syrian safe house, where they discovered hair clippings, later proven to be Nezar's, hair dye and fingerprints, including Nezar's. This was the first proof of Syrian diplomatic involvement, as the house had been let to Mouna, known to be a Syrian 'diplomat'.

Nezar, meanwhile, protested his innocence. He knew that he had been carrying out an illegal act, but he maintained that he believed that he had set Ann-Marie up to smuggle drugs. That aside, the rest of the story that Nezar gave the police may have been true. He certainly gave a very clear account of the degree to which Syria had been involved in the plot. He provided names and addresses, he sketched maps and drew flow charts; the police found that Nezar appeared willing to tell all, presumably in the naïve hope of reducing his sentence. That said, above all else, he wanted to ensure that the British did not hand him over to the Israeli authorities. Eventually, he even admitted that he knew Ann-Marie was carrying a bomb.

Ann-Marie was released but placed in protective custody since she was to be the key prosecution witness. In Berlin, the German authorities removed Heiderose, Hazi's flatmate, to a secret venue for similar reasons.

On 24 October, Nezar Hindawi stood in the dock at the Old Bailey, where he was sentenced to 45 years in prison for his actions. Mr Justice Mars-Jones delivered the longest prison sentence ever given by a British court. When asked about his relationship with Ann-Marie Murphy during the trial, Nezar had said, 'I still love her. I will love her forever.' Despite this, he seemed unperturbed by the sentence given. One observer said that this reaction was due to Nezar thinking the judge had said 'four to five years'; how accurate this is remains unclear.

What is certain is that within hours of the verdict having been given, Britain severed diplomatic ties with Syria. Sir Geoffrey Howe set out the facts to the House of Commons, providing the irrefutable proof that the Syrian state sponsored terrorism. Irrefutable that is, to the British. The Syrians obviously felt otherwise and strongly rejected any claims as to their complicity in the affair. Yet British MI5 had had the Syrian Embassy under surveillance for some time and had bugged their telephone lines. So when Dr Haidar made his call to Damascus following Nezar's arrival at the embassy on the day of the attack, the British were listening in. The Soviets also thought otherwise and having earlier condemned Britain for allowing its airfields to be used as launch pads for American 'terrorist' forces in their attack against Libya in April, they now felt duty bound to rush to the aid of their other partner in the Middle East, Syria. The Soviet news agency TASS described Britain's action as 'a provocative action based on groundless accusations'. Israel, predictably, thought the world of the British courts and the subsequent governmental action.

In their counterclaims, Syria did suggest that Israel's Mossad had plotted the bombing. The exercise, they claimed, could have been an attempt by Israel to discredit Syria. Nezar, today, supports this view, while hotly denying his being a Mossad agent himself. He claims that either the El Al security guard placed the bomb in the bag himself or knew that a bomb would arrive at Heathrow that day.

If Nezar had been working for Mossad, maybe they had told Nezar to go to the Syrian Embassy straight away in order to implicate them. Why else should he have run to the embassy rather than go underground? Nezar claimed during his trial that he believed that he had been set up by the Israelis; that he was a spy-for-hire is not totally out of the realms of possibility and there are those in the Jordanian establishment that claim Nezar worked for anybody who was prepared to pay him, including Mossad. Nezar's father is also understood to have been a Mossad agent whose undercover activities, while employed as a chef at the Jordanian Embassy in London, resulted in him being given the death sentence by a Jordanian court *in absentia*; he never returned to Jordan.

While almost anything is possible, all these claims exist with a complete absence of proof. Meanwhile, it remains undisputed that Nezar was in Britain on a false Syrian service passport, applied for by the Syrian Foreign Ministry. It is known that he was welcomed to the Syrian Embassy by the ambassador himself the day of the attack. British intelligence were able to prove that the Syrian Ambassador had initially recommended Nezar to Syrian Intelligence and further contacted them after the event had failed. Nezar was put in a house rented by a Syrian diplomat the night of the attack. Nezar had stayed at the Royal Garden Hotel posing as a member of a Syrian Arab Airlines crew.

Even granted these facts, it is possible that President Assad himself was unaware of the plot. Perhaps even probable. While officially at war with Israel, the last thing Syria needed was the ceasefire to be broken and for open hostilities to recommence.

Senior officials in the Syrian establishment, including their ambassador to London and the Syrian Air Force Intelligence Directorate, were, however, proven to be party to the crime.

Hindawi continues to protest his innocence and in an interview with Ian Black of *The Guardian* he seemed to be in no hurry to be released: 'I am prepared to do all 45 years, until the very last minute.' In 2013, the Parole Board decided that Hindawi could be released having served 26 years of his sentence, but that he was to remain in custody until he could be deported to Jordan. In January 2016 he continued to languish in Whitemoor prison.

For the other protagonists, although this is no fairy tale, there is still a happy ending. Theresa Leonard and Khalid Hassi were married and Ann-Marie gave birth to a baby girl, Caoimhe, whom she raised in Sallynoggin, Ireland.

PROFILING WORKS AGAIN

It was not only women who were being duped. On 26 June 1986, Isaias Manuel Jalafe checked in at Madrid's Barajas Airport for an El Al flight to Tel Aviv. His behaviour aroused suspicion, prompting screeners to search his baggage. As his suitcase was opened, it started to smoke. The El Al officer on duty, Nir Ran, screamed at people to take cover and grabbed a fire extinguisher and directed the foam at the case. The bomb detonated, seriously injuring Ran and 12 other people in the vicinity of the blast.

The device actually had a timing mechanism, utilising a modified wristwatch, and was designed to detonate mid-way through the flight to Israel.

Jalafe was a seasoned criminal and had been persuaded to smuggle the case onto the El Al flight by Nasser Hassan al-Ali, having been convinced that he was on a drug run. Al-Ali had been in Madrid since 17 April, the day the El Al flight in London had been targeted by Nezar Hindawi. He had met Jalafe in town and managed to convince him, in exchange for US$1,000, to effect part of his plan.

Inside the suitcase were two bottles, concealed in a toiletry bag. In the bottles was a mixture of potassium chlorate, sugar and phosphorus, attached to a timer.

Al-Ali was arrested the next day and admitted to his involvement in the plot.

TIGERS ON THE LOOSE

On 3 May 1986 members of the Tamil Tigers infiltrated a device onto an Air Lanka aircraft at Colombo Airport while it was being prepared for departure to the Maldives; the IED was concealed in crates of meat and vegetables being shipped to Male. 21 people were killed in the explosion but the death toll would have been far higher had the aircraft departed on time as the IED utilised a timing device. As it was, the explosion took place on the ground.

THE HEROISM OF NEERJA BHANOT

On 5 September 1986, a Pan Am aircraft was preparing to depart from Karachi Airport in Pakistan when it was stormed by four members of the Abu Nidal Organisation dressed as airport security guards. It was exceptionally rare for a Boeing 747 to be hijacked as generally terrorists targeted smaller aircraft, which were easier to control.

The pilots of the Pan Am flight actually escaped from the aircraft before the hijackers even made it to the cockpit, utilising the escape hatch and benefiting from the fact that, with the flight deck located on the upper deck of a B-747, they had a longer time in which to consider their response. While many criticised them for 'abandoning a sinking ship', the general advice given in the industry is that a hijacked plane is safer on the ground than in the skies and that if there is a way to ensure take off is not possible then that is the preferable option.

The hijackers were immediately forced to negotiate for a replacement crew, through one of the passengers who they forced to kneel at the doorway of the aircraft with his hands behind his head. When negotiations failed and a replacement crew was not provided, Rajesh Kumar was executed. The crew were ordered to collect passports and one of the flight attendants, Neerja Bhanot, managed to dispose of all of the American passports she had collected.

During the night, the auxiliary power unit shut down and all the lighting turned off. The passengers were ordered to the centre of the aircraft and one of the hijackers decided he wanted to bring the incident to an end by detonating the explosives on board and killing everyone, including themselves. Many of the passengers tried to evacuate from the aircraft once the shooting began and Bhanot, the flight attendant who had earlier disposed of the American passports, threw herself over three children, saving their lives but sacrificing her own life in doing so.

The story of the Pan Am hijack and, in particular, the heroism of Neerja Bhanot was immortalised in a film, appropriately entitled *Neerja*, released in February 2016.

CHRISTMAS IN IRAQ

Christmas Day may not be a big day in the Middle East, but the 25 December 1986 was certainly a significant date for four Middle Eastern hijackers. To this day, there is considerable speculation as to the actual identities and nationalities of those who hijacked Iraqi Airways flight 163 en route from Baghdad to Amman, with various organisations claiming responsibility and different states in the region quick to blame their neighbours. What we do know is that when the hijackers decided to try to take control of the aircraft, armed sky marshals attempted to prevent the team making it into the flight deck. A grenade was hurled in the cabin and the pilots initiated a rapid descent as a gun battle broke out behind them.

One of the hijackers still managed to enter the flight deck, albeit having to crawl in on his knees, and, no sooner had he done so, then there was an explosion as one of his grenades detonated.

In the passenger cabin, a fire erupted towards the rear of the aircraft and there was a considerable amount of smoke. The situation was now escalating out of control. Some of the survivors would later report hearing shots being fired in the cockpit. The aircraft eventually crash-landed in the sand at Arar, Saudi Arabia, just short of the town's airfield; the aircraft broke in two and caught fire.

Then the accusations began. Unsurprisingly, given that the incident took place in the midst of the Iran-Iraq war, Iraq initially blamed Iran, although it later blamed a domestic Iraqi dissident group as well. Various Shiite groups claimed they were responsible. Saudi Arabia was warned not to turn over any surviving hijackers to Iraq; furthermore, it was urged to release any hijackers. In Kuwait, the blame was placed on the Zaynab Organisation. The general consensus in the western world is that the actions were orchestrated by Islamic Jihad (aka Hezbollah).

Whoever was to blame, 63 of the 106 passengers and crew on board perished.

ASSAULT ON AIR AFRIQUE

On 24 July 1987, an Air Afrique aircraft was hijacked by Hussain Ali Mohammed Hariri, who had been released two years earlier from an Israeli prison when Israel had released 1,050 Arab prisoners in exchange for three Israeli soldiers. While the aircraft was flying from Brazzaville in the Congo to Paris, Hariri opened fire and demanded to be flown to Beirut.

Hariri was told there was insufficient fuel and that the aircraft would have to continue to Paris as planned, but Hariri then changed the destination to Geneva, where the Air Afrique jet eventually landed. The passengers' passports were collected and examined by Hariri, who then returned them all to the holders, except those belonging to French citizens. He identified one of the passengers, Xavier Beaulieu, and executed him by shooting him in the mouth, and then said that he would kill a second passenger if the aircraft was not granted permission to take off.

The head of the PLO's office in Geneva actually dissuaded Hariri from executing any further people. When the remaining French passengers on board saw Beaulieu's body being removed from the aircraft they started to evacuate the aircraft by opening the rear door and deploying the escape chute; the

Swiss authorities used this opportunity to storm the aircraft and subdue the hijacker.

There had been some concern by Swiss officials that French passengers were being targeted due to the breakdown in diplomatic relations between France and Iran. Accordingly the Swiss government with the agreement of both France and the Ivory Coast – the state of registration for Air Afrique – had agreed that the aircraft would not be allowed to depart. In the final assault on the aircraft by the police, an Air Afrique flight attendant from the Congo was shot in the stomach as he tried to overpower the hijacker.

THE TEARS OF MY SOUL

In 1987 North Korea was feeling somewhat peeved that South Korea was set to host the Olympic Games in 1988. Against this backdrop, a plan was initiated to destroy a Korean Air flight. The perpetrators were to be two North Korean agents, Kim Hyon-Hui and Kim Sung-Il.

Kim Sung-Il was a 70-year-old special agent of the research department of the Central Committee of the North Korean Workers Party, yet had had considerable experience living overseas. Kim Hyon-Hui was a 26-year-old woman, whose father was an employee of the North Korean foreign ministry. She had been identified as showing great potential for 'special operations' at an early age, and her natural beauty, command of the Japanese language, academic ability and family background simply added to her suitability. She was a regular recipient of medals demonstrating her commitment and talent.

Kim Hyon-Hui and Kim Sung-Il were paired up together in a 'father and daughter' act in 1984, and were sent on numerous overseas missions, travelling as Japanese passengers in the West and as North Koreans within the Eastern Bloc.

The decision to destroy Korean Air flight 858 was allegedly taken by President Kim Jong-Il himself on 7 October 1987 and so it was that Kim Hyon-Hui and Kim Sung-Il embarked upon six weeks preparation and training for their mission.

The agents travelled a circuitous route to Baghdad, starting on 12 November 1987. They initially travelled to Moscow, and then to Budapest and from there, six days later, by car to Vienna. Using forged Japanese passports, and travelling under the names Mayumi Hachiya and Shinchi Hachiya, they purchased flights to Belgrade with onward connections to Baghdad, Abu Dhabi and Bahrain. On 27 November, they were provided with the bomb and they travelled from Belgrade to Baghdad on Iraqi Airways. In Baghdad, they boarded Korean Air flight 858 to Bangkok via Abu Dhabi. They disembarked the flight in Abu Dhabi leaving the bomb in the overhead locker above their seats, 7B and 7C.

The bomb itself was triggered by a timing mechanism, which Kim Sung-Il set twenty minutes before boarding the flight. The delay was nine hours. The main charge consisted of both 350 g of C4 concealed, along with the detonator and timer, inside a Panasonic radio and Picatinny liquid explosive (PLX) disguised within a whisky bottle. The radio and bottle were placed in a vinyl shopping bag along with cartons of cigarettes.

In Abu Dhabi, they tried to board an Alitalia flight to Amman, Jordan, but there were problems with their visas so they elected to fly to Bahrain instead, where their Japanese passports were identified as counterfeit. Meanwhile flight KAL 858 had exploded over the Andaman Sea, killing all 115 people on board. Kim Hyon-Hui and Kim Sung-Il both tried to commit suicide by swallowing hydrocyanic acid gas capsules hidden inside their cigarettes. Kim Sung-Il died, but Kim Hyon-Hui survived and was sent to Seoul. For a while Kim Hyon-

Hui refused to speak, partially due to the effects of the poison she had consumed. When she did, she initially claimed to be Chinese but as time passed, and she watched television (which depicted a very different picture of life in South Korea to that which she had been taught back in Pyongyang), she began to relax and eventually confessed.

She was initially sentenced to death, but was later given a presidential pardon as it was apparent she had been brainwashed. She wrote her autobiography, *The Tears of My Soul*, and eventually married a South Korean agent who had been her bodyguard. Today she often appears on television and provides expert comment on North Korean affairs.

'I'M THE PROBLEM'

Another flight at the end of 1987 that culminated with the loss of all souls on board was Pacific Southwest Airlines flight 1771. This time the person responsible died on board.

David Burke had been dismissed from Pacific Southwest for the theft of $69 from in-flight cocktail receipts. Following a meeting with his boss, Ray Thomson, Burke had pleaded to keep his job, but to no avail. Burke decided that he was not going to be humiliated by the man. Knowing that Thomson commuted daily from San Francisco to Los Angeles, Burke bought himself a ticket for their evening flight back to San Francisco. Using his airport ID, which was still in his possession, he was able to bypass security checks, and smuggle a .44 Magnum which he had borrowed from a colleague onto the flight.

Nobody knows exactly what happened on board, but it is thought that Burke first shot Thomson – there were bullet holes in the seat he had been assigned. The pilots certainly reported that shots had been heard in the cabin and the cockpit voice recorder shows that Debra Neil, the flight attendant, opened the flight deck door and told the pilots, 'We have a problem.' Captain Gregg Lindamood can be heard to respond, 'What kind of problem?' before another shot was fired, presumably at Debra Neil. The last voice to be heard is that of Burke himself, responding to Lindamood's question with, 'I'm the problem.'

Two more shots were then fired, presumably at the captain and first officer, before the aircraft was put into a steep dive. There was one more shot fired before the aircraft crashed. Again, nobody knows who it was at – possibly Burke committing suicide prior to impact or perhaps at another passenger who was trying to overpower him.

The insider threat was, once again, proven to be something to be taken exceptionally seriously.

CHAPTER IX
1988—1995

ALL THAT JAZZ

Families travelling as a group are not normally suspected of being potential hijackers. But the 11 members of the Ovechkin family proved that there is an exception to every rule.

The family, most of whom were musicians and members of a jazz band called the Seven Simeons, had decided to seek a more liberal community where they would be rewarded for their artistic abilities. The impetus had been a tour of Japan. Until then they had played to packed theatres in the Soviet Union but had received very little pay. On their overseas concert tour they realised that life in a country that embraced Western democratic values offered greater prospects... and food.

And so, on 8 March 1988, they boarded Aeroflot flight 3739, en route from Irkutsk to Leningrad via Kurgan, having infiltrated weapons and explosives into the aircraft cabin in a double bass which the authorities had not been able to screen due to its size. Furthermore, the family were of celebrity status in Irkutsk and the airport personnel believed that they would be travelling to Leningrad for their next concert. They attempted to hijack the flight to London and gave the flight attendant a note which, according to *Izvestia*, said:

> ❝ Fly to a Capitalist country [London]. Don't fly any lower. Otherwise we'll explode a bomb. ❞

The hijackers did agree to the aircraft refuelling in Finland and they believed that they were landing in Kotka, but as the aircraft was about to land at the Soviet air force base in Veshchevo, the hijackers realised that they had been duped; the Cyrillic writing on a refuelling truck gave the game away.

Immediately, Dimitry Ovechkin shot and killed one of the flight attendants, Tamara Zharkaya, and ordered the captain to take off. The stand-off lasted two hours, following which the aircraft was stormed by a commando team, prompting a firefight. The mother, Ninel Ovechkin, ordered one of her sons to shoot her as she did not want to be captured. In fact, the entire family had agreed ahead of the hijacking that, should they fail in their mission, they would commit suicide rather than give up.

Alexander Ovechkin detonated the IED he was carrying and died from the blast. Realising they were never going to reach England, three other family members, Dimitry, Vasely and Oleg Ovechkin, all committed suicide using the single shotgun that they had – killing themselves in order from oldest to youngest. By then, the aircraft was on fire and passengers and crew were forced to escape the aircraft. Six members of the Ovechkin family, ranging from ages nine to 28, survived either because they had been too young to commit suicide or even realise what was happening, or because they simply had not had the time to grab the shotgun and fire the fatal shot before the aircraft caught fire. In addition to Tamara Zharkaya, three other passengers were killed when the aircraft was stormed.

ROYAL HOSTAGES

Arab carriers are not immune from the threat of hijacking. On 5 April 1988, a Kuwaiti airliner carrying three members of the Kuwaiti Royal Family on board was hijacked by a group of eight men, whose weapons had been concealed in food trays in the catering trolleys or left for the hijack team to collect from the aircraft's toilets.

The aircraft was diverted to Mashad in north-east Iran, where all the foreign hostages were released, yet where additional weapons and explosives were supplied to the hijackers. Once refuelled, the aircraft departed for Beirut, where the authorities refused it permission to land. Eventually, short of fuel, the Kuwaiti airliner landed in Larnaca, Cyprus. As negotiations for a full fuel load stalled, a Kuwaiti army officer was executed and his body thrown onto the tarmac. Two days later, still in Cyprus, a Kuwaiti fireman was executed, an action that forced the authorities to refuel the aircraft. As a token of goodwill, 12 hostages were released.

Rumours began to circulate that the British SAS had arrived in Larnaca and were preparing an assault on the aircraft, so, in order to stave off any action, the hijackers' associates in Beirut made it clear that any intervention in Larnaca would result in the deaths of hostages being held in Lebanon – including Terry Anderson and Jean-Paul Kauffmann. The aircraft was allowed to depart for Algiers, where the hijackers disappeared into the night sixteen days after the aircraft had been seized.

LOCKERBIE

The town of Lockerbie in Scotland was unheard of to most British and American nationals prior to the events of 21 December 1988. It was a sleepy rural Scottish town, nowhere near an airport, most of whose residents would have been blissfully ignorant of the fact that their homes lay beneath one of the multitude of flight paths for aircraft operating from European cities to American and Canadian airports. That was to change with shocking effect shortly after 7 p.m. on a wintry night as residents were preparing for Christmas – the season of goodwill to all men.

Lockerbie is now a name which will forever be associated with terrorism, where the only thing people know about the place is that it was the crash site of Pan Am flight 103. Major terrorist atrocities have taken place in Paris, New York, London, Moscow, Jerusalem, Madrid, Boston, Bangkok and Bali, yet these locations are regarded as popular tourist destinations and their names are synonymous with a multitude of positives – culture, history, architecture, cuisine, sport, beaches – but not so Lockerbie.

Both the media and the aviation industry have been fixated on the events of that fateful night for almost thirty years, with the tragedy only starting to take its place in history after 11 September 2001. There were three reasons for this – graphic imagery, media bias and politics.

In terms of imagery, the graphic pictures of the impact of an air disaster on an unwitting town generated fear in all that viewed them; we could all become victims of air crashes, regardless of cause. Eleven residents of the town of Lockerbie, or more specifically inhabitants of the now infamous Sherwood Crescent, died as their homes were obliterated by a fireball caused by the impact of the Pan Am 747's fuel tanks. Furthermore, with most bombings taking place over the sea, as was the probable intention of the Pan Am bombers, wreckage and bodies were not normally to be found on the doorsteps of people's homes or on the surrounding green hills of the Scottish countryside.

Media bias has also driven the almost fanatical focus on the Lockerbie incident. With so many of the world's key news providers being based in the United Kingdom and the United States, the fact that Pan Am flight 103 was en route from London Heathrow to New York made the story global headline news for far longer than would have been the case had the attack been on a route in the developing part of the world. Indeed, measure up the column inches on the coverage of the Air India bombing off the coast of Ireland in 1985, the UTA bombing over Niger in 1989, the Avianca bombing in Colombia also in 1989, the Xiamen Airlines disaster of 1990 and, more recently, the twin bombings of the two aircraft departing Moscow's Domodedovo airport in 2004 (where many, even in the industry, cannot name the airlines involved) with that of Pan Am 103; there is no comparison. And it is not only fascination with the investigation; the UTA bombing was, after all, supposed to have been carried out by the same team responsible for Pan Am 103. Quite simply, news coverage of a flight blowing up en route from London to New York has far greater commercial value than one operating from Brazzaville to Paris via N'Djamena.

It is, however, the political angle which is most disturbing – when governments make the decision to respond to, or ignore, a plot or attack for political expediency. The international standards for aviation security are, in general, spelled out in Annex 17 to the Chicago Convention – a document which most member states of the International Civil Aviation Organisation have signed up to. There are standards and recommended practices against which any member state can be audited and these rarely change in the aftermath of a terrorist attack which has not impacted upon the United States – Lockerbie, 9/11 (see p.241), the shoe bomber (see p.267), the liquid explosive plot (see p.283) and the underpants bomber (see p.288) all being classic examples. Attacks elsewhere have generally not resulted in policy change, however much they have demonstrated the fallibilities of our approach to aviation security – the China Northern arson attack (see p.269), the Qantas hijacking (see p.274), the Domodedovo bombings (see p.275), the actions of a suicidal pilot on an LAM flight to Angola (see p.306) and the hijacking, by a crew member, of an Ethiopian Airlines flight (see p.305) being cases in point. The impact of the probable bombing of a Metrojet flight (see p.310) in October 2015 remains to be seen, but if an insider was responsible, wholescale changes may be needed in the United States, where most staff are not screened as they go to work each day... unless, of course, the incident is quickly filed in aviation history as not pertinent to global aviation security!

One can praise and criticise the United States for this – praise, inasmuch as they have forced the global community to react to new challenges America has encountered first hand, and criticise, inasmuch as they have resisted attempts to increase security standards on the basis of incidents occurring elsewhere. The global aviation community has allowed itself to be dictated to by a country which has chosen to downplay or ignore the security implications of incidents occurring outside its domain.

The counterterrorist agenda, vis-à-vis aviation, has clearly been written with specific threats in mind – those faced by the West. This is most apparent when one looks at the industry's case references, which pay considerable attention to the Palestinian hijacking and bombings of US and European airliners in the 1960s, 1970s and 1980s, yet almost ignore the same groups' actions against Arab carriers. The lessons which can be learned from the bombing of Avianca flight 203 in

Colombia in 1989, the hijacking of a Qantas flight en route to Tasmania in 2003, the Domodedovo bombings of 2004 and, most tellingly, the bombing of a Cubana flight en route from Barbados to Jamaica in 1976 (see p.129), are many, but rarely told. Indeed, it's amazing – or perhaps not – that the Cubana bombing has almost been wiped from history completely.

The investigation into the loss of Pan Am 103 is carrying on to this day. One man has been convicted for his role in the attack and Libya has paid compensation to the families of the victims, yet many remain doubtful that the true perpetrators will ever be brought to justice. Even the details as to how the bomb was loaded onto the flight are questioned. All in all, Lockerbie, like the events of 11 September almost thirteen years later, is the subject of numerous conspiracy theories. Libya and Iran, with the support of either Hezbollah or the PFLP-GC, have both been in the dock.

What we do know is that Pan Am 103 was destroyed by a bomb concealed in a suitcase, which detonated at 31,000 ft. The issue of suitcase bombs had been a concern for some time. There had, of course, already been the attempted bombings of El Al flights in the early 1970s (see p.90), but, in the early 1980s, European security agencies were extremely concerned that more suitcase bombs were in circulation and that they had fallen into the hands of the PFLP-GC. They were showing up with disturbing regularity.

On 21 April 1980, a 26-year-old German passenger by the name of Andreas Raak was identified by El Al security at Zurich Airport as being in possession of one such suitcase bomb. It was his nervous disposition that had given him away. Raak had been given the suitcase by another German, 32-year-old Uwe Rabe. Raak was not nervous because he thought he was about to bomb the flight bound for Tel Aviv, rather that the diamonds he believed he was smuggling would be identified. The two men both had criminal backgrounds and had been cellmates in prison; following their release, Rabe contacted Raak, who had been in prison for theft and burglary, with a lucrative 'project'. Luckily for Raak, the alert El Al security officer prevented the barometrically controlled device, concealed in the false bottom of the case, from making it onto the flight. Rabe handed himself into the police in Berlin four months after the attack; in the interim he had been in Baghdad.

Also in Baghdad had been a man by the name of Abu Saif. Saif was arrested in 1982 after another suitcase bomb was detected in Geneva – this time in the hotel room of Adnan Awad. The bomb consisted of 2.7 kg of nitropenta (another name for PETN) in sheet explosive. Abu Saif later testified that he knew of ten suitcase devices being held in the offices of bomb-maker Abu Ibrahim, then head of the 15 May Organisation.

One of these devices showed up in Istanbul on 29 December 1983. The device was concealed within a carton of cigarettes and was checked in by a woman, who was never identified, for an Alitalia flight which was to connect with a Pan Am flight departing Rome later in the day. The Turkish authorities identified the bomb as a result of a process known as positive passenger-bag reconciliation; there was one passenger missing on boarding and, as such, her bag was offloaded.

At the same time, and as a result of yet another attempt to dupe a British woman into infiltrating a bomb onto a flight, a bomb was transported from Athens to Tel Aviv, then from Tel Aviv to London and from London back to Tel Aviv – undetected on all three flights. The device comprised of 250 g of pentrite, which should have been activated by an e-cell timer; the device failed. It is believed that this was another 15 May Organisation attack and the target had been the El Al flight from Tel Aviv to London. The female passenger, Diana Codling, had been persuaded by her 'boyfriend', Fuad Hussein Shara, to transport religious artefacts from the Holy Land and, at the same time, to take the opportunity, at his expense, to visit her family in England. She arrived back in Greece in January 1984 with the bomb still concealed in the lining of her case.

On 15 October 1985, two more suitcase bombs were discovered in Rome, this time due to the olfactory capabilities of Customs' canines, which identified one of the devices in the luggage of a man, travelling on a Moroccan passport, who had just landed in Italy on an Iraqi Airways flight from Baghdad. His 'colleague' was arrested in the centre of town as he disembarked an airport bus.

By the end of 1985, the 15 May Organisation had ceased its operations. The remaining suitcases, however, had now fallen into the hands of the PFLP-GC. If, as many suspect, the PFLP-GC was indeed responsible for Lockerbie, and the subsequent bombing of a UTA airliner over Niger in 1989, these could well have been the weapons used.

In respect of Pan Am 103, the Samsonite Silhouette suitcase could have been introduced into the system in one of three locations. The widely accepted viewpoint, which makes sense if one accepts that the Libyan intelligence agent Abdelbaset Ali Mohmed al-Megrahi was indeed responsible for the bombing, is that the bag was checked onto Pan Am 103 in Malta. This would have meant that the bag travelled, unaccompanied, on an Air Malta flight to Frankfurt, where it was transferred onto a Pan Am Boeing 727 – one of the feeder flights for the Boeing 747 operating from London to New York. The second option, which few believe, is that the suitcase was introduced in Frankfurt. Others, however, maintain that the bomb was infiltrated on board Pan Am 103 at London Heathrow.

The result for those on board was the same: the bomb, concealed inside a Toshiba BomBeat radio cassette recorder, detonated, resulting in the deaths of all 259 passengers and crew on board, as well as 11 residents of the town of Lockerbie.

If the PFLP-GC was responsible, it was a mission likely carried out at the behest of Iran, which was certainly the prime suspect in the first few months after the disaster. It could well have been an act of retribution against the United States for the downing of Iran Air flight 655 in the Strait of Hormuz in the Persian Gulf on 3 July 1987. The flight, operating from Tehran to Dubai with 290 passengers and crew on board, was mistaken for a military aircraft by the crew of the USS *Vincennes*. At the time, the American cruiser had just entered Iranian territorial waters, after Iranian gunboats had fired a warning shot at one of its helicopters.

As time passed after the loss of flight 103, and with no proof of guilt established, Libya became the focus of the investigation – arguably because it was politically expedient to do so at the time. As a result, two Libyan intelligence officers – the aforementioned al-Megrahi and Lamin Khalifah Fhimah – were arrested and, following three years of negotiations with the Gaddafi regime, sent to stand trial at Camp Zeist in The Netherlands, albeit to be judged in accordance with Scottish law. Fhimah was found innocent, but, on 31 January 2001, more than 12 years after the bombing, al-Megrahi was found guilty and sent to prison in Scotland – for life.

Many, including Nelson Mandela, were to campaign later for his release. Pressure increased when it was announced that al-Megrahi was dying from prostate cancer. Eventually, in 2009, with supposedly only weeks to live, he was returned to Libya, where he received a hero's welcome. He died two years and nine months later.

Libya, meanwhile, did accept responsibility for the loss of Pan Am 103 and the subsequent bombing of the UTA airliner. The Gaddafi government paid up in full, but with sanctions against Libya in place, it may well have been a financially worthwhile investment to make.

Whether al-Megrahi was actually just the fall guy remains to be seen.

Almost thirty years on, the Lockerbie saga continues. In October 2015, Mohammed Abouajela Masud and Abdullah al-Senussi were named as new suspects. Masud is an explosives expert, and al-Senussi is Colonel Qaddafi's brother-in-law and a former intelligence chief. Both men are still in Libya and, at the time of writing, in prison.

DEATH IN THE TÉNÉRÉ DESERT

The loss of UTA flight 772 has, somewhat unjustly, been eclipsed by the loss of Pan Am flight 103 over Lockerbie. On 19 September 1989, a Union de Transports Aeriens DC-10 took off from Brazzaville Airport in Congo, heading for Paris via N'djamena, Niger, with 170 passengers and crew on board. While the Pan Am passengers were to rain down on a Scottish town in the middle of winter, the UTA victims were to end their lives in the brutal, hot and sandy Ténéré desert, miles from any populated area. The bombing was, and remains, the most deadly terrorist attack perpetrated against France, even taking into consideration the coordinated attacks on Paris in November 2015.

Libya has been held responsible for the atrocity, although the method of attack was somewhat different to that of Pan Am. With flight 103, the bag containing the bomb was loaded onto the flight without any accompanying passenger; in respect of flight 772, it is believed that a Libyan secret service agent managed to manipulate a Congolese opposition member, and persuaded him to travel to Paris on an important mission. He probably did not know that the Samsonite suitcase he had checked in was lined with PETN.

Ten years after the bombing, six members of the Libyan secret service were tried *in absentia* in France. They were sentenced to life imprisonment but they have to be found before they can serve their sentences.

One of the reasons French aircraft were regarded as potential targets for the Gaddafi regime was the fact that, in 1980, a French aircraft had shot down an Aerolinee Itavia flight (see p.143), mistaking it for Gaddafi's personal jet. They may have failed to hit their target, but their intention had been clear.

Guillaume Denoix de Saint Marc, who lost his father in the attack, established the Association of the Angry Families of the UTA DC-10 in March 2002. While the association has focused most of its energies on ensuring justice is done, it has also spearheaded efforts to erect a permanent memorial to the victims. Now constructed at the crash site in Niger, and utilising a wing from the aircraft, it bears the names of the 170 souls on board. Built from black desert stone, sand and broken mirrors tethered to the ground, the memorial has the shape of the silhouette of a DC-10 and was designed to be visible from the sky by planes flying overhead. It is also visible on Google Earth.

THE UNWITTING BOMBER

On 27 November 1989, an Avianca flight operating a domestic Colombian route between Bogata and Cali exploded seven minutes after take-off, killing 107 people on board and three on the ground as a result of falling debris. This time terrorism was not the cause, rather the actions of the Medellin drug cartel ('the Extraditables'), who it is believed were intending to assassinate Colombian presidential candidate Cesar Gaviria, who was not actually on board the aircraft.

The Avianca bombing is one of the few examples whereby a passenger on board the aircraft seemingly unwittingly detonated the device, having been duped. Julio Santodomingo purchased one-way tickets to Cali in cash for himself and an 18-year-old boy, Alberto Prieto, at the Avianca ticket counter in Bogota the night before the attack; both were using false identities.

On 27 November, Santodomingo checked in first and requested seats 15E and 15F, which were located over the wing of the aircraft. Prieto arrived later and the two men made their way, boarding passes in hand, to the departure gate together. However, Santodomingo elected not to fly at the last moment; there was no checked luggage to offload. It is thought that he feigned receiving a message on his beeper instructing him that he was needed elsewhere. He left Prieto with a black bag containing a tape recorder. In all probability, and based on the forensic evidence following the crash, Prieto took seat 15E and seat 15F remained empty.

Prieto had been told that his mission was to record the conversations of passengers on the aircraft, but not to do so until the aircraft had completed its climb since using the tape recorder could interfere with the communication between the air traffic control and the flight deck at a critical stage of flight. It would appear that Prieto followed his instructions and depressed the 'Record' button when the aircraft was at 14,000 ft, initiating the detonation of the Semtex-H concealed within the tape recorder. With Prieto in a window seat over the wings of the aircraft, the proximity of the fuel tanks meant that the passengers and crew stood no chance of survival.

The details as to what actually happened were provided in 1993 by one of the Medellin drug cartel's senior figures, Carlos Mario Alzate Urquijo, as part of a plea bargain; he further implicated the drug baron Pablo Escobar as being the mission's mastermind. Alzate Urquijo was given an eight-year sentence for his involvement in the attack.

Cesar Gaviria was elected president of Colombia in 1990 and set about tackling the drug barons. Pablo Escabar declared war on the Colombian government and was killed in a gun battle in 1993.

Two of those killed on board the Avianca flight were American citizens and so the Federal Bureau of Investigation took a huge interest in the case, determined not only to avenge the deaths of its own nationals but to support the fight against drug barons. And so it was that Dandeny Mounoz Mosquera, better known as 'La Quica', was arrested in New York in 1991 and was sentenced to six years in prison for other crimes. He was later sentenced in relation to the bombing of the Avianca flight and given ten life sentences and 45 years. The Colombian government has, however, expressed its doubt as to whether 'La Quica' was behind the atrocity.

Nobody knows who Alberto Prieto actually was. His body remains unclaimed and it would seem that he was just an unwitting individual sacrificed in an act of mass murder.

MOON FESTIVAL GIFTS FOR A XIAMEN AIRLINES CAPTAIN

On 2 October 1990, Jiang Xiofeng boarded Xiamen Airlines flight 8301 from Xiamen to Guangzhou. Shortly into the flight, Jiang Xiofeng requested to be allowed to visit the cockpit as he wished to give the pilot some flowers as a gift in honour of China's autumn Moon Festival. Once inside the cockpit, he revealed that he was carrying 7 kg of explosives strapped to his body, ordered the co-pilot out and commanded the captain to fly to Taiwan. The captain claimed to have insufficient fuel to make that journey but eventually agreed with the hijacker that they would head for Hong Kong.

Running out of fuel, the captain eventually decided to land in Guangzhou and at the very last second Jiang Xiofeng tried to grab the controls of the aircraft, resulting in the captain losing control and hitting a China South West Airlines aircraft parked on the ground and a China Southern aircraft preparing to depart for Shanghai. 82 people died on board the Xiamen Airlines flight, 46 on the China Southern and there were significant injuries on both aircraft and on the China South West Airlines flight.

THE PERFECT SWAT

SWAT teams around the world now routinely train to respond to hijackings, but rarely get the opportunity to test their ability outside of training exercises. Singapore's Special Operations Force (SOF) was given the opportunity to demonstrate its prowess when, on 26 March 1991, a Singapore Airlines flight en route from Kuala Lumpur to Singapore was seized by four Pakistani passengers. They had all been seated together in seats 35A, 35B, 35C and 35D and had acted in unison. A 40-minute journey, regarded in the region as more of a bus journey, became a terrifying nine-hour ordeal.

The hijackers, who claimed to be members of the Pakistan People's Party, demanded the release of nine prisoners held in Pakistani prisons, including the husband of Benazir Bhutto. They also demanded that the aircraft fly to Sydney, Australia and to be patched through to Benazir Bhutto herself by telephone.

The crew managed to convince them that the aircraft would have to land in Singapore to refuel, given its original short flight plan. On the ground, the Singaporean negotiating team swung into action, managing to delay the refuelling process for as long as possible.

As minutes became hours, the hijackers vented their frustration on the four male flight attendants, who were being held hostage together at the rear of the aircraft. One of them, Bernard Tam, was eventually forced to drink a glass of water which contained a sedative – presumably to make him compliant. A few minutes later the hijackers made him stand up, dragged him to the door of the aircraft and threw his body to the ground; the rest of the crew were told that he had died. In reality, albeit suffering spinal injuries, he survived the fall and was able to give the authorities mission-critical information regarding the state of mind of the hijackers, the fact that they only seemed to be armed with knives, canisters and lighters, and that there was no indication that they had booby-trapped the doors of the aircraft in order to prevent SWAT team intervention.

The hijackers had proven that they were prepared to kill and, as the aircraft had not been refuelled and they had not been able to speak with anybody in Pakistan, let alone Benazir Bhutto, they threatened to set fire to the aircraft and started pouring alcohol from the galley carts throughout the cabin. In order to exert pressure on the Singaporean government to accede to their demands, a second flight attendant, chief flight steward Philip Cheong, was thrown from the aircraft without being sedated beforehand. He too survived the fall, but those on board thought that two of the crew had now been executed.

The lead hijacker, Shahid Hussain Soomro, became increasingly desperate and even tried to start a fire on the flight deck. Negotiations had, by now, totally stalled and the hijackers issued a five-minute deadline, after which, they claimed, they would start executing passengers.

Permission to refuel the aircraft was granted, and, during the process, the SOF assembled. Now all that was needed was a diversion. Up until that point all negotiations had been conducted in English, but at the eleventh hour and with the SOF alongside the aircraft, an Urdu-speaking policeman started speaking with Soomro, who summoned at least one of his fellow hijackers to the cockpit due to the change of personality; they initially thought that they had finally been patched through to Pakistan by telephone.

The SOF acted swiftly and stormed the aircraft, killing the four hijackers and securing the release of all passengers and crew unharmed. It is widely regarded as one of the most effective counterterrorist actions of all time... and was completed, according to most reports, in only 30 seconds.

FED UP WITH FEDEX

The 'insider threat' was exemplified on board a FedEx flight en route from Memphis, Tennessee, to San Jose, California, on 7 April 1994.

Auburn Calloway, an employee of the company, was facing disciplinary charges and potential subsequent dismissal for having lied about his working hours. Rather than face the humiliation of the hearing, he decided to kill himself in a way that would enable his family to benefit from his $2.5 million life insurance policy – hijacking an aircraft and crashing it as if it were an accident.

On the day in question, he boarded the flight as a passenger and, being a flight engineer himself, was able to surreptitiously disengage the cockpit voice recorder prior to take-off, so that, later on, there would be no record of his having killed the crew; one of the crew realised it was off and reset it.

Calloway attacked the pilots 20 minutes into the flight with a hammer, inflicting blows that were to fracture the skulls of both the first officer, James Tucker, and flight engineer, Andrew Peterson. Captain David Sanders and Peterson both tried to get out of their seats to overpower Calloway, who in turn managed to retrieve a spear gun from a guitar case he had carried onto the flight. As the captain and the engineer fought with Calloway, Tucker, despite his horrific injuries, performed a steep climb, a 140-degree bank, and a 'split-S' manoeuvre – aerial movements designed to try to throw Calloway off balance.

Calloway was, however, still fighting and managed to hit Sanders in the head with the hammer. Sanders and Peterson continued to fight back and eventually got control of Calloway. At this point, Tucker engaged the autopilot so that he could leave his seat to try to help and because he was almost unable to fly the aircraft himself due to losing the use of one arm as a result of the initial hammer blow.

Captain Sanders eventually landed the aircraft. All three pilots are regarded as true heroes, yet they suffered such severe injuries that none of them have ever flown an aircraft since.

THE SUICIDAL TERRORIST MAKES HIS ENTRY ON ALAS CHIRICANAS

Many consider the events of 11 September 2001 as the day that suicidal terrorism commenced in the aviation industry. It wasn't.

On 19 July 1994, one day after the Argentine Israelite Mutual Association had become the subject of a terrorist attack in Buenos Aires killing 85 people, an Alas Chiricanas flight was blown up while operating a domestic flight in Panama. On board were a group of 12 Jewish businessmen and a Lebanese man by the name of Jamal Lya.

The explosion took place ten minutes after Captain Edmundo Delgado had taken off from Colon, bound for Panama City. The Semtex/EGDN-based device itself was later determined to have been activated by a P-500 Motorola radio.

The subsequent investigation led the American authorities to believe that Lya had detonated a device that he had carried onto the aircraft himself, and that the attack was linked to the Buenos Aires bombing. Others are of the belief that Lya was actually connected to a Colombian drug cartel, given the similarity of the bomb used in the incident with that used in the 1989 Avianca bombing, and that it was purely coincidental that the Alas Chiricanas flight had been targeted so close to the Buenos Aires atrocity.

Supporters of both theories agree that Lya was the likely perpetrator and that whoever had manipulated him had done so in the knowledge that he was mentally challenged: his was the only body not to be claimed by relatives after the bombing.

The FBI are still seeking information regarding Lya, who is described as having been (back in 1994), 'a Middle Eastern male, 25 to 28 years old, approximately 5'9" tall and weighing 160 pounds. He had a white complexion, thick eyebrows, light brown eyes, black hair and short sideburns. He reportedly wore black or dark green pants and a short-sleeve shirt with a dark pattern. He did not speak English or Spanish, however he possibly spoke Arabic. In order to communicate instructions to people he used hand signals or wrote notes.'

One group did claim responsibility for both the Alas Chiricanas bombing and the attack on the Jewish cultural centre – Ansar Allah, which is believed to be a splinter group of Hezbollah.

OPLAN BOJINKJA

The sea change in terrorist tactics came on 11 December 1994, when Ramzi Yousef tested out his so-called 'X-ray proof' bomb on Philippine Airlines flight 434 operating from Manila to Tokyo via Cebu.

Before the attack in the air, he had already tested the nitroglycerine-based device twice on the ground – once in a shopping centre in Cebu City and once in a cinema in Manila. It seemed to work; he was now set for the test run of an attack against aviation which, had it succeeded, would have resulted in the loss of more lives than 9/11 – and all of them in the air.

On 11 December, Yousef boarded the Philippine Airlines flight in Manila under the assumed name of Arnaldo Forlani, which also happened to be the name of one of Italy's prime ministers in the early 1980s. He was seated in 26K. During the flight, Yousef went to the toilet, where it is believed he put the device together, using components he had smuggled on board in his shoes, and set the timer – a modified Casio wristwatch which he had worn – so that the explosion would take place four hours later. The main charge was nitroglycerine, which he had taken on board in bottles of contact lens solution.

Yousef disembarked in Cebu, having placed the IED in the life jacket beneath his seat, and it was on the next leg of the flight that the explosion took place. A 24-year-old Japanese engineer, Haruki Ikegami, was now seated in 26K and his body absorbed much of the blast. The aircraft itself remained intact and, while ten other passengers had been injured, initially the crew thought that Ikegami would also survive.

Fernando Bayot, the assistant purser and lead flight attendant in the economy cabin, was the first on the scene. Noticing the hole beneath Ikegami's seat, he tried to extricate him from it, as he appeared to have dropped down into it. It was at this point that they realised the explosion may well have been a bomb, rather than a structural collapse of the floor beneath row 26; Ikegami had not fallen into the hole at all, rather his entire body from the waist down had been decimated by the blast. He was still alive. The other passengers were moved away while Bayot and other crew tended to Ikegami as his life ebbed away. Following his death, they put an oxygen mask on him in order that other passengers would not be overly panicked by the situation.

On the flight deck, Captain Ed Reyes had felt the blast and initially thought he was losing control of the aircraft, but with the fuselage still intact he was able to safely land the damaged plane at Naha Airport in Okinawa.

Yousef planned to use considerably more nitroglycerine in his subsequent attacks against aviation – part of a broader plot named Oplan Bojinka – which included not only the destruction of 11 aircraft operating, primarily, trans-Pacific routes from Asian cities to the western seaboard of the USA, but also the assassination of Pope John Paul II on his visit to the Philippines. The third part of the plan was for one of Yousef's team, Abdul Hakim Murad, to fly an aircraft into the CIA's Langley HQ; he had already acquired a pilot's licence in the United States.

Five terrorists were to have carried out the multiple aircraft bombings planned for the 21 and 22 January 1995. All the flights were American carriers, but which had intra-Asian legs prior to their trans-Pacific, or otherwise onward, flights. This meant that the men could purchase tickets to go to other Asian cities, without needing visas for the United States. It also meant that they could fly to Pakistan having left their IEDs on board the targeted flights. All the terrorists had code names and both their names and the flights they were to bomb were outlined in an article in the *Philippine Star*:

(1) 'Mirqas' was to plant a bomb on a United Airlines flight from Manila to Seoul and leave the flight in South Korea. The aircraft, proceeding to San Francisco, would explode over the Pacific. Mirqas would further plant a bomb on a Delta flight from Seoul to Taipei, which would explode on the next leg of the flight to Bangkok, but by then, Mirqas would have left the plane and flown away to safety, then home to Karachi, Pakistan.

(2) 'Markoa' would plant a bomb on a Northwest Airlines flight from Manila to Tokyo, then get off the plane. The plane was 'timed' to blow up while en route onwards to Chicago. In the interim, Markoa would have boarded a Northwest flight from Tokyo (Narita) to Hong Kong and planted a bomb timed to explode over the Pacific as the plane was on its way to New York City. Markoa, getting off in Hong Kong, would fly to Singapore and then home to Pakistan.

(3) 'Obaid' was to plant a bomb on the United Airlines flight from Singapore to Hong Kong, which would detonate when the aircraft was flying onwards to Los Angeles. Obaid, having exited, would then board another United flight bound from Hong Kong to Singapore and embedded a bomb timed to explode on the return leg to Hong Kong. Exiting the plane after the second bomb-planting, Obaid would then fly directly home from Singapore. Home where? To Pakistan, of course.

(4) Terrorist 'Majbos' would board the United Airlines flight from Taipei to Tokyo and leave a bomb set to go

off as the airliner headed onwards to Los Angeles. He would later fly from Tokyo to Hong Kong and conceal a bomb aboard another United airlines flight, set to explode as the jet flew from Tokyo to New York.

(5) 'Zyed' was slated to fly [from Manila] by Northwest to Seoul, hide a bomb under his seat and descend from the aircraft; the bomb would then detonate on the Seoul to Los Angeles portion. It is believed that 'Zyed' was Yousef himself. Flying on to Taipei on United, 'Zyed' would plant a bomb set to explode on the Taipei– Honolulu portion of the flight. 'Zyed' would then fly to Bangkok on United, and leave the plane in Bangkok, after having concealed a bomb which would explode when the same aircraft was flying onwards to San Francisco. The terrorist would then fly to Karachi.

Youssef was not the sole mastermind; he was working in conjunction with his uncle, Khalid Sheikh Mohammed, the chief orchestrator of the attacks in the United States seven years later. The scale of Oplan Bojinka was discovered fortuitously when a fire started in Yousef and Mohammed's Manila apartment on the night of 6 January 1995, while Murad was mixing chemicals there.

Murad and Yousef both initially fled the building, but Murad returned in order to try and retrieve the laptop containing the incriminating evidence. By then, the police were on the scene and Murad tried, in vain, to bribe policewoman Aida Fariscal to allow him to depart with the laptop; she refused and Murad was arrested.

The evidence was damning and Murad's subsequent confession provided the security agencies of the world with a goldmine of information, not only about Oplan Bojinka itself, but also the capabilities and mindset of al-Qaeda. Oplan Bojinka utilised IEDs infiltrated in shoes and liquid explosives in bottles of contact lens solution, and involved flying an aircraft on a suicidal mission into the heart of the United States' intelligence community. It behoves us to question why we were so surprised by 9/11, the shoe bomber and the liquid explosive plot in the following decade.

Aida Fariscal may well have saved the lives of 4,000 passengers and crew, as well as the life of Pope John Paul II.

CHRISTMAS: THE SEASON OF BAD WILL TO ALL MEN

The season of goodwill to all men is not something that is recognised by certain members of the international community and the legendary accounts of enemies laying down their arms on Christmas Day to play football matches are probably ridiculed by terrorists of the modern era.

Indeed, Christmas has long been associated with terrorist attacks against civil aviation. It may be that the absence of other major news stories in the last two weeks of any calendar year provides the terrorist with a greater opportunity to exploit the news media, and additionally there is, even in the non-Christian parts of the world, a sense of Christmas spirit, with airports having to cope with a larger number of passengers, some carrying unusual packages.

On 24 December 1994, an Air France aircraft was preparing to depart from Algiers to Paris, when a group of armed men dressed as Algerian police officers approached the aircraft and commandeered it on the ground. They ordered the aircraft to depart, but the Algerian authorities tried to stall the departure by refusing to remove the stairs. In response, they identified one passenger who actually was an Algerian police officer and executed him. Then they identified and executed a second passenger by the name of Bui Giang To, who worked at the Vietnamese Embassy in Algiers. On Christmas Day, with the French authorities trying to persuade their Algerian counterparts not to permit the aircraft to depart, another passenger was executed, this time a cook from the French Embassy in Algiers. This forced the Algerians to capitulate, not wanting further deaths to take place on Algerian soil, but they only gave the aircraft sufficient fuel to reach the southern French city of Marseille, which it did in the early hours of 26 December.

The hijackers ordered the aircraft to be refuelled to capacity and the French authorities became extremely suspicious as to the reasons for requesting the fuel tanks be filled for a relatively short flight to Paris. As the intelligence services were investigating the background of the perpetrators, who appeared to be members of the Armed Islamic Group of Algeria (GIA), they stumbled across intelligence that indicated the plan was to fly the aircraft into the Eiffel Tower on Christmas Day in a suicidal mission.

In Marseille, a fourth passenger was about to be executed, prompting the French National Gendarmerie Intervention Group (GIGN) to conclude that the only way to resolve the crisis was to storm the aircraft. They practised on board an Airbus similar to that which had been hijacked and, once they felt ready, initiated the assault.

It almost went terribly wrong when they rolled the stairs up to the aircraft and tried to open the door to the Airbus, only to find that the height of the stairs blocked the outward opening process. The GIGN had been practicing on an empty Airbus with no passengers, no cargo and no fuel; consequently the practice aircraft was less heavy and so the door was higher off the ground than that of the hijacked aircraft. Despite this initial error, the GIGN did eventually gain access.

By the end of the 22-minute gun battle, all four terrorists had been killed and ten members of the GIGN had been injured. The first officer, Jean-Paul Borderie, escaped from the aircraft when the assault began by jumping from the window of the cockpit, breaking his leg as he landed; he pushed through the pain and staggered away from the aircraft. All the passengers and crew who had been on board when the GIGN moved in were to survive. Overall, the incident is regarded as one of the most professional stormings of an aircraft ever carried out. From the perspective of the hijackers, it was a failed mission to use an aircraft as a weapon of mass destruction. They would try again.

THE FLIGHT ATTENDANT WHO BECAME A HIJACKER WHO BECAME A SHOE SALESMAN

Most hijackings are perpetrated by individuals or families wishing to use the aircraft as a means of escape and thereby claiming political asylum in another country. Generally the perpetrators of such incidents are passengers, yet as we saw in 1950, when pilots hijacked their own aircraft from Czechoslovakia to Germany, there are times when crew members can be the perpetrators.

On 19 September 1995, flight attendant Reza Jabbari hijacked a Kish Air flight he was operating from Tehran to Kish Island. He ordered the aircraft to head to Europe, but the aircraft had insufficient fuel given that it was only operating a domestic flight within Iran. He told the captain to fly to Saudi Arabia, where it was denied permission to land. It was also refused by the Jordanian authorities.

With the aircraft running out of fuel, the aircraft was eventually permitted to land in Israel at Ovda Air Force base, located the Negev desert. This was somewhat of a surprise location for the passengers, almost all of whom were Iranian and were, consequently, disturbed to be on Israeli soil.

Jabbari had actually been a colonel in the Iranian army, but he was trying to escape from Iran because he considered it to be an oppressive regime. In Ovda, Jabbari surrendered within an hour of landing and claimed asylum. Five of the other 174 passengers and crew also claimed asylum but, on 20 September, were ordered to leave the country on the same aircraft on which they had arrived.

Iran demanded the extradition of Jabbari, and Hezbollah threatened to conduct suicidal attacks against Israeli aircraft if Jabbari was granted asylum. However, he was sentenced to eight years in prison and then freed after serving half his sentence, only to become a shoe salesman on the beaches of Eilat, Israel's resort city on the Red Sea. He was later granted Israeli citizenship and converted to Judaism.

CHAPTER X
1996–2000

DURESS OF CIRCUMSTANCE?

There are not that many hijacked aircraft which have ended up on British soil, but in 1996 a Sudan Airways aircraft hijacked by a team led by Adnan Hoshan did just that. Oddly, it was the legal battle in the aftermath of the incident that proved the most controversial aspect of the case.

On 26 August 1996, the Sudan Airways aircraft departed Khartoum for Amman, Jordan. On board were 196 passengers, seven of whom did not intend to end their journey in the Middle East. Adnan Hoshan and his six compatriots were Shiite Muslims from Iraq and all bar one were fugitives of the Saddam Hussein regime, where they were wanted for a range of offences. Now living in Sudan and having failed both to secure genuine visas to travel to Europe and to exit Sudan using forged documents, their real passports were seized by Sudanese immigration officials, making imminent deportation all the more likely. Their passports were recovered by Hoshan upon payment of bribes and his assurance that the group would leave the country. Deportation to Iraq had to be avoided at all costs as only a date with the gallows awaited them there. Hijacking an aircraft to Europe seemed to be the only practical solution.

All of the hijack team had plastic knives, which would not have been detectable by any archway metal detector at

Khartoum Airport, and plastic mustard bottles filled with salt; once airborne, the hijackers wrapped these bottles in black tape and added plasticine in order to make them look like hand grenades.

The hijack commenced in Egyptian airspace when one of the hijackers grabbed a flight attendant and threatened her with a plastic knife. He was immediately overpowered by a sky marshal who thought he was acting alone.

With the sky marshals identified, the other hijackers could now act; one stood up, holding what looked like a grenade and threatened to blow up the aircraft. The sky marshals released their captive, who then went to the cockpit and ordered the captain to comply with their demands. With a knife to his throat, and the threat of a bomb on board, he did.

A butcher was also travelling on the flight and had a set of genuine professional knives with him. It is unclear whether this person had been part of the planning, but the hijackers seemed to know about the knives and Adnan Hoshan distributed them among his team.

One of the team backed out of the plot in-flight. Sabah Nagi ended up being tied up and gagged by his colleagues after he refused to tie up a female flight attendant.

The crew took no chances and the aircraft landed in Larnaca, Cyprus, to refuel before continuing to London, where it landed at Stansted in the early hours of 27 August. The siege did not last long; within eight hours, the hijackers had surrendered and claimed asylum.

Subsequently they were sentenced at the Old Bailey for terms of between five and nine years. Mr Justice Wright justified his decision by saying that:

> It is of the highest degree of importance that I should pass sentences on you that deter others from following a similar course.

Adnan Hoshan is reported to have been quite happy to start his sentence, saying that had he returned to Iraq, 'I would be in a prison if I was lucky! It does not cost more than 50p for a bullet.'

In 1998, the Court of Appeal cleared and freed the hijackers on the grounds that they had been acting under 'duress of circumstance'. Lord Justice Rose said:

> If Anne Frank had stolen a car to escape from Amsterdam and had been charged with theft, the tenets of English law would not have denied her the defence of duress of circumstances on the ground that she should have awaited the Gestapo's knock at the door.

Nick Hardwick, the chief executive of the Refugee Council, said,

> We would never condone hijacking, but these were not callous terrorists but desperate people in fear of their lives. This shows the drastic steps people will take to flee persecution. Increasingly refugees are putting their own lives at risk by resorting to ever more desperate measures to escape and every year in Europe alone hundreds die in an attempt to reach safety.

That was the view in 1998. In 2016, this human tragedy continues to be played out, with heart-wrenching imagery, on our television screens. The extent to which we condone illegal acts when perpetrated out of 'duress of circumstance' is a conundrum we all have to consider.

JET-SKIING IN THE COMOROS

On all commercial flights, passengers sit through a flight safety briefing during which crew members explain how to utilise lifejackets and life rafts in the event of the aircraft ditching at sea. The last recorded ditching of a wide-bodied aircraft at sea was actually the result of an aircraft hijacking and most of those who died lost their lives as a result of the failure to obey one of the basic rules of aircraft evacuation – not to inflate the lifejacket before leaving the aircraft.

At the controls of Ethiopian Airlines flight 961 was Captain Leul Abate, who has the misfortune to have been involved in two earlier hijackings; one on 12 April 1992, when he was ordered to fly to Nairobi, and another on 17 March 1995, when he was ordered to fly to Sweden.

His final flight as captain was on 23 November 1996 when he was flying from Addis Ababa to Nairobi and with onward service to Brazzaville, Lagos and Abidjan. The aircraft was seized by three Ethiopian men who demanded to be flown to Australia, but the aircraft did not have sufficient fuel to meet their demands, given that it was only operating a regional route. The hijackers claimed to be armed with explosives, and they did not believe the crew's claims, as they had read the in-flight magazine, which showed the range of the Boeing 767 aircraft on which they were flying.

First Officer Yonas Mekuria, was forced from his seat and one of the hijackers replaced him. Meanwhile, the captain decided to fly along the African coast, as he feared running out of fuel, but the hijackers, noticing land, ordered the aircraft to fly in an easterly direction, which Captain Abate did, albeit tracking towards the Comoros Islands. The aircraft was now out of fuel but the intoxicated hijackers refused to allow the captain to land the aircraft.

A fight started during which Mekuria was attacked by the hijackers with an axe, which was subsequently used to destroy the aircraft's communication system. While Mekuria was fighting with the hijackers, Abate tried to ditch the aircraft in the sea as close to land as possible, and ended up only 500 metres away from Le Galawa Beach Hotel on the Comoros Islands. Guests at the hotel videoed the aircraft attempting to ditch. All was going well in the 200 mph landing in the shallow waters, until one of the engines caught a coral reef hidden just below the surface of the sea. The aircraft summersaulted and broke into three parts. Some passengers managed to escape, but many were trapped inside the fuselage having already inflated their lifejackets in preparation for the water landing.

Holidaymakers rushed to try help survivors ashore but only 50 people, including Abate and Mekuria made it. One hundred and twenty-five people died including the three hijackers, who were later named as Alemayehu Bekeli Belayneh, Mathias Solomon Belay and Sultan Ali Hussein. The incident is certainly the most significant to have been caused by former convicts seeking asylum. They had used alcohol as a way to calm their nerves, and also as their 'bomb': the bomb that they claimed to have was actually just a bottle of alcohol wrapped in a cloth.

THE 19-MONTH HIJACK ORDEAL

The longest hijacking on record started on 12 April 1999 when an Avianca flight operating a domestic route from Bucaramanga to Bogata was hijacked by six members of the National Liberation Army (ELN). For 35 of the passengers and crew on board, freedom remained out of reach for more than a year. The hijacking of the Fokker 50 began shortly after the seatbelt sign had been turned off.

One of the passengers, a priest who had earlier been blessing his fellow passengers, is reported to have donned a balaclava and ordered the plane to land at a jungle clearing in the Colombian province of Bolivar. There, the passengers and crew were then loaded into canoes and sailed down the Magdalena River to an ELN camp.

The hijack was effected by the 'Heroes of Santa Rosa' front of the ELN in order to pressurise the Colombian government into recognising the ELN as an equal partner in peace negotiations which were ongoing at the time with the larger of Colombia's guerrilla groups – the Revolutionary Armed Forces of Colombia (FARC). The ELN felt that it was being side-lined and had to demonstrate its power. The hijacking won them few friends and the government refused to negotiate, thereby forcing the ELN to alter its course of action and make individual ransom demands for each of the hostages. This worked; by the end of 1999, 25 passengers had been released, generally as a result of their families making payments.

For the remaining hostages, and all of the crew, captivity would continue into the year 2000 and the last of the hostages, Gloria Amaya de Alfonso, was not to be released until 22 November, 19 months after she had departed Bucaramanga.

One of the hostages died in captivity of a heart attack. The hijackers were eventually arrested and given lengthy prison sentences of between 30 and 39 years.

The hijack was allegedly masterminded by Maria Orlinda Guerrero, also known as 'the Black Yesenia', who was killed in 2011 during an assault on an ELN stronghold by the Colombian air force and national police.

RAINBOW BRIDGE

There are any number of objectives that might seem to be reasonably rational to justify hijacking aircraft: securing the release of political comrades from prison; escaping with large sums of money; gaining publicity for a particular cause; or, perhaps, using an aircraft as a means of escaping one country and using it as a form of transport to another. However, hijacking a Boeing 747 simply to see if you can fly it under the Rainbow Bridge in Tokyo is pushing the boundaries of rationality to the extreme! That is what 28-year-old Yuji Nishizawa, a computer games aficionado, wanted to do on 23 July 1999. He'd done it using a flight simulator programme so now he wanted to try to do it for real.

Nishizawa boarded the All Nippon Airways aircraft in Tokyo, along with 502 other passengers and 14 crew members, for its domestic flight to Chitose. Twenty-five minutes into the flight he used a 20-centimetre-long kitchen knife to compel a flight attendant to take him to the cockpit. Co-pilot Kazuyuki Koga was forced to leave the flight deck but, during the commotion, Captain Naoyuki Nagashima managed to switch the transponder to 7500, thereby alerting air traffic control to the fact that the aircraft was being hijacked.

Nishizawa wanted to fly the plane himself, and had every confidence in his ability to do so. Initially he ordered Nagashima to head for the US Air Force base of Yokota, near Tokyo. Permission was granted for landing, but Nishizawa still wanted to fly the plane under the Rainbow Bridge himself, so ordered Nagsahima to leave his seat. Naturally, the captain refused to do so, prompting Nishizawa to stab Nagashima in the neck, shoulder and chest. The captain's screams prompted other crew members, including the co-pilot, to force their way back into the cockpit, where they managed to overpower

Nishizawa. Koga assumed control of the aircraft, which, according to the *Japan Times*, was then flying at an altitude of only 300 m, and landed the aircraft at Haneda Airport five minutes later – indicative of both the altitude of the aircraft and its proximity to built-up areas.

Tragically, Nagashima did not survive and Nishizawa was arrested and charged with murder, as well as hijacking a commercial airliner.

During the trial, the defence team ordered a psychiatric evaluation which determined that Nishizawa was suffering from Asperger's syndrome, a disorder in which a person of normal intelligence and language ability exhibits autistic-like behaviour. A second evaluation was requested by the prosecution which concluded that Nishizawa was 'under significant influence of antidepressant drugs and was in a state of diminished capability at the time of the crime'. As a result, the judge determined that Nishizawa could only be held partly responsible for his crimes and, so, he was sentenced to life imprisonment instead of facing execution, being the maximum penalty in Japan for a hijacking resulting in a fatality.

IC814: THE LAST EVENT OF THE LAST CENTURY... ALMOST

Many considered that traditional hijacking was no longer a worthwhile strategy for terrorists groups in the 1990s to pursue, but the events of Christmas 1999 served as a reminder of the threat posed to civil aviation when an Indian Airlines aircraft was hijacked while en route from Kathmandu in Nepal to New Delhi. The hijackers, acting in the name of Harkat-ul-Mujahideen – an al-Qaeda affiliate based in Pakistan – seized the aircraft and initially ordered it to fly to Amritsar, and so began an eight-day hijacking that was to end on the eve of the new millennium.

The perpetrators were an extremely well trained, ruthless group of five men, whose goal was the release of prisoners from Indian jails. The atmosphere on board the aircraft was extremely tense throughout the hijacking with the passengers being warned many times that they should say their prayers as they were all about to die. Some of the passengers were separated from their loved ones; only one was executed – Rupen Katayal – who had been on his honeymoon in Nepal. His wife was not aware of the fact that her new husband had been killed until after the incident ended.

The takeover started just as the aircraft entered Indian airspace. Captain Devi Sharan used the transponder to notify air traffic control that the aircraft had been hijacked, but he used the wrong code. The crew flew, as instructed, to Amritsar, where the hijackers instructed the pilots to keep the aircraft taxiing on the runway. They demanded fuel but took off before it arrived as the hijackers feared that the Indian government was planning to storm the aircraft.

IC814 was perilously low on fuel, yet the hijackers were keen not to allow the crew to land at any other Indian airport. They elected to go to Lahore, in Pakistan, but the authorities there denied them permission to land and plunged the airport into darkness. The hijackers and, by now, the crew, knew that the aircraft was about to run out of fuel, so visually searched for the airfield. Eventually they saw what appeared to be landing lights and made their final approach. At the last moment the pilots aborted the landing when they realised that they were about to land the Airbus on a road. The near miss did, however, convince the Pakistani authorities that they had to permit the aircraft to land.

Once refuelled, IC814 departed for Dubai. The hijackers had given permission for some of the women and children on board to disembark in Lahore, but the Pakistani authorities had refused to accept any of the passengers. It was, therefore, only when the aircraft reached Dubai that the first passengers were to be released – 27, plus the body of Rupen Katyal.

Again refuelled, the aircraft soon departed for Qandahar, Afghanistan, where the aircraft remained until negotiations were completed. In the end, the Indian government approved the release of three – Mushtaq Ahmed Zargar, Ahmed Omar Saeed Sheikh and Maulana Masood Azhar – rather than the 200 prisoners originally demanded by the hijackers, and on 31 December 1999 another Indian Airlines aircraft, with a fresh crew, was brought in to fly the hostages home to Delhi. The hijacked aircraft was also flown back and quickly put back into service, as were the crew members who, despite their eight-day ordeal, were not given compassionate leave.

The release of the hostages on New Year's Eve should have been the last big news story of the twentieth century. It would have been had Boris Yeltsin not resigned as President of Russia even closer to midnight!

While the events of Christmas 1999 were clearly perpetrated with terroristic intent, there were numerous bizarre incidents that took place in the first year of the twenty-first century, the motives for which were not always clearly defined.

On 6 February 2000, an Ariana Afghan flight was operating a domestic route when a group of 12 individuals hijacked the aircraft and forced it to fly to London. The aircraft initially landed in Moscow to refuel before being granted permission to fly to Stanstead, where a three-day stand-off began. At first it was unclear what the aims of the hijackers were, but the aircraft clearly wasn't going anywhere and, for those who had any doubt, when the captain and first officer escaped the aircraft while the hijackers were in the aircraft cabin, London was clearly going the be the last port of call. Eventually it became apparent the hijackers simply wished to claim asylum and indeed were granted the right to remain in the United Kingdom following the incident. One of the hijackers even managed to get a job as a cleaner at British Airways' facilities near Heathrow.

HELPING A HIJACKER OUT

In May 2000, Reginald Chua, who had been jilted by his bride, decided to become a parajacker on board a Philippine Airlines flight operating a domestic route from Davao to Manila. Rather than ask the authorities for money, he simply collected money from all of the passengers on board before ordering the crew to descend to 6,000 ft and open the rear door of the aircraft in flight. He then donned a home-made parachute, but hesitated before jumping. One of the crew members, Frances Cabel, decided to 'help' the hijacker with his decision by kicking him out of the door of the aircraft. Chua died on impact.

TAKE ME TO ANTARCTICA... THE CABAL ARE CLONING HUMANS THERE

On 27 July 2000, Aaron Amartei Commey, armed with a 9-mm handgun, simply ran through the security checks at JFK Airport and boarded a National Airlines aircraft that was preparing for its departure to Los Angeles. He demanded to be flown south. The authorities, realising they had an individual who was psychologically disturbed yet armed, commenced negotiations with the hijacker who kept changing his preferred destination from Miami to Buenos Aires to Antarctica. At times he referred to his concern that human cloning was taking place in Antarctica. He surrendered six hours later.

During the medical evaluation to determine his competency to stand trial, Commey told psychiatrists that he had wanted to parachute into Antarctica in order to destroy the secret base of an organisation called the 'Cabal'.

The Cabal, according to Commey, was a secret group which wished to take over the world through mass destruction. It became apparent that Commey had been concerned about the Cabal for some time and was determined to get to Antarctica to weed them out. In 1998, Commey had travelled to Buenos Aires with two firearms – planning to get to Antarctica via the Argentinian capital – but had been arrested at the airport on suspicion of weapons smuggling. He was held in custody in Argentina for one month, where he underwent a psychiatric evaluation that resulted in the opinion that he exhibited symptoms of 'delirious syndrome', whereby one becomes delusional and experiences hallucinatory phenomena.

THE FOZ DO IGUAÇU HEIST

Escaping with cash-in-transit was the objective of the five men (travelling as Julio Ribeiro, Robson Santana, Erasmus Zapoluti, Carlos Oliveira and Antonio Manfrini Junior) who hijacked a VASP flight operating from Foz do Iguaçu, via Curitaba, to Brazil on 16 August 2000. The cash was in the cargo hold and was being transported for the Bank of Brazil under the supervision of TGV employee Joelson Goes Maciel.

The takeover was swift and the assailants quickly neutralised the crew. That said, a Chinese tourist, who had spent the day visiting the spectacular Iguaçu Falls, panicked and tried to open the emergency exit while the aircraft was in-flight; the unruly hostage had to be restrained by the hijackers.

During the initial stages of the hijack, perhaps as a result of the Chinese passenger's action, one of the hijackers accidentally fired his weapon; the bullet narrowly missed the chief flight attendant Victoria Regina Simas and lodged in a curtain rail that separated sections of the passenger cabin.

Maciel was identified as the official escort of the cash, who then produced documentation which revealed the amount to be five million Brazilian reals (approx. US$1.25 million) – far less than they had anticipated.

Captain Sergio Carmo dos Santos was instructed to turn off the radio and transponder and alter his course for the city of Porecatu. The captain initially argued that the aircraft could not land there safely, but the hijackers were well prepared and knew that the runway was more than sufficient. On arrival, the aircraft was greeted – with some surprise – by two pilots, a security guard and a mechanic who were the only people at the airport at the time. They too were taken hostage by the armed assailants and ordered to assist in unloading the cash into two Ford Ranger trucks, which had been parked at the airport earlier.

After the hijackers disappeared by road, the aircraft departed and the captain notified the authorities of the heist and landed in Londrina, 90 km away from Porecatu.

Marcelo Moacir Borelli was quickly identified as the likely gang leader. He had a track record of heists, having been held responsible for the theft of 61 kg of gold from the cargo hold of an aircraft at Brasilia Airport earlier the same year. While the police were trying to find him, a sickening video was posted online that clearly demonstrated Borelli's dangerous, heartless, depraved nature. Borelli was involved with a woman who had previously had a daughter with another man, somebody Borelli considered his enemy. In order to humiliate him, Borelli videoed himself abusing the 3-year-old – kicking her, subjecting her to electric shocks, forcing her to defecate and then eat her own faeces.

He was eventually arrested and on 11 January 2007, while serving a sentence of 177 years in prison in Piraquara state penitentiary, he died of AIDS, aged 39.

TRUST A SECURITY GUARD... TO HIJACK A PLANE

It doesn't help when the security guards become hijackers. On 14 October 2000, a Saudia flight, en route from Jeddah to London was hijacked by a security guard and his friend who demanded to be flown to Baghdad. Following the fall of Saddam Hussein's regime the perpetrators were returned to Saudi Arabia to stand trial.

CONFUSED SECURITY ON VNUKOVO AIRLINES

A Vnukovo Airlines flight operating from Dagestan to Moscow almost ended in disaster, not because of the hijack itself but because of the response on board from the security services. Akhmed Amirkhanov was the sole hijacker, but when he tried to take control of the aircraft, claiming to be carrying a bomb, some members of the Federal Security Service (FSB) who were also on board the aircraft, and were armed, tried to subdue other people in the cabin who were looking suspicious! The only problem was that the FSB officers were suspicious of the six government security guards who were travelling with the Dagestani finance minister, Abdusamad Gamidov. The hijacker himself was almost a bystander in the events that unfolded.

Colonel Oleg Lutsenko of the FSB ordered everybody to raise their hands and keep their heads down; he was brandishing a firearm which he should have handed over to the authorities before boarding the flight. Fortunately, the six security guards had handed in their weapons, albeit only to the aircraft's captain who had retained them in the flight deck. Consequently, once Amirkhanov had made it into the cockpit with his fake bomb, he found genuine, loaded weapons there at his disposal. Meanwhile, the Dagestani security agents thought that the FSB colonel and his colleague were part of the hijack team!

The aircraft itself landed initially in Baku, Azerbaijan and then continued to Ovda, in Israel, where the hijacker surrendered.

Amikharnov's rationale for the hijacking was somewhat questionable; it was, he later claimed, to express his concern over the 'white race' facing domination by Asians.

ROXY MUSIC'S ROCKY FLIGHT

The threat posed by psychotic individuals became very apparent to the passengers and crew of a British Airways flight operating from London Gatwick to Nairobi on 29 December 2000.

Paul Kefa Mukonyi, a 27-year-old tourism student based in Lyon, France, was travelling from Lyon to Nairobi via London. Even before boarding his flight in Lyon, Mukonyi is reported to have been behaving strangely and told French police that he was nervous of boarding the plane. On board, he asked a flight attendant whether the plane could be hijacked and, at one point, even tried to use the galley intercom in order to call the police himself, as he thought it was a normal telephone. The captain radioed ahead to Gatwick and asked for an escort to take Mukonyi to his connecting flight to Nairobi.

Once at Gate 54 in Gatwick for his flight to Nairobi, Mukonyi asked British Airways ground staff if he could speak to police. Two officers were called to the gate and he expressed fears that he was being followed and that there might be an explosive device on board. Despite the police feeling he was a troubled individual, they actually escorted him onto the aircraft, notifying the crew of the situation. Ultimately, given that he had committed no offence, it was down to the airline as to whether or not he could fly.

The passenger list also included two celebrities, Bryan Ferry of the band Roxy Music and Jemima Khan, then wife of Pakistani cricketer Imran Khan and sister of the British Conservative politician (and 2016 candidate for Mayor of London) Zac Goldsmith.

Five hours into the flight, in Sudanese airspace, Mukonyi got up from his seat and entered the flight deck. Captain William Hagan had exited the cockpit for a break, and was asleep in his bunk, leaving First Officer Phil Watson at the controls. At that time, the flight deck door had to be locked for take off and landing but not for cruising in-flight. Mukonyi leaned over Watson's shoulders and grabbed the controls, forcing the aircraft into a dive so extreme that the aircraft stalled as it plunged downwards towards the African continent.

Hagan, awoken by the unusual aircraft movement, rushed back to the flight deck and struggled to overpower Mukonyi. Initially all his efforts failed and as the aircraft's speed exceeded the maximum rate of descent for a Boeing 747 it seemed inevitable that the aircraft would crash. In a last-ditch effort, Hagan plunged his thumb into Mukonyi's eye and Mukonyi released his grip on the controls and started fighting with Hagan at the rear of the flight deck. Watson, miraculously, regained control of the aircraft more than 10,000 ft lower than when the assault had begun, and landed, as planned, in Nairobi.

Mukonyi was hospitalised for about two months before being returned to France – albeit on Emirates rather than British Airways – in order to resume his studies at Université Lumière Lyon.

CHAPTER XI
2001–2002

CONSPIRACY THEORIES

For those who love a good conspiracy theory, look no further than Bangkok and the events of 3 March 2001, when an explosion took place on board a Thai Airways B-737 aircraft 35 minutes before its scheduled departure to Chiang Mai. One of the intended passengers was Prime Minister Thaksin Shinawatra. He was to be accompanied by his son and they had been given seats 11A and 11B. If it was indeed a bomb, and had it detonated once the aircraft had been airborne, there is no doubt the aircraft and all 149 passengers on board would have been killed. Seven airline staff were injured and Kampol Meerlap, the flight attendant preparing the Business Class section of the aircraft for departure, was killed. But, perhaps it was *just* a spark in a fuel tank.

The Thai incident is subject to claim and counterclaim… much like the loss of Malév Hungarian Airlines flight 240 back in 1975 on which all 50 passengers and ten crew died when the flight, operating from Budapest to Beirut, crashed prior to landing. No official statement has ever been made and, accordingly, there is significant speculation that it was politically expedient to cover up the cause and, if the result of an attack, the identity of the perpetrator.

On 27 September 2007, György Szilvásy, then Minister of Civil Intelligence Services wrote in a letter to Róbert Répássy, member of the Hungarian parliament, that the Hungarian Office of National Security had produced a report on the crash in 2003. To summarise the report, there are no available original (secret service) documents concerning the case. The report remains top secret, for reasons not connected to the crash.

On 14 January 2009, Erik Meijer asked the European Commission, in writing, for information which would help solve the mystery. He entitled the letter 'Ending of secrecy surrounding the crash on 30 September 1975 of the Malév flight from Budapest to Beirut and the graves of 17 of the 60 victims', and wrote (according to *De Volkskrant*):

> 1. Is the Commission aware that on the evening of Tuesday, 30 September 1975 an aircraft of the Hungarian Malév airline on a flight from Budapest to the Lebanese capital Beirut crashed into the sea close to Beirut Airport, that none of the 50 passengers and crew of 10 survived the crash and that after a week Malév informed bereaved relatives that the cause of the crash was unknown, that the black box and the mortal remains of the victims could not be found on the sea-bed and that audio recordings were missing from air traffic control?
>
> 2. Is the Commission aware that the complete lack of information on the crash described in Question 1 has meant that the victims' relatives of various European nationalities (including the Hungarian Laszlo Nemeth and the Dutchwoman Francine van der Velde) are still now continuing to enquire about inconsistencies in the details that have since become known, the possible causes of the crash

and, above all, the place where the passengers killed in the crash might have been buried?

3. Is the Commission aware that there are photos showing Lebanese recovering bodies from the sea, and that a 1975 secret investigation report by the International Civil Aviation Organisation exists, showing that immediately after the crash 37 of the 60 bodies were recovered, of whom 20 were identified by Lebanese relatives while 17 other bodies that could not be identified were buried in an unknown location in Lebanon?

4. Is the Commission aware that an inquiry by the Netherlands Embassy in Lebanon in the spring of 2007 at the request of the victims' relatives obtained the information that the 17 unidentified bodies are probably located in mass graves, but that the military authorities do not want to provide any information on this, while the relatives have also learned that a Hungarian Government inquiry into the crash in 2003 produced a document that has been kept secret until now?

5. Is the Commission prepared to take action to ensure that this still unresolved question, which is probably related to past events such as the Cold War, the civil war in Lebanon and the conflict between Israel and the PLO, is no longer deliberately kept secret but, in the interest of all the relatives and to prevent inaccurate rumour, is publicly cleared up once and for all? 🙾

The response was given on 3 March 2009 by Ms Ferrero-Waldner on behalf of the Commission: 'The Commission has no jurisdiction to deal with the question asked, which is [sic] a matter solely for the national authorities concerned.'

The mystery seems set to continue…

THE DESTRUCTION OF HALF SRILANKAN'S FLEET

One of the most significant attacks against aviation occurred in Sri Lanka in the early hours of 24 July 2001, an event subsequently overshadowed by the al-Qaeda attacks in the United States less than two months later. The Liberation Tigers of Tamil Eelam (LTTE) were, like al-Qaeda, orchestrators of spectacular events.

Under the cover of darkness, 14 members of LTTE's Black Tigers, a highly trained squad of suicidal commandos, all of whom carry cyanide tablets in case they should fail their mission, attacked Sri Lanka Air Force Base Katunayake and then Colombo's Bandaranaike International Airport. By the end of the night, all the Black Tigers were dead but they had succeeded in destroying two helicopter gunships, three jet trainers and three fighter jets at the base and three of SriLankan Airlines' Airbus fleet at Bandaranaike. A further five jet trainers and six fighter jets were significantly damaged in Katunayake, as were two other SriLankan Airlines Airbus aircraft. Of SriLankan's fleet of twelve Airbus aircraft, almost half were put out of commission and the airport, gateway to what was generally considered a tourist's paradise, looked like it was in the midst of a war zone.

The Black Tigers, armed with rocket propelled grenades, anti-tank weaponry, assault rifles and explosives, attacked the air force base first, partly in the knowledge that they would have to neutralise any military intervention. They arrived at the airfield on the evening of 23 July on a bus, posing as a group of friends going on a picnic. Casually dressed, they offloaded bags which concealed their weaponry and then sat down and started to eat, drink and sing Sinhalese songs. Some local residents reported their presence and soldiers from the base came to inspect but found nothing to be concerned about.

It was customary for there to be power cuts in the area as part of the government's attempts at reducing electricity consumption; these normally lasted each evening from 9.45 p.m. until 11.15 p.m. and plunged the area into darkness. When the lights went out, and having had their last supper, the Black Tigers changed into military uniform and approached the electrified perimeter fence of the air force base. They knew that the fence worked off a generator and power cut or no power cut they could not simply scale it. However, their earlier intelligence gathering had also revealed that there was a drainage canal that traversed, partly underground, the secure area beyond the fence through to the exterior of the restricted zone; this had been built to prevent flooding of the runways and tarmac during the rainy season. Soldiers based at Katunayake were known to have exploited this drain in the dry season in order to make covert visits to 'women of the night' in a nearby residential district.

Being dry on 23 July 2001, a few of the Black Tigers crawled through the drain in order to deactivate the fence to allow the rest of the group to get onto the base with all their weaponry, still under the cover of darkness.

At around 3.30 a.m., the Tigers then detonated the electrical transformers and plunged the rest of the base into darkness. The response was muted given the frequency of power cuts and electricians were sent out to restore power. Meanwhile the Black Tigers approached the military aircraft parked both in the hangars and on the tarmac, set their charges and at 3.50

a.m. commenced their detonation. By now, everybody realised that the base was under attack.

Three of the Tigers took up a position on top of the air traffic control tower and were able, from a height, to monitor the response from the Sri Lankan army. In the early stages of the assault, the Tigers' focus was on the air force base, as their primary objective was to destroy the military aircraft, which were being used to target their enclaves – sophisticated aircraft, which included Israeli Kfir and Russian MiG fighters, which could never be attacked while airborne. Having achieved that goal, some of the Tigers made their way across the runway towards Bandaranaike's international passenger terminal. The aim was not to kill civilians – miraculously none died despite there being more than 1,000 people in the building at the time – but rather to inflict a psychological blow which would impact upon Sri Lanka's economy and dissuade tourists from visiting.

In all, it was later estimated that the LTTE had inflicted $350 million worth of material damage and, as per their brief, degraded the Sri Lankan Air Force's capability to mount operations against the LTTE. They had filmed the initial stages of the attack, footage which was released to the world's media, utilising a marketing opportunity that al-Qaeda, and more recently Daesh, have exploited to even greater aplomb.

THE MILE HIGH CLUB

On 10 August 2001 one of the most bizarre hijackings of all time took place. It was perpetrated, allegedly, by a Cuban couple in their sixties and who booked themselves onto a flight with the Key West Mile High Club, which offered speciality flights for people who wanted to have sex in the skies and get a video recording of their experience.

Pilot Thomas Hayashi was the owner of the company and was, seemingly, not the best at passenger profiling. According to Hayashi, the couple demanded to be flown to Cuba but, during a struggle in the cockpit, the male hijacker allegedly fell forward, causing Hayashi to lose control of the aircraft and crash into the sea. Hayashi managed to issue a mayday call and to escape the aircraft himself, but the Cubans had inflated their lifejackets inside the aircraft and allegedly sank with the aircraft.

There is some scepticism about whether the events took place, as neither the wreckage nor the bodies of the so-called hijackers have ever been found. Some people questioned whether Hayashi had invented the whole story in order to claim on insurance, but assuming the hijack really did happen then the hijackers certainly went down with a bang, albeit not the bang they'd been sold the flight for!

One can look at the events of August 2001 with a degree of humour; the same cannot be said for the events of September 2001.

11 SEPTEMBER 2001

Six years earlier, in 1994, the industry had been alerted to the reality of the threat of suicidal terrorism on board aircraft (exemplified by Jamal Lya on board the Alas Chiricanas flight in Panama), the planning of spectacular terrorist atrocities (as evidenced by Ramzi Youssef's Oplan Bojinka in the Philippines), and the possibility of an aircraft itself being used as a weapon of mass destruction (with the GIA's hijacking of an Air France flight with the intention of flying it into the Eiffel Tower). Nonetheless, the reality of the attacks of 11 September 2001 came as a shock.

We had seen orchestrated hijackings involving multiple aircraft and how the transmission of images by the media can be exploited to instil fear, but it is hard, even for those with a knowledge of al-Qaeda tactics, to imagine training groups of individuals to be able to pilot aircraft for the sole purpose of coolly flying them into densely populated areas in downtown New York and Washington DC.

The day is often regarded as having changed the world as we know it, and many of the security protocols that we see in place today are in response to those attacks. However powerful the imagery of commercial aircraft hitting the World Trade Centre, people jumping from buildings to their certain deaths and iconic structures being transformed to dust before our very eyes, it is important for those in developing aviation security protocols to recognise that, as horrific as those attacks were, they were, to date, a one-off terror spectacular.

Part of the reason for al-Qaeda perpetrating the attacks in the first place was not to cause the deaths of the people on board the aircraft but rather to create a climate of fear and to change our daily lives.

Reams have been written about the rationale behind the attacks and detailed analyses have been performed regarding the individuals who perpetrated them. In a book that covers the entire history of attacks against civil aviation, any discussion of these events will inevitably lack depth and analysis. Suffice to say, the actions of 19 hijackers on board four aircraft astounded even the most hardened of security professionals, not only for the ability of so many human beings to sink to such depths of depravity and have such conviction in their cause as to be able to carry out their mission without detection, but also with the sheer brilliance and simplicity of the plan in the first place.

The subsequent investigation into al-Qaeda's network revealed the competence and intelligence of the organisation's operators, communicating using social media and using code words and phrases reminiscent of the Cold War era. The perpetrators were far from disillusioned youth who had lost their homes and were living in poverty; they were highly educated, from professional, reasonably well-to-do backgrounds and were nationals of independent states; 15 of the 19 were from Saudi Arabia.

In this account, we shall focus on the attacks themselves rather than the ideology of al-Qaeda or the political ramifications, and fallout, of the day which became known as 9/11.

Conspiracy theories are aplenty and the Internet is abuzz with blogs and discussions questioning whether the attacks even took place and apportioning blame to the innocent; social media has afforded the theorists the oxygen of publicity for their warped viewpoints and enabled them to construct and 'prove' scenarios which show little respect for the 2,977 (a number which excludes the hijackers themselves) innocent people who were to lose their lives as a result of fundamentalist ideology. While, quite possibly, not the perfect source, this account relies almost exclusively on the 9/11 Report, being the output of the National Commission on Terrorist Attacks Upon the United States, as its source, and, unashamedly, quotes extensively therefrom.

Tapes of Osama bin Laden released by the US in the aftermath of the attacks would seem to indicate that he had full knowledge of the plots and believed that they 'benefited Islam greatly'. He is reported to have watched them on television and been pleasantly surprised at the impact on the buildings after the aircraft struck. He was, however, not the mastermind. That dubious accolade goes to Khalid Sheikh Mohammed, or KSM as he is often called, the uncle of Ramzi Youssef who was responsible for Oplan Bojinka (see p.211) in 1994. KSM allegedly confessed to his involvement in 2007 when he claimed that he was, 'responsible for the 9/11 operation from A to Z'; he was, by then, being held captive in Guantanamo Bay.

The plot's coordinator was Ramzi bin al-Shibh, the 'twentieth hijacker'. The original plan was that there would be five hijackers on each flight and, indeed, it is notable that the only aircraft which failed to hit its intended target was United Airlines flight 93, the one with only four hijackers on board. Ramzi bin al-Shibh had become friendly with Mohamed Atta, who was to become – at bin Laden's request – the lead hijacker on 9/11 itself, while they were studying in Hamburg in 1997. Also in Hamburg at the time were Marwan al-Shehhi, who was later to take control of United Airlines flight 175 and Ziad Jarrah, lead hijacker of United Airlines flight 93; together they became known as the Hamburg Cell.

Over the years between 1997 and 2001, the cell underwent training, met with Osama bin Laden and, thereafter, began to concoct the plot. This included recruiting fellow ideologues and, of course, learning to fly.

The entire cell applied for and received visas to enter the United States – except al-Shibh. It was because of this that he, being completely familiar with and sympathetic to KSM's plan, became the go-between between the hijackers and the al-Qaeda leadership. It was al-Shibh who relayed information and al-Shibh who transferred money to the team as and when it was required. With al-Shibh unable to participate in the attack personally, another hijacker was required. The cell called upon the services of Zacarias Moussaoui, a French-born man of Moroccan origin.

Moussaoui was not included in the final 'go team'. He was regarded by his colleagues as flaky and the team was confident they could succeed without his input. Another man, Mohamed al Kahtani, had also been identified as a potential pilot (although he was later denied entry to the US and so could not participate in the operations). Moussaoui was considered as a replacement pilot for Ziad Jarrah who had shown signs of frustration during the summer of 2001 and was known not to get along with Mohamed Atta. However, Moussaoui had failed the various pilot training courses he had attended and, on 16 August 2001, he was arrested by the FBI on visa violation charges. According to the 'Statement of Facts' presented by the US government at his subsequent trial:

> At the time of his arrest, Moussaoui possessed the following items: two knives; flight manuals for the Boeing 747 Model 400; a flight simulator computer program; fighting gloves and shin guards; a piece of paper referring to a handheld Global Positioning System; software that could be used to review pilot procedures for the Boeing 747 Model 400; and a hand-held aviation radio.

The arrest was made after Moussaoui had enrolled at the Pan Am International Flight Academy in Minnesota, requesting to learn how to fly a Boeing 747. It was his instructor, Clarence Provost, who contacted the authorities because, according to the 9/11 Report: 'It was unusual for a student with so little training to be learning to fly large jets without any intention of obtaining a pilot's license or other goal.'

By the summer of 2001, with angst increasing between team members, Moussaoui under arrest and 19 hijackers now in the United States with cover stories, the al-Qaeda hierarchy was keen to execute their plan. There was no doubt about the primary targets – the World Trade Center and the Pentagon, but bin Laden was keen that the third target be the White House.

Given the relatively small size of this building, compared to the others, Atta was concerned that they would not succeed and, hence, opted for the US Capitol.

According to the 9/11 Report, at a meeting in Spain in July 2001 between Atta and al-Shibh:

> Atta explained that Hanjour was assigned to attack the Pentagon, Jarrah the Capitol, and that both Atta and Shehhi would hit the World Trade Center. If any pilot could not reach his intended target, he was to crash the plane. If Atta could not strike the World Trade Center, he planned to crash his aircraft directly into the streets of New York. Atta told al-Shibh that each pilot had volunteered for his assigned target, and that the assignments were subject to change.

Atta also explained how the attacks would be carried out and that, 'he, Shehhi, and Jarrah had encountered no problems carrying box cutters on cross-country surveillance flights. The best time to storm the cockpit would be about 10–15 minutes after take off, when the cockpit doors typically were opened for the first time. Atta did not believe they would need any other weapons. He had no firm contingency plan in case the cockpit door was locked. While he mentioned general ideas such as using a hostage or claiming to have a bomb, he was confident the cockpit doors would be opened and did not consider breaking them down a viable idea.' He further explained that, 'he wanted to select planes departing on long flights because they would be full of fuel, and that he wanted to hijack Boeing aircraft because he believed them easier to fly than Airbus aircraft, which he understood had an autopilot feature that did not allow them to be crashed into the ground.'

By August, the plans were well underway. On 3 August, Atta and al-Shibh reportedly conferred with each other over how each the operative should purchase plane tickets and who should be assigned to provide the 'muscle' in each team. 'Atta and al-Shibh also revisited the question of whether to target the White House. They discussed targets in coded language, pretending to be students discussing various fields of study: "architecture" referred to the World Trade Center, "arts" the Pentagon, "law" the Capitol, and "politics" the White House.'

It was at this time that the two men agreed that the White House should be the third target, but that the Capitol would be kept 'as an alternate target in case the White House proved too difficult'.

The team carried out a number of surveillance flights in August 2001. 'Each flew in first class on the same type of aircraft they would hijack on 9/11.'

> All 19 tickets were booked and purchased between August 25 and September 5. It therefore appears that the attack date was selected by the third week of August. This timing is confirmed by al-Shibh, who claims Atta called him with the date in mid-August. According to al-Shibh, Atta used a riddle to convey the date in code – a message of two branches, a slash, and a lollipop (to non-Americans, 11/9 would be interpreted as September 11).

As the attack date approached, 'al-Shibh and Atta kept in contact by phone, email, and instant messaging. Although Atta had forbidden the hijackers to contact their families, he apparently placed one last call to his own father on 9 September. Atta also asked al-Shibh to contact the family of one hijacker, pass along goodbyes from others, and give regards to KSM. Jarrah alone appears to have left a written farewell – a sentimental letter to Aysel Senguen'. Senguen was Jarrah's girlfriend.

In the days before 9/11, the hijackers are known to have returned any remaining funds to al-Qaeda by wire transfer. They then assembled at their points of departure, where they stayed in budget hotels and carried out 'normal' activities – going to the gym, eating fast food and even watching pornographic videos. One can only imagine how Jarrah felt when he received a speeding ticket on the northbound I-95 in Maryland, in the early hours of 9 September.

On 11 September itself, Mohamed Atta and Abdulaziz al-Omari boarded the 6 a.m. shuttle flight from Portland, Maine, to Boston. Atta was selected for additional screening by the Computer Assisted Passenger Prescreening System (CAPPS). This system had been created 'to identify passengers who should be subject to special security measures. Under [the] security rules in place at the time, the only consequence of Atta's selection by CAPPS was that his checked bags were held off the plane until it was confirmed that he had boarded the aircraft.'

In Boston, Atta and al-Omari met up with their fellow hijackers, Satam al-Suqami, Wail al-Shehri, and Waleed al-Shehri, and checked in and boarded American Airlines flight 11, bound for Los Angeles and scheduled to depart at 7.45 a.m. 'Atta, Omari, and al-Suqami took their seats in business class (seats 8D, 8G, and 10B, respectively).The Shehri brothers had adjacent seats in row 2 (Wail in 2A, Waleed in 2B), in the first class cabin.

Captain John Ogonowski and First Officer Thomas McGuinness were at the controls of flight 11, which was also carrying nine flight attendants and 81 passengers. The plane took off at 7.59 a.m.

Marwan al-Shehhi spoke to Atta on the phone, prior to their boarding, from another terminal at Boston's Logan Airport, where he, together with his fellow hijackers, Fayez Banihammad, Mohand al-Shehri, Ahmed al-Ghamdi and Hamza al-Ghamdi, had checked in for United Airlines flight 175, also bound for Los Angeles and due to depart 15 minutes after American Airlines flight 11. 'Banihammad [was seated] in 2A, Shehri in 2B, Shehhi in 6C, Hamza al-Ghamdi in 9C and Ahmed al-Ghamdi in 9D).'

Captain Victor Saracini and First Officer Michael Horrocks were at the controls of flight 175, which was also carrying seven flight attendants and 56 passengers. The plane took off at 8.14 a.m.

At Washington Dulles, Hani Hanjour checked in for American Airlines flight 77, once again bound for Los Angeles. He was accompanied by Khalid al-Mihdhar, Majed Moqed and brothers Nawaf and Salem al-Hazmi. 'The Hazmi brothers were also selected for extra scrutiny by the airline's customer service representative at the check-in counter. He did so because one of the brothers did not have photo identification nor could he understand English, and because the agent found both of the passengers to be suspicious. [Once again, the] only consequence of their selection was that their checked bags were held off the plane until it was confirmed that they had boarded the aircraft.' On board, Hani Hanjour was in seat 1B, the Hazmi brothers in 5E and 5F, while Moqed and al-Mihdhar were seated in 12A and 12B in the Economy cabin.

Captain Charles F. Burlingame and First Officer David Charlebois were at the controls of flight 77, which was also carrying four flight attendants and 58 passengers. The plane took off at 8.20 a.m.

In Newark, New Jersey, Ziad Jarrah and his smaller team, comprising Saeed al-Ghamdi, Ahmed al-Nami and Ahmad al-Haznawi, checked in for United Airlines flight 93 to San Francisco. All four had seats in First Class.

Captain Jason Dahl and First Officer Leroy Homer were at the controls of flight 93, which was also carrying five flight attendants and 37 passengers. The flight was delayed, so instead of departing on schedule at 8 a.m., the flight took off at 8.42 a.m.

By 8 a.m., all 19 hijackers were on board their respective aircraft. By 8.42, all were airborne. However, 25 minutes before that, the first hijacking had been initiated. All outside communication with American Airlines flight 11 ceased after 8.14 a.m.

The 9/11 Report gives the best and most accurate account as to what happened on board the four aircraft.

> *American Airlines flight 11*: Betty Ong and Madeline 'Amy' Sweeney, tell us most of what we know about how the hijacking happened. As it began, some of the hijackers – most likely Wail al-Shehri and Waleed al-Shehri, who were seated in row 2 in first class – stabbed the two unarmed flight attendants who would have been preparing for cabin service.
>
> We do not know exactly how the hijackers gained access to the cockpit; FAA rules required that the doors remain closed and locked during flight. Ong speculated that they had 'jammed their way' in. Perhaps the terrorists stabbed the flight attendants to get a cockpit key, to force one of them to open

the cockpit door, or to lure the captain or first officer out of the cockpit. Or the flight attendants may just have been in their way. At the same time or shortly thereafter, Atta – the only terrorist on board trained to fly a jet – would have moved to the cockpit from his business-class seat, possibly accompanied by Omari.

As this was happening, passenger Daniel Lewin, who was seated in the row just behind Atta and Omari, was [also] stabbed by one of the hijackers – probably Satam al-Suqami, who was seated directly behind Lewin. Lewin had served four years as an officer in the Israeli military. He may have made an attempt to stop the hijackers in front of him, not realizing that another was sitting behind him.

The hijackers quickly gained control and sprayed Mace, pepper spray, or some other irritant in the first-class cabin, in order to force the passengers and flight attendants toward the rear of the plane. They claimed they had a bomb.

About five minutes after the hijacking began, Betty Ong contacted the American Airlines Southeastern Reservations Office in Cary, North Carolina, via an AT&T airphone to report an emergency aboard the flight. This was the first of several occasions on 9/11 when flight attendants took action outside the scope of their training, which emphasized that in a hijacking, they were to communicate with the cockpit crew. The emergency call lasted approximately 25 minutes, as Ong calmly and professionally relayed information about events taking place aboard the airplane to authorities on the ground.

At 8.19, Ong reported: 'The cockpit is not answering, somebody's stabbed in business class – and I think there's Mace – that [sic] we can't breathe – I don't know, I think we're getting hijacked.' She then told of the stabbings of the two flight attendants.

At 8.21, one of the American employees receiving Ong's call in North Carolina, Nydia Gonzalez, alerted the American Airlines operations center in Fort Worth, Texas, reaching Craig Marquis, the manager on duty. Marquis soon realized this was an emergency and instructed the airline's dispatcher responsible for the flight to contact the cockpit. At 8.23, the dispatcher tried unsuccessfully to contact the aircraft. Six minutes later, the air traffic control specialist in American's operations center contacted the FAA's Boston Air Traffic Control Center about the flight. The center was already aware of the problem.

Boston Center knew of a problem on the flight in part because just before 8.25 the hijackers had attempted to communicate with the passengers. The microphone was keyed, and immediately one of the hijackers said, 'Nobody move. Everything will be okay. If you try to make any moves, you'll endanger yourself and the airplane. Just stay quiet.' Air traffic controllers heard the transmission; Ong did not. The hijackers probably did not know how to operate the cockpit radio communication system correctly, and thus inadvertently broadcast their message over the air traffic control channel instead of the cabin public-address channel. Also at 8.25, and again at 8.29, Amy Sweeney got through to the American Flight Services Office in Boston but was cut off after she reported someone was hurt aboard the flight.

Three minutes later, Sweeney was reconnected to the office and began relaying updates to the manager, Michael Woodward.

At 8.26, Ong reported that the plane was 'flying erratically.' A minute later, Flight 11 turned south. American also began getting identifications of the hijackers, as Ong and then Sweeney passed on some of the seat numbers of those who had gained unauthorized access to the cockpit.

Sweeney calmly reported on her line that the plane had been hijacked; a man in first class had his throat slashed; two flight attendants had been stabbed – one was seriously hurt and was on oxygen while the other's wounds seemed minor; a doctor had been requested; the flight attendants were unable to contact the cockpit; and there was a bomb in the cockpit. Sweeney told Woodward that she and Ong were trying to relay as much information as they could to people on the ground.

At 8.38, Ong told Gonzalez that the plane was flying erratically again. Around this time Sweeney told Woodward that the hijackers were Middle Easterners, naming three of their seat numbers. One spoke very little English and one spoke excellent English. The hijackers had gained entry to the cockpit, and she did not know how. The aircraft was in a rapid descent.

At 8.41, Sweeney told Woodward that passengers in coach were under the impression that there was a routine medical emergency in first class. Other flight attendants were busy at duties such as getting medical supplies while Ong and Sweeney were reporting the events.

At 8.41, in American's operations center, a colleague told Marquis that the air traffic controllers declared Flight 11 a hijacking and [that they] 'think he's [American 11] headed toward Kennedy [airport in New York City]. They're moving everybody out of the way. They seem to have him on a primary radar. They seem to think that he is descending.'

At 8.44, Gonzalez reported losing phone contact with Ong. About this same time Sweeney reported to Woodward, 'Something is wrong. We are in a rapid descent ... we are all over the place.' Woodward asked Sweeney to look out the window to see if she could determine where they were. Sweeney responded: 'We are flying low. We are flying very, very low. We are flying way too low.' Seconds later she said, 'Oh my God, we are way too low.' The phone call ended.

At 8.46.40, American 11 crashed into the North Tower of the World Trade Center in New York City.'

United Airlines flight 175: By 8.33, it had reached its assigned cruising altitude of 31,000 ft. The flight attendants would have begun their cabin service. The flight had taken off just as American 11 was being hijacked, and at 8.42 the United 175 flight crew completed their report on a 'suspicious transmission' overheard from another plane (which turned out to have been Flight 11) just after take off. This was United 175's last communication with the ground.

The hijackers attacked sometime between 8.42 and 8.46. They used knives (as reported by two passengers and a flight attendant), Mace (reported by one passenger), and the threat of a bomb (reported by the same passenger).They stabbed members of the flight crew (reported by a flight attendant and one passenger). Both pilots had been killed (reported by one flight attendant). The eyewitness accounts came from calls made from the rear of the plane, from passengers originally seated further forward in the cabin, a sign that passengers and perhaps crew had been moved to the back of the aircraft. Given similarities to American 11 in hijacker seating and in eyewitness reports of tactics and weapons, as well as the contact between the presumed team leaders, Atta and Shehhi, we believe the tactics were similar on both flights.

The first operational evidence that something was abnormal on United 175 came at 8.47, when the aircraft changed beacon codes twice within a minute. At 8.51, the flight deviated from its assigned altitude, and a minute later New York air traffic controllers began repeatedly and unsuccessfully trying to contact it.

At 8.52, in Easton, Connecticut, a man named Lee Hanson received a phone call from his son Peter, a passenger on United 175. His son told him: 'I think they've taken over the cockpit – An attendant has been stabbed – and someone else up front may have been killed. The plane is making strange moves. Call United Airlines – Tell them it's Flight 175, Boston to LA.' Lee Hanson then called the Easton Police Department and relayed what he had heard.

Also at 8.52, a male flight attendant called a United office in San Francisco, reaching Marc Policastro. The flight attendant reported that the flight had been hijacked, both pilots had been killed, a flight attendant had been stabbed, and the hijackers were probably flying the plane. The call lasted about two minutes, after which Policastro and a colleague tried unsuccessfully to contact the flight.

At 8.58, the flight took a heading toward New York City. At 8.59, Flight 175 passenger Brian David Sweeney tried to call his wife, Julie. He left a message on their home answering machine that the plane had been hijacked. He then called his mother, Louise Sweeney, told her the flight had been hijacked, and added that the passengers were thinking about storming the cockpit to take control of the plane away from the hijackers.

At 9.00, Lee Hanson received a second call from his son Peter:

'It's getting bad, Dad – A stewardess was stabbed – They seem to have knives and Mace – They said they have a bomb – It's getting very bad on the plane – Passengers are throwing up and getting sick – The plane is making jerky movements – I don't think the pilot is flying the plane – I think we are going down – I think they intend to go to Chicago or someplace and fly into a building – Don't worry, Dad – If it happens, it'll be very fast – My God, my God.'

The call ended abruptly. Lee Hanson had heard a woman scream just before it cut off. He turned on a television, and in her home so did Louise Sweeney. Both then saw the second aircraft hit the World Trade Center.

At 9.03.11, United Airlines Flight 175 struck the South Tower of the World Trade Center.

American Airlines flight 77: At 8.51, American 77 transmitted its last routine radio communication. The hijacking began between 8.51 and 8.54. As on American 11 and United 175, the hijackers used knives (reported by one passenger) and moved all the passengers (and possibly crew) to the rear of the aircraft (reported by one flight attendant and one passenger). Unlike the earlier flights, the Flight 77 hijackers were reported by a passenger to have box cutters. Finally, a passenger reported that an announcement had been made by the 'pilot' that the plane had been hijacked. Neither of the firsthand [sic] accounts mentioned any stabbings or the threat or use of either a bomb or Mace, though both witnesses began the flight in the first-class cabin.

At 8.54, the aircraft deviated from its assigned course, turning south. Two minutes later the transponder was turned off and even primary radar contact with the aircraft was lost. The Indianapolis Air Traffic Control Center repeatedly tried and failed to contact the aircraft. American Airlines dispatchers also tried, without success.

At 9.00, American Airlines Executive Vice President Gerard Arpey learned that communications had been lost with American 77. This was now the second American aircraft in trouble. He ordered all American Airlines flights in the Northeast that had not taken off to remain on the ground. Shortly before 9.10, suspecting that American 77 had been hijacked, American headquarters concluded that the second aircraft to hit the World Trade Center might have been Flight 77. After learning that United Airlines was missing a plane,

American Airlines headquarters extended the ground stop nationwide.

At 9.12, Renee May called her mother, Nancy May, in Las Vegas. She said her flight was being hijacked by six individuals who had moved them to the rear of the plane. She asked her mother to alert American Airlines. Nancy May and her husband promptly did so.

At some point between 9.16 and 9.26, Barbara Olson called her husband, Ted Olson, the solicitor general of the United States. She reported that the flight had been hijacked, and the hijackers had knives and box cutters. She further indicated that the hijackers were not aware of her phone call, and that they had put all the passengers in the back of the plane. About a minute into the conversation, the call was cut off. Solicitor General Olson tried unsuccessfully to reach Attorney General John Ashcroft.

Shortly after the first call, Barbara Olson reached her husband again. She reported that the pilot had announced that the flight had been hijacked, and she asked her husband what she should tell the captain to do. Ted Olson asked for her location and she replied that the aircraft was then flying over houses. Another passenger told her they were traveling northeast. The Solicitor General then informed his wife of the two previous hijackings and crashes. She did not display signs of panic and did not indicate any awareness of an impending crash. At that point, the second call was cut off.

At 9.29, the autopilot on American 77 was disengaged; the aircraft was at 7,000 ft and approximately 38 miles west of the Pentagon. At 9.32, controllers at the

Dulles Terminal Radar Approach Control 'observed a primary radar target tracking eastbound at a high rate of speed'. This was later determined to have been Flight 77.

At 9.34, Ronald Reagan Washington National Airport advised the Secret Service of an unknown aircraft heading in the direction of the White House. American 77 was then 5 miles west-southwest of the Pentagon and began a 330-degree turn. At the end of the turn, it was descending through 2,200 ft, pointed toward the Pentagon and downtown Washington. The hijacker pilot then advanced the throttles to maximum power and dove [sic] toward the Pentagon.

At 9.37.46, American Airlines Flight 77 crashed into the Pentagon.

United Airlines flight 93: United's first decisive action to notify its airborne aircraft to take defensive action did not come until 9.19, when a United flight dispatcher, Ed Ballinger, took the initiative to begin transmitting warnings to his 16 transcontinental flights: 'Beware any cockpit intrusion – Two a/c [aircraft] hit World Trade Center.' One of the flights that received the warning was United 93. Because Ballinger was still responsible for his other flights as well as Flight 175, his warning message was not transmitted to Flight 93 until 9.23.

By all accounts, the first 46 minutes of Flight 93's cross-country trip proceeded routinely. Radio communications from the plane were normal. Heading, speed, and altitude ran according to plan. At 9.24, Ballinger's warning to United 93 was received in the cockpit. Within two minutes, at 9.26, the pilot, Jason

Dahl, responded with a note of puzzlement: 'Ed, confirm latest mssg plz – Jason.'

The hijackers attacked at 9.28. While traveling 35,000 ft above eastern Ohio, United 93 suddenly dropped 700 ft. Eleven seconds into the descent, the FAA's air traffic control center in Cleveland received the first of two radio transmissions from the aircraft. During the first broadcast, the captain or first officer could be heard declaring 'Mayday' amid the sounds of a physical struggle in the cockpit. The second radio transmission, 35 seconds later, indicated that the fight was continuing. The captain or first officer could be heard shouting: 'Hey, get out of here – get out of here – get out of here.'

Because several passengers on United 93 described three hijackers on the plane, not four, some have wondered whether one of the hijackers had been able to use the cockpit jump seat from the outset of the flight. FAA rules allow use of this seat by documented and approved individuals, usually air carrier or FAA personnel. We have found no evidence indicating that one of the hijackers, or anyone else, sat there on this flight. All the hijackers had assigned seats in first class, and they seem to have used them. We believe it is more likely that Jarrah, the crucial pilot-trained member of their team, remained seated and inconspicuous until after the cockpit was seized; and once inside, he would not have been visible to the passengers.

At 9.32, a hijacker, probably Jarrah, made or attempted to make the following announcement to the passengers of Flight 93: 'Ladies and [g]entlemen: Here the captain [sic], please sit down keep remaining sitting. We have a bomb on board. So, sit.' The flight data recorder (also recovered) indicates that Jarrah then instructed the plane's autopilot to turn the aircraft around and head east.

The cockpit voice recorder data indicate that a woman, most likely a flight attendant, was being held captive in the cockpit. She struggled with one of the hijackers who killed or otherwise silenced her.

Shortly thereafter, the passengers and flight crew began a series of calls from GTE airphones and cellular phones. These calls between family, friends, and colleagues took place until the end of the flight and provided those on the ground with firsthand [sic] accounts. They enabled the passengers to gain critical information, including the news that two aircraft had slammed into the World Trade Center.

At 9.39, the FAA's Cleveland Air Route Traffic Control Center overheard a second announcement indicating that there was a bomb on board, that the plane was returning to the airport, and that they should remain seated. While it apparently was not heard by the passengers, this announcement, like those on Flight 11 and Flight 77, was intended to deceive them. Jarrah, like Atta earlier, may have inadvertently broadcast the message [to the control centre] because he did not know how to operate the radio and the intercom. To our knowledge none of them had ever flown an actual airliner before.

At least two callers from the flight reported that the hijackers knew that passengers were making calls but did not seem to care. It is quite possible Jarrah knew of the success of the assault on the World Trade

Center. He could have learned of this from messages being sent by United Airlines to the cockpits of its transcontinental flights, including Flight 93, warning of cockpit intrusion and telling of the New York attacks. But even without them, he would certainly have understood that the attacks on the World Trade Center would already have unfolded, given Flight 93's tardy departure from Newark. If Jarrah did know that the passengers were making calls, it might not have occurred to him that they were certain to learn what had happened in New York, thereby defeating his attempts at deception.

At least ten passengers and two crew members shared vital information with family, friends, colleagues, or others on the ground. All understood the plane had been hijacked. They said the hijackers wielded knives and claimed to have a bomb. The hijackers were wearing red bandanas, and they forced the passengers to the back of the aircraft.

Callers reported that a passenger had been stabbed and that two people were lying on the floor of the cabin, injured or dead – possibly the captain and first officer. One caller reported that a flight attendant had been killed.

One of the callers from United 93 also reported that he thought the hijackers might possess a gun. But none of the other callers reported the presence of a firearm. One recipient of a call from the aircraft recounted specifically asking her caller whether the hijackers had guns. The passenger replied that he did not see one. No evidence of firearms or of their identifiable remains was found at the aircraft's crash site, and the cockpit voice recorder gives no indication of a gun being fired or mentioned at any time. We believe that if the hijackers had possessed a gun, they would have used it in the flight's last minutes as the passengers fought back.

Passengers on three flights reported the hijackers' claim of having a bomb. The FBI told us they found no trace of explosives at the crash sites. One of the passengers who mentioned a bomb expressed his belief that it was not real. Lacking any evidence that the hijackers attempted to smuggle such illegal items past the security screening checkpoints, we believe the bombs were probably fake.

During at least five of the passengers' phone calls, information was shared about the attacks that had occurred earlier that morning at the World Trade Center. Five calls described the intent of passengers and surviving crew members to revolt against the hijackers. According to one call, they voted on whether to rush the terrorists in an attempt to retake the plane. They decided, and acted.

At 9.57, the passenger assault began. Several passengers had terminated phone calls with loved ones in order to join the revolt. One of the callers ended her message as follows: 'Everyone's running up to first class. I've got to go. Bye.'

The cockpit voice recorder captured the sounds of the passenger assault muffled by the intervening cockpit door. Some family members who listened to the recording report that they can hear the voice of a loved one among the din. We cannot identify whose voices can be heard. But the assault was sustained.

In response, Jarrah immediately began to roll the airplane to the left and right, attempting to knock the passengers off balance. At 9.58.57, Jarrah told another hijacker in the cockpit to block the door. Jarrah continued to roll the airplane sharply left and right, but the assault continued. At 9.59.52, Jarrah changed tactics and pitched the nose of the airplane up and down to disrupt the assault. The recorder captured the sounds of loud thumps, crashes, shouts, and breaking glasses and plates. At 10.00.03, Jarrah stabilized the airplane.

Five seconds later, Jarrah asked, 'Is that it? Shall we finish it off?' A hijacker responded, 'No. Not yet. When they all come, we finish it off.' The sounds of fighting continued outside the cockpit. Again, Jarrah pitched the nose of the aircraft up and down. At 10.00.26, a passenger in the background said, 'In the cockpit. If we don't we'll die!' Sixteen seconds later, a passenger yelled, 'Roll it!' Jarrah stopped the violent maneuvers at about 10.01.00 and said, 'Allah is the greatest! Allah is the greatest!' He then asked another hijacker in the cockpit, 'Is that it? I mean, shall we put it down?' to which the other replied, 'Yes, put it in it, and pull it down.'

The passengers continued their assault and at 10.02.23, a hijacker said, 'Pull it down! Pull it down!' The hijackers remained at the controls but must have judged that the passengers were only seconds from overcoming them. The airplane headed down; the control wheel was turned hard to the right. The airplane rolled onto its back, and one of the hijackers began shouting, 'Allah is the greatest. Allah is the greatest.'

> With the sounds of the passenger counterattack continuing, the aircraft plowed [sic] into an empty field in Shanksville, Pennsylvania, at 580 miles per hour, about 20 minutes' flying time from Washington, DC.
>
> Jarrah's objective was to crash his airliner into symbols of the American Republic, the Capitol or the White House. He was defeated by the alerted, unarmed passengers of United 93.

It is nigh on impossible to calculate the financial or emotional impact of that day given the huge loss of life. The hijackings had not only claimed the lives of the passengers and crew but, as with Lockerbie, albeit in incomparable numbers, the lives of innocent people unconnected with aviation going about their normal working lives on the ground.

At 9.58.49 the South Tower of the World Trade Center collapsed, followed at 10.28.22 by the North Tower. Images of the towers disintegrating will forever be engrained on the minds of all that witnessed the atrocities either in person or on television, as, no doubt, al-Qaeda had intended. Like the assassination of JFK, the Apollo moon landing and the death of Princess Diana, everybody old enough knows where they were when they heard the news of 9/11. We bore witness to the horror experienced by employees trapped in their offices, engulfed by smoke and flames, of people taking to the rooftops of the towers in the hope of aerial rescue and of the 200 or so people who had no option but to jump.

2,606 people died at the World Trade Centre, and a further 125 at the Pentagon. It is thought that 1,609 people lost a spouse or partner and 3,051 children lost a parent. Many of those who perished were the heroes who rushed to the crash sites in order to rescue others – 343 firemen, 37 Port Authority police officers, 23 New York Police Department officers and two paramedics.

Flying was never to be the same again.

The 11 September 2001 is certainly one which will be a landmark in aviation security history. However, unlike the abundance of hijackings for financial gain, political expression or even as a result of mental illness, we should avoid dwelling excessively on the events of that day. A knee-jerk reaction is neither good for security nor is it an appropriate response for society as a whole, as, in effect, that is exactly what the perpetrators' intentions were – to disrupt our daily lives.

What is more telling is the fact that despite the raft of security measures put in place as a response to 9/11, we have not achieved security in the skies. Indeed, in the 14 years subsequent to 11 September 2001 there were more successful attacks against aviation than those in the same period prior to that day.

UKRAINE SHOOTS DOWN SIBERIA AIRLINES FLIGHT

While the world started to worry about commercial airliners overflying conflict zones in 2014, following the loss of Malaysia Airlines flight 17 over the Ukraine while it was en route from Amsterdam to Kuala Lumpur (see p.303), another aircraft had been shot down in the same region in 2001.

Siberia Airlines flight 1812 was operating from Tel Aviv, Israel, to Novosibirsk in Russia on 4 October 2001, when, at an altitude of 36,000 ft and somewhere over the Black Sea, it disappeared off the radar. Less than a month had passed since the 9/11 attacks, so it was immediately assumed that a bomb was the cause.

The investigation showed otherwise. It emerged that the 66 passengers and 12 crew members had been shot out of the sky as a result of a Ukrainian military training exercise gone badly wrong. In an attempt to shoot down a drone, they missed their target and the missile locked onto the Siberia Airlines flight, which was 250 km away, instead.

Ukraine eventually paid compensation to the victims' families, although never actually admitted guilt. It also banned the testing of all missile systems, including the Buk which we now believe was responsible for the downing of MH17.

THE SHOE BOMBER

On 21 December 2001, little more than two months after the 11 September attacks, Richard Reid – today known as the 'Shoe Bomber' – arrived at Paris' Charles De Gaulle Airport. His intent was to board an American Airlines flight bound for Miami and to detonate the IED contained in his shoes to bring down the aircraft. Fortunately, for those passengers flying on, coincidentally, the anniversary of the Lockerbie disaster, Reid was identified as a possible threat to the flight and did not manage to board.

An ICTS (the contract security company providing American Airlines with profiling services) security agent flagged Reid as being a person of concern given his absence of checked luggage for a purported trip to Antigua, via Miami, in order to spend the holiday season with family. Furthermore, Reid appeared scruffy, yet was holding a brand new British passport, which had been issued at the British consulate in Brussels on 7 December. Once questioned by ICTS, he was referred to the French police and, by the time they had finished questioning him, his flight had departed. Reid was put up at the Copthorne Hotel at American Airlines' expense.

It was a cold and damp night in Paris and that may have been one of the contributory factors to Reid's failure to destroy the airliner the following day, as the fuse in his shoe had become damp and therefore hard to light; the sweat from his feet may have also contributed to the moisture on the fuse. It must have been a rather strange night for Reid secreted in a hotel room when he thought he would be dead, partying with 72 virgins.

When he returned to the airport the following morning he was allowed to board the flight – despite ICTS agents' concerns – partly because people felt sorry that he'd missed his flight the day before. Midway through the flight he tried to ignite the fuse; the power source was a match. Flight attendant Hermis Moutardier saw him strike the match and thought that he was about to light a cigarette; she warned him that smoking was not permitted on board. A few minutes later, Moutardier found Reid crouched over and, having got his attention, was horrified to see that he was now holding a shoe in his hand and another lit match. She summoned the assistance of her colleague Cristina Jones and they tried to overpower him. Passengers came to the rescue, but not before Reid had bitten Jones' thumb. Once Reid was restrained, the aircraft diverted to Boston, where he was arrested.

Reid was certainly not acting alone. In the run up to the attacks, he had travelled the world, his globetrotting interspersed by regular trips to Pakistan. All without a permanent job. On 6 July 2001, he flew from Karachi to Amsterdam, where he claimed to have lost his passport and had a fresh one, without any incriminating Pakistani stamps, issued at the British consulate. On 12 July, he flew El Al to Israel, and experienced the depth of the legendary Israeli passenger profiling process; he was searched from head to toe. His surveillance trip proved that El Al flights were unlikely to be successfully targeted by shoe-bombers. He left Israel by land to Egypt, crossing into the Sinai desert, before eventually making his way back to Holland.

That autumn, Reid made further visits to Pakistan and Afghanistan; this time accompanied by Sajid Badat. In early December, Reid visited Brussels, where he once again 'lost' his British passport and had a new one issued, keen to cover up his trail. On 16 December, he took the train to Paris, where, the next day, he bought his ticket for American Airlines flight 63 at the Voyage Myriam travel agency. He was to fly on a round trip ticket to Antigua, via Miami; his departure date was 21 December. He paid 1,981 euros for his ticket... in cash.

Badat, meanwhile, had travelled home to the UK. He was to fly from Manchester to Amsterdam and then board a flight to the United States wearing a similar pair of shoes to those worn by Reid; the fuse wire was later found to be cut from the same batch. In the now typical al-Qaeda fashion, two aircraft were to have been bombed mid-Atlantic simultaneously. Badat, however, had a change of heart and, at the last minute, notified his handler that Reid would be acting alone. According to *The Times*, an email was sent stating, 'You will have to tell Van Damme that he could be on his own.'

Badat tried to renounce his jihadi past. He took the shoes back to his parents' house in Gloucestershire, where they were found in a police raid two years later.

Reid's actions spawned the removal of shoes and boots at airport security checkpoints around the world.

ZHANG PILIN'S SUICIDE... OR BO XILAI'S COVER STORY?

Less well known are the probable actions of Zhang Pilin on 7 May 2002. Pilin took out seven life insurance policies that day with a total value of around $170,000. Some of the policies were taken out in Dalian in the morning before he flew to Beijing, and others were taken out in Beijing Capital International Airport before his return trip the same day to Dalian on a China Northern Airlines flight. Zhang Pilin was carrying gasoline and he set fire to the aircraft prior to its landing in Dalian. All 103 passengers and nine crew were killed when the aircraft crashed into the sea. The subsequent investigation showed it was not the fire itself that had caused the plane to crash but, rather, the fact that the fire had been set at a critical stage of the flight: on its final approach to Dalian Zhoushuizi International Airport, the ensuing panic, with passengers jumping from their seats and running away from the fire, destabilised the aircraft, thereby causing the pilot to lose control.

The motive for Zhang Pilin's actions is unclear, with some reports indicating he was in debt and suffering from cancer. However, more recently it has been speculated that the naming of Zhang Pilin as the culprit was merely a cover-up for the actions of the former Chongqing Communist Party secretary Bo Xilai and his wife, Gu Kailai, in their attempt to kill the wife of one of Bo Xilai's political opponents, Han Xiaoguang. Li Yan Feng was a passenger on board who had travelled to Beijing in order to try and get her husband released from prison.

It is interesting to note that the cockpit voice recorder data has never been released and yet it is almost inconceivable that the black box was not discovered when the aircraft wreckage was successfully salvaged. To add to the mystery, Li Yan Feng's name did not appear on the passenger list.

INDEPENDENCE DAY SHOOTING AT LAX

Many passengers worry about aviation security and fear a terrorist attack on board an aircraft, yet, as we have seen, incidents can take place at airports as well. It was on US Independence Day, 4 July 2002 that Hesham Mohammed Hadayet opened fire at the El Al check in counter at Los Angeles International Airport killing El Al ticketing agent Vicky Chen and a bystander, Yaakov Yaminov. Hadayet was armed with a .45-calibre handgun, a 9-mm gun and a 6-inch knife; he was shot dead by an El Al security guard patrolling the check-in area.

'I'D RATHER DRINK YOUR BLOOD'

The desperation of people attempting to migrate, or to avoid deportation, has been demonstrated numerous times throughout history. Even now in the twenty-first century, political turmoil, famine and an absence of hope can cause people to risk their own lives, and those of their families, to embark on high-risk voyages, where the possibility of dying en route is outweighed by the greater risk of staying put. Reaching greener pastures and then being turned back is not an option. On 29 August 2002, a Montenegro Airlines flight was chartered specifically to deport a large group of ethnic Albanians from Düsseldorf, Germany, to Pristina, Kosovo. One of the deportees was 20-year-old Shaban Isufi and he had no wish to leave Germany.

Despite the presence of Montenegrin police on board, at one point during the flight he requested to use the toilets. While inside the closet, Isufi removed his shoelaces from his trainers and then returned to his seat. When flight attendant Irena Radonjic was performing the drinks service and asked him what he wanted, he jumped from his seat, placed the laces around her throat and is reported to have said, 'I'd rather drink your blood.' He threatened to strangle her if the aircraft did not return to Germany.

One of the 15 police escorts quickly overpowered Isufi, who required hospital treatment in Kosovo when the aircraft landed. Radonjic escaped with shock, a few bruises to her neck and a story to tell.

ISRAELI INTERESTS TARGETED AGAIN

The Israeli profiling system proved somewhat wanting on 17 November 2002, when Tawfiq Fuqra, an Israeli Arab, tried to hijack an El Al flight en route from Tel Aviv to Istanbul. Fuqra tried to stab a flight attendant and gain access to the flight deck, allegedly with the intention of crashing the aircraft 9/11-style, but he was subdued by sky marshals on board the flight. While Fuqra had managed to bring the weapon on board, the Israeli authorities were keen to emphasise that they operate a layered approach to security and that no one element is foolproof; that's why there were sky marshals on board. The attack did, in the end, fail.

Only 11 days later, on 29 November 2002, the fifty-fifth anniversary of the United Nations resolution that called for the division of Palestine into separate Jewish and Arab states, an Arkia Israel Airlines flight was targeted as it departed Mombasa's airport in Kenya bound for Tel Aviv. This time the attack was external with the firing of two Strela heat-seeking missiles at the aircraft; the launchers were later found 2 km away. It is believed the attack failed because the missiles were fired too close to the aircraft and did not allow sufficient time for them to be able to lock on to the aircraft's heat source – the engines.

While the events of 11 September 2001 alerted the industry to the threat posed by a hijacker willing to take his or her own life, the emphasis within the industry was on the terrorist with suicidal intent. Yet not all suicidal individuals with a desire to target aviation are terrorists.

CHAPTER XII
2003—2013

TASMANIA'S WHERE THE DEVIL LIVES

It was on 29 May 2003 that David Mark Robinson tried to enter the flight deck of a Qantas flight en route from Melbourne to Launceston, Tasmania. His intent was to overpower the pilots and fly the aircraft into Cradle Mountain in the Walls of Jerusalem National Park in north west Tasmania, as he felt that by sacrificing himself and the passengers and crew of the Qantas flight he would be able to release the Devil and bring about Armageddon.

Robinson got up from his seat in row 7 of the Boeing 717 as soon as the seatbelt signs were turned off. The crew were starting to prepare to serve refreshments on the very short flight to Tasmania. Robinson took out two sharpened wooden stakes, each 15 cm in length and bizarrely with tape wrapped around the handles to prevent splinters (even though he was planning to die!), and attacked Denise Hickson, the flight attendant nearest to him. He then made his way forward.

Robinson was prevented from gaining access to the flight deck by the heroic actions of the Qantas Cabin Manager Greg Khan, who despite receiving several stab wounds to the head, managed to overpower Robinson; four passengers – Domenic Bordin, Keith Charlton, Gregory Martin and Garry Stewart –

then helped restrain him while the flight deck crew announced that they had an emergency situation on board and requested an immediate return to Melbourne.

It emerged that, in an era that pre-dated restrictions on the carriage of aerosols in cabin baggage, Robinson was also carrying a number of aerosols and a cigarette lighter which, combined, he planned to use as flame throwers.

The aviation industry can learn much from this attack. Firstly, it was perpetrated on a route that almost all security consultants would deem to be low risk – this was a domestic route. Secondly, the hijacker understood the limitations of archway metal detectors and therefore used home-made wooden stakes, which he secreted in his jacket pocket knowing that the metal detectors would not identify them. Thirdly, the attack on the flight to Launceston was not the first time that Robinson had tried to to enter the cockpit of a commercial flight; in January 2003, he had flown from Hobart to Melbourne and had to be escorted to his seat by a female flight attendant after he had tried to gain access to the cockpit.

He was later diagnosed to be suffering from paranoid schizophrenia.

RUSSIA'S 9/11

Suicidal terrorism had been embraced as a modus operandi by Chechen terrorists for a number of years, but the incidents were often afterthoughts in global media coverage. That was set to change in the summer of 2004.

What became known as 'Russia's 9/11' occurred on 24 August 2004, when two aircraft were destroyed within three minutes of each other by Chechen Black Widows who had travelled to Moscow that morning from cities in the Northern Caucas. Bribery, corruption and, what can best be described as gross professional negligence, had enabled the terrorists to achieve their goal.

Aminat Nagayeva and Satsita Dzhebirkhanova were flatmates in the town of Grozny, where they both worked as market traders. The two women left home on 22 August, telling their relatives that they were going to Baku in order to purchase school goods; they were accompanied by Rosa Nagayeva – Aminat's sister – and a friend of Dzhebirkhanova, Mariam Taburova. The foursome arrived in Moscow's Domodedovo Airport at 7.45 p.m. on a flight from Makhachkala (although some reports indicate they may have travelled by train). Airport police stopped the women and pulled them aside for further inspection, actually demonstrating, once again, the advantages of profiling techniques. Their documents were handed over to an airport police captain, Mikhail Artamonov, who was supposed to instigate a baggage, body and background check on them. Seemingly, he released them without further inspection. Artamonov was later arrested and sentenced to nine years in jail for the way in which he had compromised security at the airport.

The four women proceeded to buy tickets from a ticket tout, Armen Arutyunov, for flights – Nagayeva on one that evening to Sochi and Dzhebirkhanova on one departing at 9 a.m. the following day to Volgograd. The tout was needed as they did not wish to present their actual IDs.

Arutyunov was paid 5,000 roubles by the women. From that sum he paid 1,000 roubles to a Siberia Airlines employee, Nikolai Korenkov, to alter Dzhebirkhanova's ticket from the 9 a.m. departure of the 25 August to one the same evening; the morning departure was a larger aircraft type and, if Nagayeva had been successful in her mission, Dzhebirkhanova might not have even got to commence hers. Dzhebirkhanova managed to check-in two minutes before the flight closed. Arutyunov also paid a bribe to get Nagayeva onto the Volga AviaExpress flight to Volgograd. The bribes were accepted in the belief that the two women were smuggling drugs.

We know that Dzhebirkhanova was seated in 19F – a window seat – on the Tu-154 aircraft. The forensic evidence indicates that her bomb was detonated in the privacy of the aircraft's toilets; her walk there was short. Nagayeva commenced her death march to the toilets of the Volga AviaExpress Tu-134 at much the same time.

They also detonated their devices almost simultaneously. The Volga AviaExpress flight crashed in Tula and, three minutes later, the Siberia Airlines flight crashed near Rostov-on-Don. There were no survivors on either aircraft. Dzhebirkhanova and Nagayeva soon became the prime suspects given that nobody came to claim their bodies and the suspicious circumstances of their ticket purchase became apparent.

Particles of hexogen were found in the wreckage of both flights. In Tula, the prosecutor reported that:

> There is not much left of the woman bomber who blew up the Tu-134. A part of her left leg (from the knee to foot) and fragments of her head and arms were found near debris from the plane's rear. Her body being blown to such fragments and the fact that they were severely burned mean that the woman was located at the epicentre of the explosion. Most likely, the explosive was attached to her body.

Visual identification of the bomber was almost impossible.

In Rostov, Kommersant (a Russian media outlet) reporters were also told that visual identification of Dzhebirkhanova had been impossible:

> Can you imagine a body which was blown up by 500 grams of trotyl and then fell from a 10 km height? All that was left of the bomber is her legs and a fragment of the head. They were found during the examination of the rear of the plane. The panelling of the plane's interior in this place is flashed, and the seats are bent, which is another proof of an explosion. The head found during the investigation did not give us any information, and the examination of the legs revealed the fact that the woman wore European size 37 shoes, regularly had pedicures and painted her toenails pink.

Rosa Nagayeva and Mariam Taburova, who had brought their friends to Moscow, became wanted women. They were to appear in Beslan one week later when, on 1 September, they were two of approximately 32 militants who took 1,100 people hostage – including 777 children – at a school on the first day of term. The incident was to end on 3 September when Russian forces stormed the building; 385 hostages were to die in the process. All but one of the militants were also killed – including Nagayeva and Taburova. The Beslan School Massacre goes down in history as one of the most callous, brutal, and depraved acts of terrorism of all time and, given that schoolchildren were the specific target, is even harder to fathom than the attacks of 11 September 2001 in the United States.

MIRACLE LANDING IN BODØ

In a similar vein to the attempted hijacking of the Qantas flight to Tasmania, another flight operating a low-risk domestic route – this time in Norway - was targeted on 29 September 2004 when an armed Algerian, Brahim Bouteraa, boarded a Kato Air flight from Narvik to Bodø. As there are no flight attendants on board Dornier 228 aircraft, it was the responsibility of the first officer to check the cabin was secure for take off; on his return to the flight deck, he reported that one of the passengers was reading an Arabic book. According to Captain Stein Magne Lian, in an interview with *Aviation Security International*, 'We didn't think more of that at the time, even though people reading Arabic books are not the norm.'

The flight usually took 35 minutes and it was as the aircraft was descending from 6,000 ft to 5,000 ft that Captain Magne Lian was struck on the head with the back of an axe. First Officer Kristian Markus Andresen was also hit but with the bladed side. The captain grabbed Bouteraa's wrist and struggled to control the aircraft which was in a steep spiral spin. One of the passengers, Odd Erikson, who was a local politician, ran up the aisle to assist, accompanied by a car salesman, Trond Frantzen. The aircraft actually missed the ground by less than 100 ft and the captain later said:

> By the time we did start to pull up, I was afraid the tail would hit the ground. It was really low. It was if we were in a ditch. We could see the ground on both sides of us.

The aircraft did eventually land in Bodø but it took 8–10 minutes for the police to reach the aircraft.

Bouteraa was later sent to prison for 15 years but released after 10 and he was deported with an armed escort to Algeria in 2014.

Bouteraa had been armed with an axe, a box cutter and a hunting knife, which were not detected as there was no screening on domestic flights in Norway at that time. It is, however, also possible to hijack aircraft with knives which are not so seemingly obvious, as was the case on 25 December 2001, when a man tried to hijack a Xiamen Airlines flight, en route from Harbin to Xiamen, to Taiwan armed only with a fruit knife.

THE WHEELCHAIR HIJACKER

One would think that hijackers would always be able-bodied people. On 12 September 2005, Porfirio Ramirez proved an exception to the rule when he hijacked an Aires aircraft which was en route from the Colombian city of Florencia bound for Bogota. Porfirio was in a wheelchair and was accompanied by his son. They had smuggled two hand grenades onto the aircraft by Porforio simply sitting on them in his wheelchair. Porfirio wanted money from the government as compensation for having been partially paralysed 14 years earlier during a drug raid in which he had been accidentally shot. Following negotiations he agreed a settlement of $43,000. He accepted payment by cheque and, in order to prove that the money had been deposited into his account, the government negotiators presented him with a receipt, following which he surrendered.

The story was later turned into a feature-length film, *Porfirio*, and was shown at the Cannes film festival in 2011. It should be noted that the receipt he was given by the government was false and that he had been given no money but he was paid for his appearance in the movie. So crime does sometimes pay.

FROM AN ALBANIAN BEAUTY PAGEANT TO AN AUDIENCE WITH THE POPE

If one thinks of Albania and about asylum seekers, one normally thinks of Albanians trying to claim asylum or migrate to countries in the European Union or the United States. Hakan Ekinci had other ideas. He had fled Turkey and claimed asylum in Albania but, knowing he was about to be deported from Tirana back to Istanbul, he decided to hijack Turkish Airlines flight TK1476 on 3 October 2006. Ekinci did not want to return to Istanbul as he considered himself to be a conscientious objector who did not want to serve in a Muslim army. Indeed, he had fled to Albania while doing his National Service in the Turkish Army. He decided that, as a Christian, he would hijack the flight to Italy and seek the assistance of the Pope.

He waited for the flight attendant, Nazenin Donder, to serve coffee to the captain shortly after take off, and then rushed into the flight deck and immediately told the captain and first officer to divert to Rome. He said that the bumbag he was wearing was packed with C4 explosives (it was actually only filled with newspaper) and that there were three hijackers on board the aircraft. Captain Mürsel Gökalp decided to follow Ekinci's instructions and fly towards Italy. Ekinci, however, had to accept that the flight would land in Brindisi as there was insufficient fuel on board to reach Rome.

For the passengers, it was all very confusing. They had not been told the aircraft had been hijacked, as Ekinci refused to permit there to be any communication from the cabin to the crew. Among the passengers were four beauty queens – Miss Singapore, Miss Malaysia, Miss Philippines and Miss India - who only became aware of the fact they had been hijacked once the aircraft was on the ground, as they couldn't understand any of the Albanian or Turkish conversations around them. It was only when they used their mobile phones to call their families that they found out that the plane they were on had actually been hijacked. Their families were watching CNN!

Mia Tan, who had been representing Singapore at the beauty pageant in Albania, explained in an article she wrote for *Aviation Security International* how the passengers first became aware that something was wrong.

During the flight there was an announcement, 'This is your captain speaking. Due to technical problems, we have to make a landing in Brindisi, in southern Italy. We should be arriving in another 20 minutes. Thank you.' A thought then occurred: here we were headed for Istanbul, Turkey, yet we were stopping in Italy, which is in the opposite direction, for technical repairs? Didn't quite make sense... unless they were seeking the Formula 1 Ferrari team to fix the plane!'

It was hours later that she found out the true cause for the diversion.

Ekinci was arrested and, much to his surprise, imprisoned, during which time he tried to commit suicide. After three years, he was released and deported back to Turkey.

THE AIR MAURITANIE HIJACKING... AND CAPTAIN LEMINE'S CUNNING PLAN

Ever since 11 September 2001, aircrew have been encouraged to take steps to overpower hijackers. One of the cleverest plans to do so was put into motion by Captain Ahmedou Mohamed Lemine on board an Air Mauritanie flight operating from Nouakchott to Las Palmas via Nouadhibou, on 15 February 2007. Lemine goes down as one of the modern-day heroes of the aviation industry.

The hijacker, Mohamed Ould Abderrahmane, 32, armed with both 9-mm and .22 semi-automatics, demanded to go to Paris, where he had intended to claim asylum. When the Moroccan authorities denied the flight permission to land and refuel in Dakhla, Western Sahara, the crew convinced him to accept the original destination, Las Palmas, as an alternative given the fuel load on board.

It was during this conversation that Lemine realised that Abderrahmane did not speak French, affording him the opportunity to tell First Officer Satvinder Virk that he was going to brake very sharply on landing, an action which he hoped would throw the hijacker off balance. And it did. The hijacker fell to the cockpit floor and dropped one of his guns, at which point Virk, supported by one of the flight attendants, Thiam El Hacen, jumped on Abderrahmane. Thiam even poured boiling water from the coffee machine in the galley onto the hijacker. He was effectively restrained and taken into custody.

Some of the passengers were slightly injured by the aggressive braking manoeuvre, but the hijack had been brought to a swift conclusion. And, for most of the passengers, they were even where they wanted to be!

LIQUIDS, AEROSOLS AND GELS

It was in the summer of 2006 that a plot to destroy airliners operating from the UK to US and Canada was identified. The perpetrators were going to be using home-made liquid explosive devices. That plot brought about restrictions on liquids, aerosols and gels being carried in hand baggage. The media and even the governments portrayed this plot as if it was the first time that liquid explosives had ever been planned to be used in an attack on civil aviation, yet, as we have seen, liquid explosives have been used to target flights since the 1930s.

From the terrorists' perspective, even though the 2006 plot had been interrupted, the aim of using liquids remained, and it was put into action on 30 June 2007. Two jihadists drove their green Jeep Cherokee into the terminal building at Glasgow Airport. The vehicle was laden with propane gas canisters.

The driver was Kafeel Ahmed, a doctor of engineering. While they were able to set the vehicle on fire, it had not exploded as intended. Worse, for Ahmed, the vehicle had not even made it into the terminal building; while bystanders tried to put the fire out, Ahmed was still making attempts to drive the Jeep inside.

Bilal Abdullah, the other attacker, was a British-born Iraqi-qualified doctor specialising in the treatment of diabetes at Glasgow's Royal Alexandra Hospital. On 30 June, however, he was simply a front-seat passenger in the Jeep; as it became caught in the door to the terminal, he jumped out and started throwing Molotov cocktails – using J2O bottles – shouting, 'Allahu Akbar,' as he did so.

Ahmed started pouring petrol out of the window of the car and then dropped a Molotov cocktail into the fuel. He then exited the vehicle, intentionally stepping into the flames. On fire, Ahmed tried to prevent anybody coming near the vehicle. He seemed not to be experiencing any pain; subsequent toxicology reports indicated that both men were pumped full of morphine.

Ahmed was eventually subdued by police officers using CS gas. Abdullah tried to escape on foot, but was tackled by passer-by Michael Kerr. Kerr's leg was broken and he lost a tooth as Abdullah lashed out, but Kerr had enabled others to tackle, and subsequently arrest, the runaway doctor.

The damage to the airport could well have been worse: had the Jeep made it into the terminal, it is quite likely that there would have been a significant number of casualties.

Ahmed died just over a month after the attack as a result of the 90 per cent burns he received. Ironically it was the medical team at the Royal Alexandra Hospital which tried to save him. Abdullah was later sentenced to 32 years in prison.

Mohammed Asha, a neurologist working at the University Hospital of North Staffordshire, was also convicted of being the plot's mastermind. He had been arrested six hours after the attack.

The Glasgow Airport attack was not supposed to be a stand-alone incident. In the early hours of the previous day, 29 June, Abdullah and Ahmed had attempted a similar attack in London. They had parked two vehicles, each containing propane gas, petrol and 2,000 nails, which were supposed to have exploded having been activated by a pay-as-you-go mobile phone, outside the Tiger Tiger nightclub.

Neither of the Tiger Tiger car bombs detonated as planned. Abdullah and Ahmed left London by train and travelled to Stoke-on-Trent to meet up with Asha in order to plan their next course of action. The meeting took place at the ambulance entrance to the Royal Infirmary's A&E department.

The men left Stoke and took another train – this time to Glasgow, where they were to spend what was supposed to be the last night of their lives at their rented house in Neuk Crescent, Paisley.

THE IMPOSSIBLE FLIGHT

There have been a number of hijackings where the hijackers have demanded to go to destinations beyond the range of their aircraft. In one such case case, Asha Ali Abdille tried to hijack an Eagle Airways flight on 8 February 2008, en route from Blenheim to Christchurch in New Zealand, and requested to be flown to Australia.

A Somali immigrant, she was known to be suffering from mental health problems; indeed, she actually had 27 convictions to her name and was on bail for threatening to kill and for possession of a weapon at the time she attempted the hijacking. She was armed with three knives and, just as in the case of the Kato Air incident a few years earlier, she took advantage of the fact there was no screening of baggage on domestic flights.

When Abdille was told the aircraft could not chart a course for Australia, she attacked the captain and first officer who were both quite seriously injured. Despite his thumb almost being severed, the captain managed to land the plane.

XINJIANG TENSION & THE EAST TURKESTAN ISLAMIC MOVEMENT

Xinjiang's independence from China is the objective of the members of the East Turkestan Islamic Movement (ETIM) and there was considerable concern during the run up to the 2008 Beijing Olympics that terrorist attacks would be perpetrated to publicise their cause.

As far as aviation was concerned it was on 7 March 2008 when, on a flight from Urumqi (the capital of Xinjiang province) to Beijing, a woman named Guzalinur Turdi infiltrated petrol onto a China Southern flight by concealing it in modified fizzy drinks cans.

Like the 9/11 hijackers, simplicity was the order of the day, with permissible everyday items utilised as potential weapons of mass destruction. The traditional improvised explosive device (IED), with its four component parts, was further consigned to the history books and replaced by a simple improvised incendiary device (IID), working on the principle of the 'Triangle of Fire': Heat + Fuel + Oxygen = Fire.

Incident reports vary, yet it would appear that our female suicide bomber was a frequent flyer, who arose from her seat and, much like the Chechen Black Widows in 2004 (see p.275), made her way to the over-wing toilets of the Boeing 757. She then closed the door behind her and emptied the contents of the cans on the floor and fittings.

According to some reports, it would appear that Turdi fortunately suffered a bout of nerves and failed to ignite her highly inflammable deposit. As she left the toilets, crew members standing by, having become concerned about the amount of time she had spent inside, noticed a distinct smell of gasoline and decided to search the toilets, where they found the empty cans in the rubbish bin. They restrained Turdi and the flight eventually diverted to Lanzhou, where she was arrested and later confessed.

It should be noted that some reports also cite an accomplice whose task it may have been to ignite the gasoline; others claim that her 'minder' did not board the flight on the day in question but had flown with her previously on two surveillance missions.

A few weeks after the hijack, China Southern Airlines gave the crew $57,000 as a reward for their efforts.

Strangely, there are no reports as to what happened to Turdi after her arrest. Usually, in such circumstances, execution would be the order of the day, and the Chinese government would be very keen to publicise the fact. In this case, the silence is deafening.

999... IS 666 UPSIDE DOWN

The significance of the 9 September 2009, otherwise written as 09/09/09, may be hard for most people to determine. Not so, however, for a Bolivian priest, Jose Mar Flores, who believed that the date was going to herald a natural disaster. Why? Because 999 upside down equates to the satanic number 666. So significant was this that the Bolivian pastor felt it was incumbent upon him to speak to the president of Mexico and warn him of a devestating forthcoming earthquake.

Armed with a Bible in one hand and a small device, which he had made out of a juice can and some fairy lights, and which looked to the flight attendant like an IED, he hijacked an Aeroméxico flight en route from Cancun to Mexico City and claimed to be accompanied by three fellow travellers – the Father, the Son and Holy Ghost. Flores remained in his seat throughout the incident and once the plane was on the ground in Mexico City was quickly taken into custody by the police.

THE UNDERPANTS BOMBER

An event that was to change the way in which passenger screening was to be conducted took place on Christmas Day 2009 when Umar Farouk Abdulmutallab, wearer of the most famous pair of underpants in the world, attempted to destroy a Northwest Airlines flight en route from Amsterdam to Detroit.

Abdulmutallab had graduated in Mechanical Engineering from University College London in 2008, but during his time in Britain he had started to become radicalised. Financially supported by his wealthy family – which, ironically, he detested, due to their capitalist mentality – he moved to Dubai and embarked upon an MBA programme there. Becoming increasingly interested in fundamentalist Islamic belief, he dropped out of university and, still at his father's expense, moved to Yemen, where he enrolled on an Arabic language course. Once again, he was not to complete the programme and his family became increasingly alarmed at the rhetoric emanating from him. It was later discovered that he was receiving training from al-Qaeda in the Arabian Peninsula (AQAP).

On 19 November 2009, his father, one of the most prominent bankers in Nigeria, was so concerned about his son's behaviour that he reported him to CIA officers at the US Embassy in Abuja. His American visa, which had been issued in London a year before, was not revoked.

Abdulmutallab travelled to Ghana via Ethiopia, on 9 December, and checked in to an airport hotel. On 16 December, he went to the KLM airport ticket office in Accra and purchased his ticket to Detroit in cash for $2,831. He was routed Lagos to Detroit, via Amsterdam for the outbound flights and Detroit to Accra, via Amsterdam, for the return on 8 January 2010. Later the same day, and presumably to avoid arousing suspicion by not booking a round-trip ticket, he changed his final destination from Accra to Lagos.

On 24 December, Abdulmutallab took a Virgin Nigeria flight to Lagos and, having spent less than an hour in his homeland, he then boarded the KLM flight to Amsterdam. He was allocated seat 20B.

On Christmas morning he arrived at Schiphol and transferred onto the Northwest flight to Detroit. His passport was checked and he was found to have a multiple-entry visa to the United States, issued in London in June 2008 and expiring in June 2010. Some of the questions posed by security agent Jafar Hosseyni were revealed at Abdulmutallab's subsequent trial and are now a matter of public record.

At no point did anybody question why a man of African origin, travelling for two weeks to Detroit in the middle of winter, would do so without any checked luggage. Abdulmutallab was, however, identified by a screener as a person of concern, yet following a discussion with one of the supervisors, he was still allowed to board the aircraft with his device concealed in his groin. He took seat 19A.

As the aircraft was about to descend into Detroit, Abdulmutallab visited the toilets. He spent twenty minutes out of sight and, on exiting, simply said that he had an upset stomach. Back in his seat, he pulled a blanket over his lap. Then there was a bang – though nothing major, other passengers described it as sounding like a firecracker. Abdulmutallab's trousers were, however, on fire.

Jasper Schuringer was the first passenger to realise that Abdulmutallab had to be overpowered. He grabbed the bomber from his seat, burning his own hands in the process, and, assisted by others, Abdulmutallab was marched up the aisle to First Class, with his trousers around his ankles – as he had taken his trousers down in order to try to activate the device. Once he was seated in 1G, the passengers and crew removed his shoes, trousers and what remained of his underpants; they covered him with a blanket.

Ramy Guirgis, a Delta employee who was travelling as a passenger on the flight, offered to sit with Abdulmutallab until the aircraft landed. As he sat with him, Guirgis asked what had happened and Abdulmutallab admitted, for the first time, that he had intended to destroy the aircraft.

All this time, the pilots were blissfully unaware as to what had happened and it was only then that lead flight attendant Elaine Christmas – aptly named, given the time of year – notified the flight deck that there had been a fire. The mention of the word 'fire' initiated an accelerated descent into Boston, possibly faster than was needed given that Abdulmutallab was by then restrained. Indeed the flight landed less than seven minutes after the bomb had been detonated and less than four minutes after they had been told of the 'fire'.

On the ground, the pilots requested that the authorities meet the aircraft 'to respond to an incident of firecrackers on board'. They still had no idea that they had almost become the victims of a terrorist bombing.

The passengers and crew of the Northwest flight were fortunate that the home-made device did not function as planned. The bomb was described in the indictment against Abdulmutallab as being:

> a device containing pentaerythritol tetranitrate (also known as and hereinafter referred to as 'PETN'), triacetone triperoxide (also known as and hereinafter referred to as 'TATP'), and other ingredients.

Abdulmuttalab had used a syringe to effect a chemical reaction which should have caused detonation. At his eventual trial, the process was described as follows:

> There was the syringe, and the syringe was designed to cause a fire. That fire would ignite another chemical. There's a small amount of a chemical called TATP. The syringe would be pushed, that would set the TATP on fire, that TATP would explode. Think of that as the first explosion. And that explosion of TATP would then trigger the main charge, the PETN, for the second explosion. So it would be fire, small explosion, big explosion. The fire is caused by mixing two chemicals, potassium permanganate and ethylene glycol, in a syringe. Those are common chemicals. Ethylene glycol is in antifreeze, and potassium permanganate is also a common chemical, and it's easily available. And when those two chemicals are mixed together, they bubble, and then they smoke and then they burst into flames, just as the passengers on flight 253 saw. When they mix together, they cause that type of fire.
>
> The bomb did actually explode, the TATP did explode, that first charge, but obviously the PETN didn't have the big explosion that they expected to bring the plane

down, and the PETN burned. Some of it burned, some of it didn't. 🙙

The total quantity of PETN was 200 g, 80 g of which was still in his underpants when the plane landed.

Some years later, the head of the Transportation Security Administration, John Pistole, indicated that the explosives had become degraded because Abdulmutallab had actually been wearing the same underwear for two weeks prior to the attack.

In 2013, the ABC news network interviewed Pistole at the Aspen Security Forum and reported that he had described, what became known as 'Underwear II' – the next generation of underpants bomb designed by AQAP. 'Underwear II' was truly innovative and utilised 'two redundant initiators filled with explosives to detonate a larger liquid charge in men's briefs.' Pistole told ABC that an AQAP double agent had provided the Department of Homeland Security with an actual device that he was supposed to have used on board an aircraft and that the ability of the aviation security system to detect the explosives would have been extremely limited because he encased the explosive in kitchen caulk, to evade bomb sniffing dogs.

Abdulmutallab is now serving multiple life sentences for his actions and will, presumably, bear the scars of his failed attack until his dying day.

SERIOUS PRINTER ERROR

The aviation industry was to be further challenged on 29 October 2010, when two computer printers were sent from Yemen to the United States via FedEx. Thanks to Saudi Arabian intelligence, the authorities picked up on the probable presence of two IEDs concealed in packages, and the intelligence was so good that even the air waybill numbers were cited, thereby providing the authorities with the details of the exact packages requiring further inspection.

The bomb which was eventually discovered in Dubai had been sent from a Federal Express agent in Sana'a, Yemen; its destination was Chicago. It was flown, first, on a Qatar Airways flight to Doha, and from there, again on Qatar Airways, to Dubai; both legs had been passenger aircraft. In Dubai, the shipment was to have been loaded onto a FedEx Express aircraft for its subsequent journey to the US and it was in the FedEx facilities at Dubai Airport that the device was eventually found.

Initially the package was screened using traditional technologies but, when no explosives were found, an alert security officer in Dubai began to question why computer printers were being shipped from Yemen to Chicago, as the cost of doing so by FedEx far exceeded the cost of simply buying a new printer in the USA. Furthermore, the destination was identified as the former address of Or Chadash, the lesbian, gay, bisexual and transgender Jewish community of Chicago. Even to an Emirati officer, this seemed somewhat strange, considering the printer had been shipped by someone in Yemen. Consequently, he ordered the package and the printer be taken apart; it was only once they had examined the printer toner cartridge that they found an IED constructed in laboratory conditions, therefore leaving no trace.

The other device, what has since become known as the East Midlands bomb, was also sent from Sana'a, but this time via UPS. It was flown to Dubai, where it was loaded onto a UPS plane to Cologne-Bonn, Germany. By the time the German authorities had been given the specific intelligence relating to the device, the UPS flight had already departed for the US. The package was thus intercepted at a refuelling stop in the East Midlands, UK. The UPS aircraft itself was searched and then allowed to depart without the bomb on board. The police effected their initial examination of the package, removing both the printer from the package and the toner cartridge from the printer. Amazingly, they had inadvertently deactivated the device, but did not actually discover the bomb and even cleared the printer for onward travel. Two hours later, based on the intelligence coming through from Dubai, and with the printer now at the Fort Halstead defence laboratory, they realised that they had been handling a real bomb throughout.

An Interpol report confirmed that the explosive charge was PETN – 400 g in the case of the device intercepted in East Midlands, and 300 g for the Dubai bomb – and that the power source was a mobile phone battery.

There is rarely any humour in an aircraft bombing, but granted that the printer toner cartridge bombs did not detonate, the investigators were able to examine not only the construction of the IEDs, but also the accompanying items packed with the printers. In one of the shipments, the bombers had included a copy of Charles Dickens' *Great Expectations*…

IN RUSSIA, CHINA AND BULGARIA

Arriving passengers at Moscow Domodedovo Airport were less fortunate. On 24 January 2011, a suicide bomber decided to target the arrivals hall rather than the check-in in a suicide attack that claimed 37 people's lives. The Imarat Kavkaz (Caucasus Emirate), at the time led by Doku Umarov, later claimed responsibility for the attack. Imarat Kavkaz is a militant jihadist organisation with the stated objective of removing Russia's presence from the North Caucasus. The bomber was 20-year-old Magomed Yevloyev.

Civil aviation was attacked for political purposes again by the East Turkestan Islamic Movement (ETIM), on 29 June 2012, as part of the Uyghyur campaign for independence in Xinjiang. The group had been unsuccessful in their attempt to bring down a China Southern flight in 2008 (see p.286). This time, they sent six hijackers to overpower the crew of a Tianjin Airlines flight en route from Hotan to Urumqi.

The perpetrators had managed to pass security at Hotan Airport with weapons and explosives concealed in the crutches of one of the group who was feigning disability. On board, however, the assailants were overpowered by the passengers and crew and two of the hijackers died of their injuries in hospital. The other four were later executed.

Finally, on 18 July 2012, five Israeli tourists and a Bulgarian bus driver were killed at Burgas Airport on the Bulgarian Black Sea coast. The man carrying the device had been wearing a wig and was seen pacing around the arrivals hall awaiting the arrival of a flight from Tel Aviv. When the Israeli passengers exited customs, he followed them to their tour bus and seemingly attempted to load the backpack he was carrying onto the bus together with the Israeli passengers' luggage. He was challenged by the Israeli passengers and the bus driver came down to see what the fuss was about. It would seem the terrorist's colleagues then remotely detonated the device killing him along with his victims. The death toll would have been much higher had the bus been full and en route to the resort.

The investigation is ongoing (at the time of writing), but in February 2013, Tsvetan Tsvetanov, the Bulgarian Minister of Interior, announced there was 'well grounded' evidence that Hezbollah was behind the attack.

CHAPTER XIII
2014—2016

THE MYSTERY OF MALAYSIA AIRLINES FLIGHT MH370

The disappearance of Malaysia Airlines flight 370 on 8 March 2014, while en route from Kuala Lumpur to Beijing, is one of the greatest aviation mysteries of all time. A terrorist hijacking? A bomb? A fire? Pilot suicide? Cyber attack? Explosive decompression? Stowaway in the avionics bay? Missile fired in a military exercise gone wrong? Unruly passenger? Total systems failure? Lithium batteries exploding? Maybe the first chemical/biological weapons incident? Had the aircraft been mysteriously flown to Diego Garcia by the Americans? Or maybe to Kazakhstan, with all the passengers being held hostage in caves by al-Qaeda terrorists? Was it a diversionary tactic orchestrated by the Russians to divert the world's attention from their 'activities' in Crimea? Or was it the North Koreans flexing their military muscle? Or, perhaps, is the real reason that MH370 was actually been abducted by aliens?

Some of the ideas are downright ridiculous, others definite possibilities. Suffice to say, the loss of MH370 has left the entire world, including the aviation community, perplexed. How could a Boeing 777 simply disappear without a trace and remain undetected for days, which became months and then years?

The result: speculation. Speculation which must be agonising for the families and friends of the passengers and crew on board the ill-fated flight, as they cling on to that faintest of possibilities that their loved ones may indeed be alive. Speculation which calls into question the integrity of crew members who, rather than being the villains of the piece, may have actually been performing their duties heroically as they desperately tried to retain control of the aircraft. Speculation which is fuelling many a blogger's addiction to conspiracy theories or desire to make banal or abusive comments. But such is the bizarre nature of this incident, we have little alternative but to speculate.

So, given the fact that Malaysia's prime minister confirmed that the loss of MH370 was almost certainly a 'deliberate act', as opposed to a mechanical or structural malfunction, what could have happened?

The chances of an improvised explosive device detonating on board have been all but eradicated by the confirmation that the flight in question seemingly continued to fly, after it had been established that communication with the aircraft had been lost, and that the transponder had been intentionally switched off. Given the fact we now know that whoever was at the controls also intentionally changed direction, we can also almost rule out any missile attack against the aircraft; nonetheless, the possibility still exists that a state misidentified MH370 as a rogue aircraft entering its airspace and tried to shoot it down when it failed to identify itself, with the captain of MH370 making desperate efforts to pilot his aircraft away from danger (as happened with Korean Air flight 007 in 1983).

The more likely scenarios however remain associated with the mindset of whoever turned off the transponder. A pilot can certainly hijack their own aircraft. One year after MH370 disappeared, Andreas Lubitz utilised the enhanced security door protecting the cockpit to provide himself with the privacy needed to intentionally crash his Germanwings aircraft into the Alps.

But even one month before the loss of MH370, the co-pilot of an Ethiopian Airlines flight (see p.305) en route from Addis Ababa to Rome decided to hijack his own flight to Geneva. He waited for the captain to exit the flight deck to use the toilets and then locked himself in the cockpit and continued to fly the aircraft to Switzerland, where he claimed asylum.

But then why turn off the transponder?

The only time that hijackers successfully seized control of an aircraft, neutralised the flight deck crew and continued to fly the aircraft was on 11 September 2001... four times over. It was that event that brought about the enhanced flight deck door – a lockable, bullet-proof protective shield designed to prevent a hijacker gaining access to the cockpit. However, as with X-ray technology for screening baggage, this is actually far more about deterring incidents than being an effective security solution. Cockpit doors open numerous times on long-haul flights and aircrew are notoriously complacent about adhering to the guidelines for operating them. The advice is that the door should be open for no more than three seconds and then only after the cabin has been checked to ensure that all passengers are seated. In the real world, this often doesn't happen.

Both Indian Airlines flight IC814 (see p.226) and Turkish Airlines flight TK1476 (see p.281) were hijacked when their cockpit doors were opened in order for flight attendants to give the pilots coffee shortly after take off.

The other concern about the post-9/11 flight deck door is that, while it may keep the bad guys out of the cockpit, it can also keep the good guys out too. Once a hijacker is ensconced in the flight deck alone, the door can be bolted to ensure that nobody gains access. This worked to the industry's benefit when, in March 2012, a JetBlue pilot locked his colleague Clayton Osbon outside the flight deck, as he was experiencing mental health problems. On the other hand, the aforementioned Ethiopian Airlines co-pilot found the door aided his plan, as it did for Andreas Lubitz too.

While it is harsh to criticise a pilot who is currently missing and, we must presume, innocent, the images that appeared of MH370's first officer in the media did little to enhance confidence in his respect of Malaysia Airlines' own internal procedures. Jonti Roos, a South African girl, provided the media with photographs of herself and a friend inside the flight deck of a Malaysia Airlines flight en route from Phuket to Kuala Lumpur three years prior to the loss of MH370; she claimed that the pilots invited them into the cockpit for the entire flight, including take off and landing, having seen them queuing up to board. Had the crew of MH370 also invited 'guests' up to the flight deck?

Then again, we might be dealing with a passenger who was suicidal but who wished to die in a specific location. That was what David Mark Robinson wanted to do when he attempted to hijack a Qantas flight en route from Melbourne to Launceston in 2003 (see p.274).

We now enter the murky realms of terrorism. The key argument against it seems to be – aside from the previously unheard of Chinese Martyrs Brigade – the lack of any claim of responsibility. But then again, previous attacks against aviation have not always been accompanied by a claim of responsibility; take Pan Am flight 103 (where even the plot's author is still debateable – see p.194) and Air India flight 182 (see p.156) as examples.

Part of the significance of the attacks of 11 September 2001 was the media spectacle – the endlessly repeated footage of aircraft flying into buildings. Perhaps, once again, we are playing our roles in a script carefully drafted by a media-savvy branch of al-Qaeda or Islamic State? In the same way that the post-9/11 media debate was not about the al-Qaeda agenda per se, and with their penchant for the spectacular, the ceaseless news reports of the missing aircraft, the angst of the family members, the wild speculation, the poor communication, the fallibility of the aviation security system may just be the sort of headlines they are aiming for?

If one does have to identify a potential terrorist group, the most likely is the ETIM. Malaysia had previously deported ethnic Uyghyurs back to China. That would provide a limited reason for such groups to target a Malaysian carrier. But could the aircraft have in fact landed and the passengers and crew be taken hostage? Well, it has happened before, albeit using a Fokker 50 aircraft and not a B-777 – on 12 April 1999 an Avianca flight was hijacked by members of the ELN and flown to a jungle landing strip (see p. 223).

The Malaysian authorities initially declared the Kazakhstan/Turkmenistan to northern Thailand air corridor a search zone, so the aircraft could have been flown into Chinese airspace, roughly in the direction of Xinjiang Province and certainly towards the multi-national area considered by some to be East Turkestan. Then again, the discovery of an aileron on the beaches of Réunion in 2015 would certainly seem to indicate that the aircraft had, indeed, crashed into the Indian Ocean.

What about flying undetected? Well, you can if you want to, just not for too long. Israeli commandos managed to rescue the hostages taken to Entebbe in 1976 (see p.119); avoiding radar detection and bypassing hostile countries, the legendary mission resulted in aircraft landing at an international airport in Uganda undetected in the middle of the night. But that was 1976.

That still leaves the fundamental question as to who flew the aircraft. There are three options: a crew member, a passenger or a stowaway.

A pilot could certainly disable the transponder and would already be inside the flight deck. It would just be a matter of waiting until the other pilot exited the flight deck for a comfort break and then locking himself into the cockpit to take unilateral control over the flight.

But let's not forget the stowaway – the passenger whose name does not appear on the flight manifest. While most stowaways tend to clamber into wheel wells, some have secreted themselves on board aircraft, often disguised as airport staff. On 7 July 2012, two stowaways managed to penetrate the perimeter at Iceland's Keflavik International Airport and then, dressed as airport staff, board an Icelandair aircraft; they were found by alert crew members prior to departure. The same cannot be said in the case of a China Airlines flight that landed in San Francisco on 22 October 2012: a passenger from Shanghai had flown from Shanghai to Taipei and on to the United States, where he claimed asylum, having boarded the aircraft wearing a cleaner's uniform and avoided detection during the stopover in Taipei by concealing himself in an electrical compartment on board.

The industry has long been concerned about the 'insider threat'. At almost every major international airport in the world, criminal activity of one type or another takes place in what are supposed to be sterile zones. It is certainly a possibility that, in an airport the size of Kuala Lumpur International Airport, individuals, with or without the knowledge of the crew of MH370, and with or without technical knowledge of how to disable an aircraft's communication systems, could have managed to secrete themselves on board.

Where on board? Well, perhaps the avionics bay. It is an area of the aircraft rarely, if ever, searched prior to a flight's departure; yet on certain aircraft, such as the B-777, it is accessible from the passenger cabin. Somebody hiding away in the avionics bay, with the technical knowhow to disengage the various control and communication systems of the aircraft, is a distinct, albeit rarely discussed, possibility.

The most likely of the security-based scenarios would, if wrong, mean the vilification of a man who could have actually been heroically trying to save the aircraft. However, many in the industry do believe that Captain Zaharie Ahmad Shah hijacked the aircraft himself when his first officer exited the flight deck for a comfort break.

One cannot argue that Captain Shah's behaviour had been typical of a pilot about to operate an international flight in the run up to the loss of MH370. Aside from the somewhat unusual YouTube clips he had posted, in which he teaches viewers to repair household appliances, Shah was politically active and had been photographed wearing a T-shirt with the slogan 'Democracy is Dead' emblazoned on it. That, alone, would not normally be cause for concern, but more relevant is that, on the day of the flight's departure, Shah was reported to have been at the court for the conviction of Malaysian Opposition Leader Anwar Ibrahim for sodomy and was, allegedly, incensed at his imprisonment. Add to the mix the reported break up of his marriage, his having wiped clean his computer simulator, the absence of any future plans, his having received a telephone call from a woman who was using a pay-as-you-go mobile phone obtained using false ID just before MH370s departure, and the reported unusual behaviour he allegedly displayed towards the guards at his residence just before leaving home for the airport, it seems that we have little choice but to consider his active involvement in the disappearance. If so, one then has to consider whether it was an act of suicide perpetrated when in the depths of despair or as a premeditated action as part of a bigger terrorist or criminal plot.

What we do know is the point at which air traffic control lost contact with the aircraft, the variances in the aircraft's altitude, the route selected and the seemingly intentional flight tactics performed in order to avoid detection by radar demonstrated flying abilities of an exemplary nature.

But there are other disturbing questions, unconnected to Captain Shah, to which there have been no answers. Why did it take Vietnamese air traffic control 17 minutes to ask their Malaysian counterparts why MH370 hadn't switched frequency after it transferred from Malaysian to Vietnamese airspace? Why was there no military intercept of the aircraft if it did depart from its intended route? While we don't have the cockpit voice recorder yet, why has the voice recording of air traffic control communications not been released? Where is the voice recording of the communications between the civilian and military air traffic controllers? Plenty of questions, very few answers.

So, for now, we must speculate. Until we find the wreckage or, by some miracle, see the hostages emerging from some remote location, it's all we can do.

THE TRAGEDY OF MALAYSIA AIRLINES FLIGHT MH17

As if the loss of MH370 was not bad enough, Malaysia Airlines was to lose another aircraft four months later. MH17 was operating from Amsterdam to Kuala Lumpur and was overflying Ukraine when it was blown out of the sky.

According to the report published by the Dutch Safety Board in October 2015, Malaysia Airlines flight MH17 crashed as a result of a Russian-made Buk missile, which exploded just above the front left-hand side of the cockpit, causing other parts to break off, killing 298 people. It is argued by Ukraine and leaders in the West that Russian-backed rebels were responsible, yet Russia claims that the evidence suggests the plane was shot down by a surface-to-air Buk missile fired by Ukrainian forces.

The report makes it clear that, given the conflict in the region, Ukraine should have closed its airspace to commercial traffic. Furthermore, Malaysia Airlines and the International Civil Aviation Organisation are alleged to have not adequately considered the risks involved in flying in that region, especially given that 16 military planes and helicopters had been shot down in eastern Ukraine in the weeks before flight MH17 was lost. On the day of the crash, 160 flights flew over the area in question.

The loss of Malaysia Airlines flight 17 now stands with the likes of Korean Air flight 007 (shot down by the Russians when it strayed off course as a result of an autopilot failure on 1 September 1983), and aforementioned strikes against El Al, Libyan Arab Airlines, Aerolinee Itavia, Iran Air and many more, as an example of the risks passengers are exposed to when flying on routes over or near conflict zones, or when their aircraft is mistaken to have hostile intent. For Ukraine, the state had just about faced up to its own responsibility for the accidental shooting down of a Siberia Airlines flight, operating from Israel to Russia, in 2001, (see p.266) when it became the graveyard for passengers and crew who had nothing to do with its own conflict with Russia.

SUICIDAL PILOTS AND AIRCREW MENTAL HEALTH

The aviation industry has had to wake up to the fact that pilots can not only hijack their own aircraft in order to reach overseas destinations but may also be experiencing mental health issues which could result in their crashing their own aircraft, despite it being laden with innocent passengers and fellow crew members.

On 17 February 2014, Hailemedhin Abera Tegegn hijacked an Ethiopian Airlines flight to Geneva, on which he was serving as first officer. Tegegn exploited the window of opportunity afforded him when the captain exited the flight deck for a comfort break, bolting the flight deck door closed from the inside in order that he could take complete command of the aircraft. When the captain tried to return to the flight deck, he found that he was locked out; he, the rest of the crew and passengers, simply prayed that Tegegn was not suicidal as they banged on the door hoping to gain access. They were lucky that Tegegn was simply seeking asylum. On 20 March 2015, Tegegn was sentenced, *in absentia*, to 19 years and 6 months in prison by the Ethiopian courts for the hijacking.

The incident highlighted three security challenges the industry faces. Firstly, the fact that the enhanced flight deck door, designed to keep potential hijackers outside the cockpit, can also prevent crew and passengers from overpowering an intruder, or pilot, should they manage to lock themselves inside. Secondly, the reality of the 'insider threat' whereby a, presumably, trusted and vetted individual can become the assailant. And, thirdly, the fact that aviation security is not just a counterterrorist operation and that, as such, we need to be able to identify negative intentions of whatever kind and wherever it can impact upon the safety and security of our operations.

Fortunately, the Ethiopian Airlines incident ended without any loss of life, but there has been no change to procedures as a result. Moreover, the fact that it was an Ethiopian airliner (as opposed to a European or American carrier), en route to Rome from Addis Ababa, resulted in less media interest and industry disregard.

The end result could have been so different. The Ethiopian hijacking took place only three months after Captain Hermino dos Santos Fernandes crashed the Mozambique Airlines aircraft he was piloting (from Maputo to Luanda, Angola) in Namibia on 29 November 2013. The cockpit voice recorder showed that the co-pilot had been locked outside the flight deck and was desperately trying to get into the cockpit when the aircraft impacted with the ground, killing all on board. Sound familiar?

There was no global response to the Mozambique Airlines incident. Why? Because it was an African carrier flying between Mozambique and Angola.

Pilot suicide is not commonplace, but it is not unheard of. The frequency is, however, far greater than the number of times suicidal terrorists have commandeered aircraft and flown them into population centres. Unstable pilots operating in the general aviation or recreational arena have often chosen to perform acts termed 'aircraft-assisted suicide'. According to a Federal Aviation Administration report on the phenomena in the United States, published in February 2014, 'From 2003–2012, there were 2,758 fatal aviation accidents; the National Transportation Safety Board (NTSB) determined that 8 were aircraft-assisted suicides (all involving the intentional crashing of an aircraft)'.

Aside from Mozambique Airlines and Germanwings, there have also been some other significant incidents impacting commercial aviation.

In 1994, Royal Air Maroc flight 630 crashed ten minutes after take off from Agadir, killing all 44 on board. The investigation found that 32-year-old Captain Younes Khayati had disengaged the autopilot and intentionally crashed the plane in an act of suicide. An examination of the aircraft's flight recorders found the co-pilot, Sofia Figugui, shout:

> Help, help, the captain is...

Then she was cut off. It was speculated that Khayati was suicidal over a failed love affair and, possibly, that he was even enamoured with, yet rebuffed by, his married first officer.

Following the December 1997 crash of SilkAir flight 185 en route from Jakarta to Singapore, there was considerable speculation and controversy over the cause; suicide/homicide on the part of the pilot, Captain Tsu Way Ming, was high on the list of possibilities. This speculation stemmed from a number of circumstances including a life insurance policy he took out with effect from the day of the crash, recent disciplinary matters and financial problems. The Singapore police found no evidence that any of the crew had suicidal tendencies or had caused the crash, but the NTSB reported that 'the accident can be explained by intentional pilot action'.

On 31 October 1999, an Egyptair flight en route from New York to Cairo crashed into the sea. Again, there was much speculation as to the cause, with the Egyptian authorities repeatedly refuting suggestions that it may have been an act of pilot suicide. However, most official reports, including that produced by the NTSB, have concluded that the crash occurred as a result of the deliberate actions of the relief First Officer Gameel al-Batouti. The cockpit voice recorder shows clear evidence that the captain left the flight deck to use the toilets and that, shortly thereafter, al-Batouti was heard to be repeatedly saying, 'I rely on God,' in Arabic. The captain rushed back to the flight deck and the conversation between the two pilots supports the NTSBs view as to the cause. That said, nobody seems sure why al-Batouti may have been suicidal in the first place.

Of course, an act of suicide is one thing, an act of mass murder something else. Aircraft have been used as instruments of war, most famously those piloted by Japanese kamikaze pilots in World War Two, and commercial aircraft were turned into weapons of mass destruction in the terrorist attacks of 2001. However, most acts of aircraft-assisted suicide have been perpetrated by pilots flying solo.

In 1976, a pilot used his An-2 aircraft in an attempt to kill his wife! Vladimir Serkov, under the influence of alcohol at the time, took off from Severny Airport in the Russian city of Novosibirsk and then intentionally crashed into a residential building where his wife and child resided. Aside from Serkov himself, three residents were killed; his wife and child were not at home at the time.

The loss of Germanwings flight 4U9525 while en route from Barcelona to Dusseldorf on 24 March 2015 is likely to be an industry game changer, primarily because it was a German carrier (owned by Lufthansa), operating from Spain and crashing in France. Within hours of the announcement that First Officer Andreas Lubitz had intentionally crashed the airliner, some carriers had begun changing their procedures so that there would, henceforth, always be two crew members on the flight deck – a long-standing recommended practice. Yet we still don't know why Lubitz crashed the aircraft and our conclusions are based on cockpit voice recorder data, which should not, at such an early stage, even have been made public; the revelations were in breach of globally accepted international accident investigation processes.

Regardless, calls from within the industry have ranged from mandating the periodic psychological assessments of pilots to considering enabling people on the ground to be able to override the door locking system.

In terms of mandatory psychological assessments, one thinks back to Japan Airlines flight 350 in 1982, when Captain Seiji Katagiri tried to crash the DC-8 aircraft he was flying while it was on its final approach into Tokyo's Haneda Airport; fellow crew members managed to overpower Katagiri. An article which appeared in *Time* magazine following the incident makes eerie reading in the aftermath of the Germanwings disaster:

> There were claims that Seiji Katagiri had been suffering from hallucinations and feelings of depression. He once summoned police to his two-story [sic] house near Tokyo because he was convinced it was bugged, but a thorough search turned up no eavesdropping devices. On three occasions, his employers had urged him to see a psychiatrist. Ever since he was granted one month's leave in November 1980 for a 'psychosomatic disorder', Katagiri's wife has worried about his neurotic behaviour.

Twenty-four people died in the Japan Airlines incident when the aircraft landed in Tokyo Bay. Katagiri himself survived. Indeed, he was arrested while trying to flee the scene of the disaster and was charged with professional negligence resulting in death; he was found not guilty by reason of insanity.

All the incidents highlighted, while shocking in their own right, have made it absolutely crystal clear to the industry that pilots could become suicidal and might be prepared to crash their aircraft. Unlikely, true... but most of the security measures we put in place at airports are to prevent the 'one in a billion' and most of the technologies we deploy are to identify the 'needle in the haystack'.

In order to plan for the future, we need to know, firstly, the full details of what took place on the flight deck of Germanwings 9525 and that information is, at the time of writing, still being gathered. Flying an aircraft directly into a mountainside in the French Alps will certainly have made it difficult, if not impossible, to effect a detailed forensic examination of Lubitz's corpse. Secondly, the best lesson we can learn from the past is that we need to avoid knee-jerk reactions.

ISLAMIC STATE PERPETRATES MASS MURDER IN THE SINAI... PROBABLY

On Halloween 2015, the sixteenth anniversary of the loss of the Egyptair flight at the hands of a suicidal pilot (see p.307), another nightmare was to befall the Egyptian aviation industry – one which was to claim the lives of the 224 passengers and crew on board Metrojet flight KGL9268 just 23 minutes after its departure from Sharm el-Sheikh bound for St. Petersburg. All the indicators are that the explosion which took place was caused by an improvised explosive device infiltrated on board by Islamic State's Sinai affiliate.

As is commonplace in the aftermath of a tragedy, there has been considerable focus on the security measures that were in place at the point of departure, and the media highlighted stories from visitors to the Red Sea resort, who were keen to relate their accounts of the inadequate security processes they had witnessed. The harsh reality is that whichever airport a doomed flight departed from, there would be similar stories.

Sharm el-Sheikh may well not be an example of best security practice, but it does not stand alone. The findings of a 2015 US Government Accountability Office report into screening at American airports showed that, in 67 out of 70 tests, inspectors were able to infiltrate prohibited items, including dummy IEDs, through security checkpoints. A 95 per cent failure rate! Furthermore, even in supposedly ultra-secure facilities, such as prisons, the authorities cannot ensure the detection of all prohibited items, despite there being next to no limit on the amount of time one spends screening prisoners, visitors and staff and no customer service issues to worry about.

At the time of writing (only weeks after the loss of KGL9268), aside from the death toll, there is no story to tell. We don't know who placed the IED on board or even where it was secreted. Islamic State's own publication, Dabiq, published pictures of the rather crude device they claim was used. It is, however, widely speculated that the bombing was facilitated by an 'insider'. That is, either somebody who knowingly obtained a job at the airport in order to effect the bombing, or an airport worker who gradually became radicalised subsequent to their employment there. Alternatively, it could have been an airport worker who accepted bribes to ensure that a bag, which they might have believed contained drugs, weapons or other restricted items, bypassed security checks – without any knowledge of their role in planting a bomb on board.

The insider threat is certainly challenging for the industry. One only has to look to the tragic events of 5 November 2009 at Fort Hood in the US, when Major Nadal Malik Hasan, a psychologist in the US military, killed 13 fellow service personnel and injured 30 others. Or of 16 September 2013, when Aaron Alexis, a civil contractor to the US Navy, killed

12 and injured three others in a shooting at the Navy Yard in Washington DC. If we can't identify the insider threat in a military environment, where everybody goes through intense screening, how can we do so in airports?

In recent years, there have been a disturbing number of plots against aviation that have been identified as involving insiders. In 2007, Russell Defreitas and Abdul Kadir conspired to blow up fuel tanks, and a fuel pipeline running beneath New York's JFK Airport. Defreitas, the plot's originator, was a cargo employee at JFK and had been carrying out a surveillance operation, videoing facilities and then taking footage to Guyana, where Kadir, who had connections with militant groups in Iran and Venezuela, was based and where the plot was being developed.

In 2009, Rajib Karim, a software engineer working at British Airways' call centre in Newcastle, UK, came into direct contact with Anwar al-Awlaki (a key player in al-Qaeda) and was discussing with him how to use his position to perform a cyber attack against his employer. Karim was also exploring ways of achieving his ultimate goal of becoming a suicide bomber and was discussing with al-Awlaki whether he should become a member of cabin crew during a strike by BA's flight attendants.

And then, in 2013, Terry Lee Loewen, a technician with Hawker Beechcraft, was arrested at Wichita Mid-Continent Airport when he was trying to infiltrate a van laden with what he believed were explosives. In actual fact, the explosives were inert and had been given to him by the FBI in a sting operation. Loewen had become a person of interest when he became a Facebook friend of somebody expressing jihadi sentiments; an FBI agent then befriended him and Loewen told him that he wanted to carry out an attack. Together they planned the mission and Loewen was arrested only when the authorities found him actually using his security clearance to enter the airport.

These three incidents actually demonstrate that, in the UK and US at least, the insider threat exists. However, they also show that effective surveillance operations can prevent plots from becoming reality. In the case of Loewen, while many might argue 'entrapment', the FBI's activities demonstrated the effectiveness of a red-teaming operation that ought to be replicated around the globe.

A March 2015 Australian Federal Police (AFP) report, marked 'For Official Use Only', was leaked to the press and its contents should serve as a reminder that some of the world's most ruthless organisations are determined to infiltrate the ranks of our pilots, and have already succeeded in doing so. The report stated that:

> On 16 March 2015, information was received by the AFP that indicated two possible Indonesian pilots, likely employees of AirAsia and Premiair, had posted information on their Facebook pages that inferred support to the Islamic State.

Hardly a week goes by without reports emerging of people with security clearance being arrested at airports for their involvement in luggage theft, extortion, human trafficking, gun running, drug trafficking or facilitating the illegal movement of people across international borders. Most notable was the arrest, in December 2014, of Eugene Harvey – a Delta Air Lines employee – for having facilitated the transport of 153 guns on 20 different flights operating between Atlanta and New York. Harvey had simply used his pass to enter airside areas at the airport – there being no screening of staff in all but a handful of US airports – and placed the guns on planes. Greed was the objective, but what if the guns had been bombs?

DAALLO AIRLINES BOMBED IN 2016

On 2 February 2016, a Daallo Airlines flight which had departed Mogadishu, Somalia, for Djibouti was forced to return to the airport after an explosion in the passenger cabin ripped a hole in the fuselage over the wing – perilously close to the fuel tanks. The blast damage to the stricken airliner bore a close resemblance to the damage caused to TWA flight 840 (see p. 165) back in 1986. The Somali authorities were able to confirm that the Daallo flight was a victim of a bombing and that one passenger, Abdullahi Abdisalam Borleh, had been the sole fatality having been sucked from the aircraft following the blast. It is unclear (at the time of writing) whether or not he was suicidal, but CCTV images released show him receiving a laptop computer from an airport-based employee after passing through the security checkpoint. It is thought likely that al-Shabab was behind the attack.

The passenger was actually ticketed on Turkish Airlines, but Turkish had cancelled their flight that day due to inclement passenger and had agreed with Daallo Airlines that they transport their passengers to Djibouti.

THE FUTURE

There is no indication that the threat to aviation is in any way diminishing. The events of the post-9/11 era have clearly demonstrated that, while the frequency of attacks may not be high, the impact and death toll can be monumental. The terrorist we are now pitted against is a far cry from the revolutionary activist of half a century ago. There is a greater preparedness by the likes of al-Qaeda, Islamic State and their affiliates, to perpetrate callous acts of unspeakable brutality, where success is measured in terms of deaths achieved, pain suffered and humiliation caused, rather than political goals reached, comrades released or finance secured.

We must now face the reality that the enemy is sophisticated, highly educated and media savvy, able to put out propaganda material in digital magazine formats that rival the quality and design of high-street fashion publications. Their use of social media and capabilities to implement cyber attacks is a growing concern; in the first half of 2015 alone, one civil aviation authority, five airlines – the worst hit being LOT Polish Airlines – and two airports have been the subject of online attacks. On 12 April 2015, supporters of Daesh (Islamic State) hacked the website of Hobart International Airport, posting a message supporting ISIS and making the website unavailable for 24 hours.

As 2016 started, the threat posed by cyberwarfare was clearly illustrated in an attack on the IT network of Kiev's Boryspil Airport. According to the Ukrainian authorities the January attack was launched from a server in Russia. Identified early, no damage was caused, but given that the network also included the airport's air traffic control, a 'successful' virus could have had devastating consequences.

When effecting hijackings or bombings on board aircraft, twenty-first century terrorists have infiltrated their weapons in different ways – shoes, underpants, fizzy drinks cans, crutches, printers – demonstrating their ability to stay one step ahead of the technologies and processes we deploy to defend the industry and its users. Each plot has been different, as they think 'outside the box'. Things we previously considered as unlikely have now become distinct possibilities – including the use of chemical/biological weapons, body bombs and terrorists infiltrating our very core as crew members and air marshals.

The industry's ability to tackle many of the inherent weaknesses head-on has been hampered by concerns over, and accusations of, perpertrating invasions of privacy and civil liberties and our desire to treat everybody as posing an equal threat – an approach that no security agency in the world would embrace. That any plots have been interrupted at all is as a result of surveillance of target groups by the security services rather than the constant scrutiny of us all.

There is no logic to racial profiling, but in the same way that customs and immigration officers identify people as having committed criminal acts when they come off aircraft by deploying behavioural analysis and risk-based screening, those responsible for pre-board inspections and staff monitoring must do likewise. All too often, the industry resorts to relying on technology with inherent limitations to do the job that, at present, only the human brain can perform effectively. Technology has its place and is an essential element of the security arsenal, but it must be used intelligently.

The stakes are high. Any single failure in security has the potential not only to result in the deaths of all those on board the aircraft in question, but also in casualties as a result of the political response to the atrocity perpetrated. Some of those consequences may equate to civilian death tolls in the tens, or hundreds, of thousands when military action is deemed appropriate. This means that an even greater investment must be made in the staff in whose hands we place our trust to identify the next attempt to hijack or bomb a flight. There is no place for security theatre.

Aside from this message of doom and gloom, there is plenty to celebrate. The aviation industry is safer now than it has been at any time in its history. The risks we are exposed to in using other forms of transport or, indeed, walking along the high street are far higher than when we board an aircraft. Millions of passengers take to the skies every day and reach their destination safely, without incident. It is the nature of aviation that when disaster strikes the whole world hears about it, while we pay little attention to the daily toll of lives which evaporate in motor vehicle accidents.

Our eyes and our ears are our best defence and, nowadays, we are all part of the security web that protects society as a whole, let alone the aviation industry. Reporting observations made in person or online has never been more important. At the same time, we cannot be held hostage to a climate of fear as then terrorists will have succeded in achieving their goal.

BIBLIOGRAPHY

PUBLICATIONS

Anders, L and K. Hayes (1998) *Hijack, Our Story of Survival*, Andre Deutch, London

Arey, A. James (1973) *The Sky Pirates*, Ian Allan, London

Gunther, Max (1985) *D. B. Cooper: What Really Happened*, Contemporary Books, USA

Hee, Kim Hyun (1993) *The Tears of My Soul*, William Morrow and Company, New York

Jiwa, Salim (1986) *The Death of Air India Flight 182*, W. H Allen & Co, London

Kean, T and L. Hamilton (2004) *The Complete Investigation: The 9/11 Report, The National Commission on Terrorist Attacks Upton the United States*, The New York Times Publishers, New York

Khaled, Leila (1973) *My People Shall Live*, Hodder & Stoughton Ltd, London

MacDonald, Eileen (1991) *Shoot The Women First*, Random House, New York

BIBLIOGRAPHY

Mickolus, F. Edward (1980) *Transnational Terrorism: A Chronology of Events, 1968–1979*, Greenwood Press, Connecticut

Mickolus, Sandler and Murdock (1989) *International Terrorism in the 1980s: A Chronology of Events, 1984–1987*, Iowa State University Press, Ames

Netanyahu, Iddo (2002) *Yoni's Last Battle: The Rescue at Entebbe*, Gefen Publishing House, Jerusalem

Newton, Michael (2002) *The Encyclopaedia of Kidnappings*, Checkmark Books, USA

Pflug, N. J. and P. J. Kizilos (1996) *Miles Before I Go To Sleep*, Hazelden, USA

Philips, David (1973) *Skyjack*, Harrap, London

Schiff, Z and R. Rothstein (1972) *Fedayeen: The Story of the Palestinian Guerrillas*, Vallentine Mitchell & Co. LTD, London

Smith, William E., 'Terror Aboard Flight 847', *Time* magazine, June 24 2001

Snow, P and D. Philips (1970) *Leila's Hijack War*, Pan Books LTD, London

Tan, Sumiko (1991) *Hijack! SQ117*, Heinemann Asia, Singapore

Tsakov, Tsvetan. 'Bulgarian Aviation in the XX c.: Triumphs and Catastrophes', (Sofia: AirGroup2000, 2000)

Vaugue, Tom (1994) *The Red Army Faction Story 1963–1993*, AK Press, UK

ONLINE SOURCES

Ahrends, Martin and Baron, Udo. 'Christel and Eckhard Wehage', Berlin Wall Memorial, http://www.berliner-mauer-gedenkstaette.de/en/1970-318,412,2.html (accessed 2015)

'Argentina celebrates 45 years of the "Condor Operation" Landing in Falklands', MercoPress, http://en.mercopress.com/2011/09/29/argentina-celebrates-45-years-of-the-condor-operation-landing-in-falklands (accessed 2015)

Australian Federal Police (AFP) report, http://www.abc.net.au/news/2015-07-09/afp-tracks-indonesian-pilots-linked-to-islamic-state/6607532

Baum, Philip. 'Germanwings 9525: the challenge of suicidal pilots behind intrusion-proof cockpit doors', *Aviation Security International*, http://www.atc-network.com/atc-news/germanwings-9525-the-challenge-of-suicidal-pilots-behind-intrusion-proof-cockpit-doors (accessed 2015)

Baum, Philip. 'Germanwings Flight 4U9525: the latest act of aircraft-assisted suicide?', A*viation Security International*, https://www.asi-mag.com/germanwings-flight-4u9525-the-latest-act-of-aircraft-assisted-suicide/ (accessed 2015)

Baum, Philip. 'Kato Airline Hijack: axe attack in the cockpit', *Aviation Security International*, http://www.avsec.com/kato_airline_hijack_axe_attack_in_the_cockpit/ (accessed 2015)

Baum, Philip. 'Leila Khaled: in her own words', Green Light Ltd, http://www.avsec.com/leila_khaled_in_her_own_words/ (accessed 2015)

Baum, Philip. 'Metrojet Flight KGL9268: A Special Report', *Aviation Security International*, https://www.asi-mag.com/metrojet-flight-kgl9268-a-special-report/ (accessed 2015)

Baum, Philip. MH 370 – a 'deliberate act' – *Aviation Security International*, https://www.asi-mag.com/mh-370-deliberate-act/ (accessed 2015)

Baum, Philip. 'Vesna Vulovic: how to survive a bombing at 33000 ft', Green Light Ltd, http://www.avsec.com/vesna_vulovic__how_to_survive_a_bombing_at_33000_feet/ (accessed 2015)

Baum, Philip. 'Zvonko & Julienne Busic: an ASI exclusive interview', *Aviation Security International*, http://www.avsec.com/zvonko_julienne_busic_an_asi_exclusive_interview/ (accessed 2015)

'Bericht über das Gespräch eines Militärstaatsanwalts und eines MfS-Mitarbeiters mit den Eltern von Christel und Eckhard Wehage', in: BStU, MfS, HA IX Nr. 10391, Bl. 168. (accessed 2015)

Dash, Mike. 'America's First Highjacking', A Blast From The Past, http://mikedashhistory.com/2014/12/30/americas-first-highjacking/ (accessed 2015)

'Ending of secrecy surrounding the crash on 30 September 1975 of the Malév flight from Budapest to Beirut and the graves of 17 of the 60 victims', http://www.europarl.europa.

eu/sides/getDoc.do?pubRef=-//EP//TEXT+WQ+E-2009-0015+0+DOC+XML+V0//EN

'FBI History–Hall of Honor: W. Carter Baum', https://www.fbi.gov/about-us/history/hallhonor/baum (accessed 2015)

'Hijacked!' [transcript], http://www.pbs.org/wgbh/amex/hijacked/filmmore/pt.html (accessed 2015)

Hijazi, Ihsan A. 'Syria Weighs Response', NYTimes, http://www.nytimes.com/1986/02/06/world/syria-weighs-response.html (accessed 2015)

'Jack Gilbert Graham', https://www.fbi.gov/about-us/history/famous-cases/jack-gilbert-graham (accessed 2015)

Klein, Daniele. Union de Transports Aeriens Flight UT 772: the Gaddafi Connection, *Aviation Security International*, https://www.asi-mag.com/union-de-transports-aeriens-flight-ut-772-the-gadaffi-connection (accessed 2015)

Laviv, Omer. Big Data: 'aiding aviation and border security' – *Aviation Security International*, https://www.asi-mag.com/big-data-aiding-aviation-border-security/ (accessed 2015)

Lednicer, David. 'Aircraft Downed During the Cold War and Thereafter', http://sw.propwashgang.org/shootdown_list.html (accessed 2015)

Morgan, Dolan. 'Fortnight Journal: Documenting the Promise of the...', http://www.fortnightjournal.com/dolan-morgan/258-the-first-hijacking-myth.html (accessed 2015)

Rokach, Livia. 'Israel's Sacred Terrorism: Contents and Foreword', https://msuweb.montclair.edu/~furrg/essays/rokach.html (accessed 2015)

Ross, Brian. 'Remember failed pantybomber Abdul Farouk Umar Abdulmutallab? Here's pantybomb 2.0', Before It's News, http://beforeitsnews.com/opinion-conservative/2013/07/remember-failed-pantybomber-abdul-farouk-umar-abdulmutallab-heres-pantybomb-2-0-2685362.html (accessed 2015)

'Sabotage!' HistoricWings, http://fly.historicwings.com/2013/03/sabotage/, quoting Ronan Hubert, Bureau of Aircraft Accidents Archives (accessed 2015)

'SAWIO Ultimatum – German Guerilla', http://germanguerilla.com/1977/10/13/sawio-ultimatum/ (accessed 2015)

Soclof, Adam. 'El Al 1992 Crash in Amsterdam was Among Worst in Dutch, Israeli Aviation History', http://www.jta.org/2012/09/21/the-archive-blog/el-al-1992-crash-in-amsterdam-was-among-worst-in-dutch-israeli-aviation-history (accessed 2015)

Tan, Mia. 'Hijacking of the beauty queens: Miss Singapore's perspective', *Aviation Security International*, http://www.avsec.com/hijacking_of_the_beauty_queens__miss_singapore_s_perspective/ (accessed 2015)

Trifonov, Vlad and Dupin, Sergey. 'Legs Tell No Tales', Kommersant Moscow, http://www.kommersant.com/page.asp?id=502083 (accessed 2015)

'Troubled Pilot', TIME, http://content.time.com/time/magazine/article/0,9171,922801,00.html (accessed 2015)

United States District Court for the Eastern District of Virginia, Statement of Agreed Facts in the Zacarias Moussaoui Trial,http://law2.umkc.edu/faculty/projects/ftrials/moussaoui/zmstatementoffacts.html (accessed 2015)

United States District Court for the Eastern District of Michigan Southern Division, Jury Trial, Volume 4, Tuesday October 11, 2011, https://www.documentcloud.org/documents/1505806-abdulmutallab-trial-transcript.html

United States Government [transcript of Hearing], US Department for Defence 15 March 2007

'Urteil des Kreisgerichts Halberstadt gegen Eckhard Wehage vom 21. Oktober 1963', in: BStU, MfS, HA IX Nr. 10389, Bl. 230–233

'World Trade Center and Pentagon Attacks', GlobalSecurity, http://www.globalsecurity.org/security/ops/911-prep.htm (accessed 2015)

Zacarias Moussaoui trial, http://law2.umkc.edu/faculty/projects/ftrials/moussaoui/zmstatementoffacts.html

ABOUT THE AUTHOR

Photo Credit: Sophie Bronze

Philip Baum is Managing Director of Green Light Ltd, a London-based aviation security training and consultancy company with a global footprint, and Editor-in-Chief of *Aviation Security International*, the industry's journal of airport and airline security.

In both a consultancy role and in an editorial capacity, Philip advocates a common-sense-based approach to risk management and rejects tick-box security methodology. He is passionate about the incorporation of profiling, in the form of behavioural analysis, into the screening process and strives to ensure that aircrew – both pilots and flight attendants – are recognised as, and trained to be, security professionals, who are part of the web which protects the industry.

The industry calls upon him to chair international symposia, speak at conferences and participate in forward-thinking working groups. The media call upon him to provide expert commentary in the aftermath of security incidents affecting aviation – hence, he is a familiar face on the BBC, Sky News and CNN. Philip was also brought in as an expert witness to the United Kingdom's House of Commons' Home Affairs Select Committee inquiry into aviation security in the aftermath of the attempted downing of an aircraft by a suicide bomber on Christmas Day 2009.

As Editor-in-Chief of *Aviation Security International* since 1997, he has interviewed persona from government ministers to crew members and passengers to hijackers, including Leila Khaled, Julienne Busic, Capt. Stein Magne Lian and Vesna Vulovic, all of whom are featured in this book.

INDEX

INDEX

INDEX

INDEX

INDEX

Have you enjoyed this book?

If so, why not write a review on your favourite website?
If you're interested in finding out more about our books,
find us on Facebook at **Summersdale Publishers** and
follow us on Twitter at **@Summersdale**.

Thanks very much for buying this Summersdale book.

www.summersdale.com